W9-ASF-221

Remember When

♥ Text by *Allen Churchill*

Remember *When* / *Text by* Allen Churchill

A Ridge Press Book ○ Golden Press

CONTENTS

Editor in Chief: *Jerry Mason*
Editor: *Adolph Suehsdorf*
Art Director: *Albert Squillace*
Project Designer: *Allan Mogel*
Art Associate: *David Namias*
Associate Editor: *Moira Duggan*
Associate Editor: *Frances Foley*
Art Production: *Doris Mullane*
Research: *Dell Byrne,*
Peter Lacey, Michael Mason,
Judy Underhill

♥

Prepared and
produced by
The Ridge Press, Inc.
Printed in the
United States of America
Published by
Golden Press, Inc.
850 Third Avenue, New York 10022
Copyright © 1967 by
Western Publishing Company, Inc. and
The Ridge Press, Inc.
All rights reserved,
including rights of reproduction
and use in any form or by any means,
including the making of copies
by any photo process, or by any
electronic or mechanical device,
printed or written or oral,
or recording for sound or visual
reproduction or for use in any
knowledge retrieval system or device,
unless permission in writing
is obtained from the copyright proprietor.
Library of Congress Catalog Card
Number 67-21146

GOLDEN PRESS® is a trademark of
Western Publishing Company, Inc.

This edition prepared
for distribution by
Crown Publishers, Inc.

♥ 1900 1905

1905 1910

1910 1915

1915 1920

1920 1925

1925 1930

1930 1935

1935 1942

Turn of the Century

♥ Not many of us alive today remember the moment at which this book begins.

For though some of us were actually living on January 1, 1900, few were old enough to take part in the nationwide celebration of the United States as Old Man Time whistled his scythe through the air, cutting off the last leaf of 1899 to reveal a pristine 1900. Already, high-spirited Americans were calling the new year Nineteen Oughty-Ought, or even Naughty-Naught. Newspaper editorials greeted the new century in words solemn and reverent.

The New York *World*, however, chose to be mordant. "The 1800's are gone forever," it said, "and brisk, bright, fresh, altogether new 1900 greets everybody today—good for a clean hundred years before 2000 comes around and everybody now alive is gone . . . "

1900! Why, even the figures had an invigorating look. The calendar might say 1900, but this was really the Twentieth Century. It made the whole spinning planet seem ancient indeed.

Altogether, the turn of the century made an exhilarating moment in history, with each citizen celebrating in his own fashion. In the United States some seventy-six million souls (including babies) were present to herald the brave new world. In the White House, benign President William McKinley issued a statement of good cheer for the New Year, then betook himself to

bed; he was to preside at a reception for foreign diplomats the next day.

The governor of New York was Theodore Roosevelt, who would turn out to be McKinley's vice-presidential running mate in the November election. Roosevelt was known as Teddy to all Americans, though he himself disliked the name. Tonight he gathered his six children around him and told them that snow was forecast for the next day. Teddy had much miscellaneous information tucked away in a teeming brain and he knew it had snowed on the turn-of-the-century morn a hundred years before. The last century had been one of rare enlightenment and progress for mankind, especially for the United States of America. So, Roosevelt vigorously assured his children, snow for tomorrow was the best omen for the next hundred years.

Great men like Thomas Alva Edison, Admiral George Dewey, Alexander Graham Bell, and J. P. Morgan welcomed the new century with serene confidence. Thirty-seven-year-old Henry Ford of Detroit nursed hopes that during the next year or two he would build a "universal car," while the Wright brothers of Dayton dreamed of flying like birds. Novelist Stephen Crane and Army doctor Walter Reed (who had sought and found the cause of yellow fever) should have been uneasy men, for this was to be their last year on earth.

The arrival of 1900 and the twentieth century was greeted with high hopes. Sticklers like Life's Father Time thought the celebration should begin New Year's Eve, 1901.

Father Time: NO YOU ARE JUST ONE YEAR TOO PREVIOUS.

Warren Gamaliel Harding and Calvin Coolidge, in their thirties, leading average lives, had no possible conception of what glory the future held for them. In New York, struggling writer Theodore Dreiser would see his first novel published during the coming year. It was *Sister Carrie,* and the gloomy Dreiser feared that few would take time to read it. In this he was absolutely correct. But when republished some years later, the book was a success.

Even the sternest of parents—and it was the fashion to be stern in 1900—allowed children to stay up as late as 1:00 A.M. to greet the New Year. Churches held midnight services, and from Rome Pope Leo XIII told Roman Catholics the world over that a midnight Mass was permissible on this exceptional Sunday night. In New York, the chateau-like mansions on Fifth Avenue were brightly lighted and the sound of muted music told of gay dancing parties within. In Boston, Chicago, San Francisco, New Orleans, and other cities, the holiday pattern was the same. The rich danced and toasted in champagne, while others celebrated as well as their pocketbooks permitted. According to newspaper accounts the next day, the mood of cross-country crowds was jolly, with fish-horns (whatever were they?), megaphones, pea whistles, and baby rattles (what has become of them?) contributing to the jollity.

Not everyone celebrated, though, for a few spoilsports held rigidly to the belief that this was not a turn of the century at all. Insisting that it was only the terminal

As much as any one man, Thomas Alva Edison transformed America, bringing it into a new era with his multitude of inventions. Here he stands with early phonograph.

year of the 1800's, they planned to hold off until December 31, 1900, before jubilating. Few Americans paid heed to such ideas. On anybody's calendar the switch from 1899 to 1900 seemed definite enough and citizens embraced the New Year as the New Century.

If a single word can be used to describe the celebrations from coast to coast, that word is *noise.* Everywhere brass bands played, church bells tolled, glee clubs sang out-of-doors. Factory whistles that hideously cut the air at 6 A.M. to waken towns seemed strangely friendly when blasting a salute to 1900. So did the whistles of riverboats and the clang of trolley bells. Whatever its size, each community made as much noise as it could.

New York, the nation's largest city, naturally produced the most. Whistles from ferry boats, factories, and ocean liners joined with bells and chimes, while men rushed into streets to shoot rifles and revolvers into the air. "From the Battery to the Bronx the chorus grew in volume," says an account, "until New York was one big toot of joy."

For all citizens this New Year celebration had a special feeling. Americans felt themselves extremely fortunate to be Americans. The United States seemed the best place on earth to live in, and its inhabitants were both proud and glad to be there. Why, America was not only the youngest nation on earth, but also the most promising. In 1900, hopes were limitless.

There were drawbacks to life in the

12

U.S.A., but the over-all feeling at the dawn of the new century was that Americans were lucky, lucky, lucky. "The United States," pontificated *The New York Times,* "is now the envy of the world." Americans had invented the telephone, the phonograph, flickering films, the electric light, the rocking chair, the games of poker and baseball, and chewing gum. There was one telephone for every sixty-six residents of the country and long-distance calls could be made from New York to Omaha. Daily newspapers recounted the exploits of the wealthy men known as the "barefoot millionaires," so-called because of their humble farm-boy origins. They were ruthless, callous, self-made men, a new breed on earth. Europe, with its encrusted class system, offered nothing like them.

Few Americans could put the national wonders into words, but it was possible to sense them all. America was the first truly self-sustaining nation. It reaped every variety of grain, grew nearly every kind of vegetable, enjoyed almost every known meat and fish. It grew enough cotton for everyone, five times as much as the rest of the world. It produced more than half the world's corn, copper, and oil, more than a third of its steel and pig iron, a third of its gold.

The great land boasted two hundred thousand miles of railroad track, the same distance in telegraph wires. Telephone lines stretched over a million miles of the land. The same flag flew over forty-five states, and all the people of this vast land mass were governed under one Constitution and its fifteen amendments, the last added in 1869. Men (but not women) voted to elect the President of the United States. Senators, however, were chosen by state legislatures, and there was democratic grumbling over this. "Let the people elect their Senators," men said. The first direct senatorial primary was scheduled for the coming September, in Minnesota.

This lusty American scene was also the home of wooden cigar-store Indians, mustache cups, barbershop quartets, livery stables, beer parlors, washboards, and icemen with tongs. The hairpin, bicycle, and horseshoe industries thrived. The Midwest was much on the national mind, for the most colorful politicians and the best novelists seemed to hail from there. Families amused themselves with stereopticons,

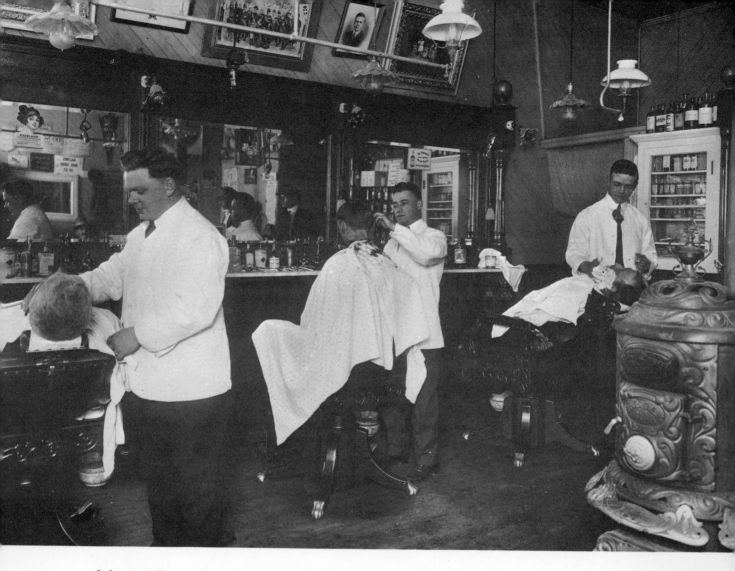

while seated in parlors decorated with wax flowers, cattails, century plants, and peacock feathers. The fad of the year was pyrography, the delicate art of burning designs into leather cushions. Traffic outside city windows went clip-clop. Only the rich had electric lights.

It was a friendly time, with much "dropping in" among neighbors, some of it of a ritual nature. When a girl married, friends and neighbors waited a discreet interval, then paid her a call. She returned the courtesy, accompanied by her mother.

Churchgoers visited newcomers in a parish as soon as they arrived. When anyone died, neighbors called on the bereaved family, bearing some small but nourishing gift as a token of sympathy. Favored for this was a jar of calf's-foot jelly flavored with wine. Or a light cake or meringue.

On New Year's Day, well-to-do wives stayed home to receive callers, while their husbands journeyed from house to house paying respects. In every house that could afford it stood a great bowl of creamy eggnog, surrounded by platters of ham and turkey, a heaping dish of scalloped oysters, a massive cheese, a proud plum pudding.

Winter vacations were unthought of. Summer was the only time for a holiday. For those unable to afford a vacation in the summertime, there were picnic grounds at the end of trolley lines. These were set up by the trolley companies themselves, to encourage business.

It was a world free of gasoline fumes, income tax, TV, radio, advertising agencies. There were no sports pages, no parcel post. Sugar cost 4¢ a pound, eggs 14¢ a dozen, potatoes 45¢ a bushel, butter 24¢ a pound. In cities a fine turkey dinner cost 20¢ and a hotel room $1 a day. Stenographers got $10 a week, salesgirls $5 to $7.50, sweatshop girls $2.50. Everyone over the age of thirty-five had been living during the Civil War, and the forty thousand veterans of the Grand Army of the Republic constituted a potent political lobby. William Jennings Bryan was the outstanding figure in the Democratic party, certain to run against McKinley in the fall. Who would be his vice-presidential running mate? Possibly it would be (it was) Adlai Ewing Stevenson of Illinois, who had been Vice President in the second Cleveland administration.

The country was big and getting bigger!

New York's Flatiron Building (opposite), a wonder in 1904, still stands, but original Madison Square Garden (right) has disappeared, as have marvellously ornate buildings of St. Louis Exposition.

14

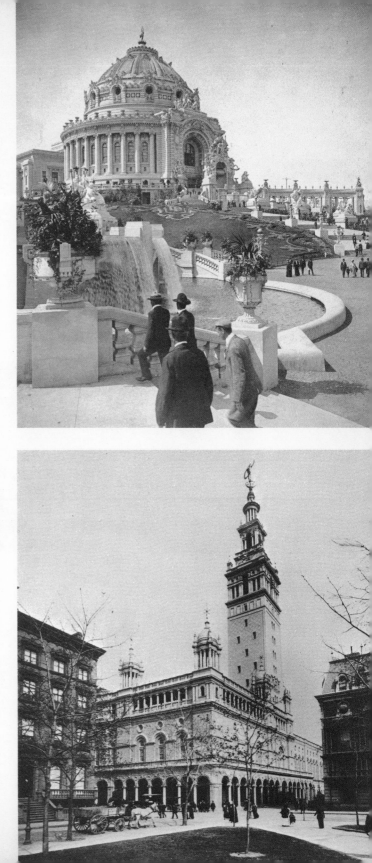

bouts, tallyhos, and other horsedrawn vehicles. There were only 13,824 autos in the land, most of them toys of the idle rich. The average American stuck by his bicycle, and during the coming twelve months one in seventy would buy a new one. But people were slowly getting the idea that the funny horseless carriage might be here to stay. The Fifth Avenue Coach Company had just added an electric Autostage. It sat eight inside, four out, and the fare was 5¢. As for airplanes, they existed only in the minds of dreamers like Samuel P. Langley and the Wright boys. Levelheaded men rejected the idea of flying as "loony."

If progress in electricity and the gasoline motor seemed temporarily slow, advances in a different field had been massive. This was the growth of the big-money monopolies, or trusts. An example was Standard Oil, whose profits for the first quarter of 1900 amounted to $17,000,000. Giant trusts hung over American life like a deadening pall. The monopolistic combines wiped out competition, stifled individual enterprise, and roped in profits staggering to the mind. They defied the Government, dictated prices, mocked the public, scorned society and pressed the national economic life into a tight, hopeless mold.

Americans resented and feared the trusts. But they had an ambivalent attitude toward the robber barons who created them. This was the Land of Opportunity, and perhaps the man who had the ability to rise above his fellow man also had the right to exploit him. When railroad builder

Yet only the Eastern seaboard had been visibly changed by the hand of man. Most of the country was still frontier territory. No one had thought of drilling for oil in Texas—in fact, few thought of Texas. Pennsylvania and Ohio were dotted by oil derricks, with Oil City, Pennsylvania, the hub of the industry. West of the Mississippi the one-street frontier town was just broadening out to become two streets, or maybe three. On the West Coast, Los Angeles proclaimed a population of one hundred two thousand.

The Sears Roebuck catalogue for 1900 carried nothing for cars, though it had sixty-seven pages crammed with harness, saddles, horse blankets, and gleaming accessories for broughams, phaetons, runa-

Fancy bonnet, lace collar, and high-button shoes were for dress-up in 1904. Flagwaver is in everyday wear of 1904. Placid Palisades picnic has 1910 Manhattan in background, across Hudson.

Collis Huntington died in 1900, he was hailed as the man who had shortened the time it took to cross the continent from six weeks to six days. Few gave a thought to the disparity between Huntington's towering wealth and the bare subsistence wages of those who had laid the track.

Medicine in 1900 was far from being a sophisticated science. People still died young; the average life span for men was forty-nine years, women fifty-one. Insulin was unknown for diabetes; there was no vaccination for typhus. Without miracle drugs, pneumonia and diphtheria were very often fatal. Cholera and small pox were common, and children died of scarlet fever. The mortality rate of babies under the age of two was high.

There was an Atlantic cable, but no wireless. (Marconi would send his first transatlantic message in 1901.) America felt isolated, but it was not altogether unaware of the rest of the world. On January 2, 1900, newspapers reported that Kaiser Wilhelm II of Germany had delivered a speech on New Year's Day promising to build up the German navy. Ranted the bellicose Kaiser: "I hope to be enabled, with a firm trust in the guidance of God, to prove the truth of the saying, *When one in this world wants to decide something with the pen, he does not do it unless supported by the strength of the sword.*"

Another portent was found in the Washington (Pennsylvania) *Reporter:* "A meeting is called for Tuesday evening, January 2, 1900, at 7:30, at the First Presbyterian Church, to consider the question of the organization of the Anti-Saloon League."

But such things hardly seemed to matter. "Nothing is too good for the American people," said a Budweiser beer ad. Americans were creating a better world. People of many nations were melding together to create a single nation of tremendous potential. Of America's population of seventy-six million only forty-one million were native born. Every nationality on the globe was represented in the great American melting pot. Immigrants still poured through Ellis Island at a rate of more than half a million a year. Their arrival was encouraged, even advertised for, by agents of the United States Government who traveled Europe describing a land of milk and honey. Steerage rates from Genoa were $12 to $20.

With such impetus the country had become a world power. It helped Cuba to establish itself as a nation, annexed the Philippines, Guam, and Puerto Rico. It had a standing army of sixty-five thousand and four first-class battleships. The national climate was changing. People were beginning to drop the handmade for the machine-made. Young people were departing the farm for the factory, while talk around cracker barrels no longer concerned the Civil War and its aftermath, but the strange new economic conditions. In colleges, educational emphasis was shifting from the classics to the sciences.

Far more than any nation in history, America was devoting itself to the betterment of living conditions. Citizens agitated for pasteurized milk, hospitals, electricity in the home. No other country had ever given so much thought to personal well-being.

It made for a proud people. A few American heiresses, daughters of money barons and their socially ambitious wives, were marrying European noblemen, heirs to ancient titles and drafty castles. Americans watched these international spectacles with mixed fascination and fury. Who would want to return to Europe, even to live in a castle?

Running in the New York theater district —widely known as the Great White Way— was a hit play called *The Man From Home,* by Booth Tarkington and Harry Leon Wilson. A leading character was a Hoosier named Daniel Voorhees Pike, as homespun as his name. Opined Dan Pike, in the course of the play, "I would not trade the State Insane Asylum for the worst ruined ruin in Europe." Every living, breathing American agreed.

In such a mood the New Century began. Where would it lead us?

Advertising—whether for boots, lamps, or the circus—was cheerful, if low key. Breweries used color calendars. On buttons, McKinley and Roosevelt battled W. J. Bryan. Miss Phoebe Snow was pet of advertising world.

18

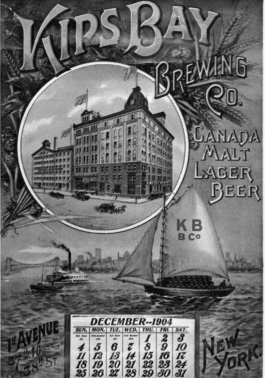

Miss Snow draws near
The cab to cheer
The level-headed
Engineer,
Whose watchful sight
Makes safe her flight
Upon the Road
of Anthracite.

Lackawanna
Railroad

A Man's World

♥ It was a man's world at the turn of the century. The man of the time was the formidable master of his house, monarch of all he surveyed from the family hearthside, respected enforcer of discipline, arbiter of dinner-table disputes. There was a solid basis for his towering importance at home. Father was the breadwinner, the only member of the family who returned home with pay in his pocket.

Moreover, a man worked hard to earn his money, for a ten-hour day was the working rule of the time. The day laborer—and the vast horde of immigrants was mostly laborers—arose at five o'clock in the morning to be at work on time with his lunch pail at seven. The factory worker was close behind and the white-collar worker just after him.

Be he bookkeeper or banker, an office worker rose at six in the morning to begin his day. Usually his first act in wintertime was to don a flannel robe and dash downstairs to the cellar to stoke a dormant furnace into morning heat. Upstairs again, he changed from nightshirt to flannel underwear. He then shaved with a straight razor and trimmed the straggle of his mustache with a pair of special shears. If he were well-to-do and believed in taking care of himself, he might devote a few precious morning minutes to a tone-up session with Dr. Bowers' Patented Neck-Stretching Machine. "Guaranteed to promote growth in the human body, dispel any diseases of eye, ear, nose and throat, and alleviate the most calamitous sickness." Dr. Bowers' machine looked as awesome as a gallows, but many men swore by it.

After this, he put on the white shirt he had worn for the past two or three days, but treated himself to a fresh, attachable celluloid collar and a pair of newly starched cuffs, also attachable. He had little difficulty deciding which suit to wear, since the average fellow owned only two, one a best, or Sunday-go-to-meetin' suit. Both were of heavy material, made for durability rather than style. One inevitably was a trusty blue serge.

Our man wore the same suits summer and winter, for there was no such thing as lightweight attire except in the Deep South. After the trousers (two pairs with each suit) and socks with garters, he put on shoes, with tops and laces or perhaps buttons. Then he knotted his necktie, or clipped a bow tie to the stiff collar.

Next came the manly ceremony of buttoning the vest. In one pocket he placed the timepiece that was a measure of his station in life. If rich, his watch was heavy gold. For the man on a lower rung of life's ladder, it was a silver Ingersoll costing $1. Through an open buttonhole of his vest he looped a heavy watch chain, anchored in an opposite pocket by a penknife or some other heavy object.

Gay blades favored gaudy bathing suits.
After a quick dip, they not only had to dry their hair,
but their ample mustaches as well.

the monarch of all he surveyed at home underwent a shrinkage at work. The average employee of the time (and even the better-than-average) stood in quaking fear of the boss. Any man could be fired at any moment, without reason or back pay. And one of the fastest ways to get bounced was to be late.

So a man arrived well before 8:00 A.M. (often the boss was the first one in) and stayed at his desk until five thirty or six. Sometimes he went out for lunch, more often he ate several of his wife's sandwiches at the desk. Only the boss always went out to lunch, carefully taking just an hour. A man worked six long days a week and felt fortunate to do so. His father had worked two Sundays a month as well.

At workday's end, he wended his way home, in cities by horsecar, in small towns on foot or bicycle, passing lamplighters in the dusk. At home, justifiably weary, a man was cheered by a wife and children who hovered over him, perhaps fetching his slippers or lighting his pipe.

It was a settled existence and a hopeful one. If our man was a native-stock American—a generation or more in the land— he had been nurtured on the books of Horatio Alger. "It's a fine thing, my lad, to be alive in the world today," Alger men kept telling Alger boys. It was a sentiment which had, in a way, brainwashed the American male. This was the Land of Opportunity—everyone knew that! The canny Alger capitalized on it. In his books poor boys broke up dog fights, stopped

Downstairs, he joined wife and offspring at the kitchen table, where the morning newspaper waited at his place. On weekdays the paper cost 1¢, Sundays 5¢. While scanning the front page, he stowed away a meal that might include oatmeal, three eggs, bacon, coffee, milk, and hot buttered muffins. Sometimes he had steak and potatoes. Then he put on a derby hat (laborers and boys wore caps) and set off for work.

♥

There were few suburbs in those days. In part, this was because people felt no need to stretch out from the not-too-populous cities. An equally important reason was that a man who had to be at work on time could not afford the hazards of what a later world called commuting. For

runaway horses, or returned lost wallets. Inevitably the dogs, horses, and wallets were owned by millionaires, and the boys were rewarded in a manner which raised them from "rags to riches."

So the American working man, earning his average $12 a week, did his long day's work feeling that one day the boss might come along and say, "You are a good man, Smith, the only one quick enough to catch that dangerous discrepancy in the books. I plan to retire soon and you will be the new president of the firm."

In the public eye were the "barefoot millionaires," who seemed to have risen almost as miraculously as any Alger hero. They hadn't, of course, but newspapers of the time treated them so tenderly that no one would doubt it. For example, few who admired multimillionaire Russell Sage knew he was so stingy that he refused to wear underwear. It was generally known, however, that Andrew Carnegie started out as a bobbin boy in a cotton factory at $1.20 a week, and John D. Rockefeller as a bookkeeper at $25 a month. Both these men had garnered untold millions. Why, Andy Carnegie was in the process of selling his Carnegie Steel Company to J. P. Morgan, a transaction which would bring the canny Scot $250,000,000.

It put a feeling of euphoria in the air. With a little luck a man might do as well as Carnegie!

Men's wear had boxy lines and full cut, but suits sold for as little as $15, coats for $35. Cigar bands, now an all-but-forgotten art, portrayed kings, poets, actresses.

22

♥ The existence of the male of the early 1900's seems as dull as the celluloid collar he wore. He had no TV, no car, no golf.

But he did have a pin-up girl. She was the Gibson Girl, who appeared nearly every week in the center fold of the humor magazine *Life*. Both male and female purchasers of the popular ten-cent magazine quickly turned to this center fold for, in addition to the beauty of the Gibson Girl, the drawing usually pictured the rugged handsomeness of the Gibson Man. There also would be a twist of deft satire on the American scene.

Most of all, however, it was the Gibson Girl, with her pompadour, wasp waist, and aloof beauty, who pulled readers. She was the undisputed goddess of a sentimental generation. Girls tried to dress like the Gibson Girl and to look like her. Males, feasting their eyes on her, imagined the Gibson Girl dropping a dainty handkerchief, her glance fleeting and tender.

The creator of the Gibson Girl was tall, hard-working Charles Dana Gibson, one of a small group of highly popular contemporary artists. The others were Frederic Remington, painter of cowboys and Indians; Maxfield Parrish, creator of high-indigo fantasy; Howard Pyle, specialist in American history; and Jessie Willcox Smith, with her sleeping, dreaming children.

Of all these, Gibson was the tops. He was at his best in sharp black and white, and could express more with a single line than any other artist of the time. His sketches appeared in both magazines and books. Before he was thirty-five, nine volumes of his drawings had been published. Gibson Girls and Gibson Men were to be found on burnt-leather cushions, plates, hardwood easels, and woven handkerchiefs. Gibson's eye was sharp and observant, and his style had bite. He lampooned social climbers, Americans abroad, and other aspects of contemporary life. Even in a drawing with only two characters, he seemed able to tell a full, satisfying story.

The fortunate Gibson was one of those rare artists who satisfied both critics and masses. His drawings appeared to pull a diffused nation into focus and to bring people a feeling of style and identity. This was especially true of the Gibson Girl, of whom the New York *World* rhapsodized: "Before Gibson synthesized his ideal woman the American girl was vague, nondescript, inchoate. There was no type of her to whom one could point and say, *That is the typical American girl.* As soon as the world saw Gibson's ideal it bowed down in admiration, saying, *Lo, at last, the typical American Girl!*"

American females of all shapes and sizes tried to ape the Gibson Girl. Artist Joseph Pennell, after a stroll, exclaimed, "Fifth Avenue is like a procession of Gibsons." Yet Gibson's effect on the American male

Every girl aspired to be a Gibson Girl. Artist Charles Dana Gibson's "Design for Wallpaper" offered several examples of how it could be done. Proud pompadour was an essential ingredient.

was no less remarkable. The Gibson Man was physically patterned on Gibson himself, with overtones of Richard Harding Davis, the romantic war correspondent, author, playwright, and man about the world. Strong-jawed and straightforward, the Gibson Man was resolutely clean shaven. Until he arrived, American males had prided themselves on lush beards and mustaches. After a few years of the Gibson Man, the facial foliage had all but vanished. Then, in an effort to duplicate the Gibson Man's broad shoulders, tailors began padding their suits.

The work of Charles Dana Gibson today provokes instant nostalgia. Just the sight of that handsome pair—the Gibson Girl and the Gibson Man—swirls us instantly back to the sweet Naughty-Naughts.

26

Gibson (above) modeled the Man partly on himself. His drawings used black and white to full effect and told charmingly romantic stories, such as "The Greatest Game in the World—His Move."

There were postcards
for every occasion. Messages
got right to
the point, illustrations
favored scenes
of wholesome jollity.

A Woman's Place

♥ It was a man's world, but women lived there! Woman's place was definitely in the home. She was neither allowed to vote nor expected to have political opinions. Only in the arts could she aspire (and sometimes reach) the heady world of earning power and freedom.

A few top actresses in the theater, a few lady novelists, a few full-bosomed divas in opera, a few beautiful girls on the musical-comedy stage—all achieved success by fighting enormous pressure from families, friends, ministers, the entire world. On all sides a girl was told that a respectable young woman must not try to earn a living or make a career for herself. Her mission on earth was to find a husband, obey him, and make him happy. Then she must replenish the human race with as many children as possible.

The well-brought-up young lady learned to play the piano, to cook, and to sew. She read polite novels and love poetry and played croquet. But for the most part she merely waited for a suitor to ask papa for her hand in marriage. Then life—as the world saw it—began.

After marriage, she had a house to take care of. If her parents were well-to-do, she received as a wedding gift a living room set of plush sofa and matching easy chairs. Or a bedroom or dining room set of golden oak. On the living room walls she hung framed pictures of landscapes and laughing cherubs. If she had a modern house with running water the sink would be waist-high, but in an older one it was lower, a hangover from pipeless days when jugs of hot water had to be lifted from stove to sink. In the city she might have a bathroom, elsewhere a privy.

As the woman in charge of her own home, she quickly learned the not-so-gay traditions remaining from the Nineties. She was expected to rise before 6:00 A.M., ahead of her husband, to prepare breakfast for him and the children. With her husband at work and the kids in school, she began shining the stove and performing countless other rituals involved in an endless round of housework. In the afternoon, she took an hour for a restful nap, then began to prepare dinner, after which she and a daughter washed the dishes.

She was a woman whose hair had not been cut since childhood (if then); she took out hairpins before going to bed and brushed her hair one hundred times, watching herself in a cheval glass. She rubbed a mixture of Vaseline and cucumber into her skin to give it tone. With no skin creams on the market, this was the latest fad.

Aside from domestic satisfactions, there were few thrills in a woman's life. Not even clothes provided much fun. When dressed up, milady wore four or five layers of clothing, all clumsy and tight. One item— the worst—was a high, tight corset with

30

Housewives rose at dawn, prepared a huge family breakfast, then varied the day of never-ending housework with such duties as shoveling coal into the furnace.

*Though clothes seemed designed for decorous immobility
(top), or perhaps a genteel game of croquet, more active sports
like tennis were coming into vogue. Long dresses only
occasionally revealed a flash of ankle.*

whalebone stays. Below this was rough underwear, over it a cotton chemise and a petticoat. Her stockings were probably black or beige cotton, unless she was that one woman in two thousand who owned silk stockings. Fashion decreed that high-top shoes ($3 a pair; $1.97 at frequent sales) be a size or two small for feminine feet, with kid gloves equally punishing to hands. Around her neck a girl wore a collar called a choker. Often she wore a veil. If young and fascinated by the social whirl, her dream in the evening was to have a waist so small it could be encircled by a man's hands. This could only be done by pulling the corset breathtakingly tight.

A great—or was it awful?—moment in a growing girl's life came when her elders decreed that hereafter she should wear the long skirts of the day. From that moment on, as far as the world was concerned, a girl had no legs. One versifier wrote a poem

called "Good-by, Legs," in which a girl laments, "I shall be legless until my death." She goes on:

> *Tomorrow I'll be sweet sixteen,*
> *No more I'll be a "girl."*
> *From that time on around you, legs,*
> *Some lengthened skirts must swirl.*

If a husband had a Sunday suit, his wife had a Sunday dress. She wore it to church on Sunday, then hastily changed before vanishing into the kitchen to cook dinner. This Sunday dress (and other good ones) comprised about ten yards of heavy material like cravenetted serge or cheviot. Tailored suits of the same materials, in vogue for weekday social activity, sold in stores for $15. However, a woman usually made her own dresses from patterns in the *Ladies' Home Journal,* or had them made by a local dressmaker. Skirts of both dresses and suits reached all the way to the ground, where they stirred up dust. As seen by author Kathleen Norris, "She wore a wide-brimmed hat that caught in the breezes, a high choking collar of satin or linen, and a flaring skirt that swept the streets on all sides. In wet weather the skirt got soaked and icy. Even in fair weather its owner had to bunch it in great folds and devote one hand to nothing else but the carrying of it."

Few changes in female attire occurred during the Nineties. But suddenly a new craze—the shirtwaist—swept the country. Its main appeal lay in the number of changes of costume it allowed a girl. The shirtwaist was like a man's celluloid collar and cuffs, only far more colorful. A girl could wear different waists with the same skirt and appear to have on something new each day. Besides, shirtwaists were cheap and much lighter than serge or cheviot. As the craze swept on, a poet wrote:

> *When gentle June displays her wares,*
> *And of her beauties boasts,*
> *The contest shows beyond a doubt,*
> *The shirtwaist's worn the most.*

It was particularly popular with a new

For working women like these in shirt factory, jobs were generally monotonous and low-paid. An early breakthrough came with typing and shorthand (left), which men did not do well.

breed known as the "office girl," for whose existence the typewriter may be thanked. For some reason men had not taken to the newfangled machine, perhaps because female fingers flew faster. Up to then, few girls could get jobs in business. Instead, those who had no family to support them had to become salesgirls at $5 a week, waitresses at 5¢ a tip—or girls of the streets, where the wages of sin, for a while at least, were higher. But thanks to the typewriter, the office girl made a beachhead in the business world.

Women were not exactly aware of it at the moment, but also in the offing was a change in tight corsets and dust-catching skirts. For this the bicycle and the refined game of tennis were responsible.

With the onset of the bicycle craze, manufacturers had designed special women's bikes with nets over the rear wheel to keep skirts from catching in the spokes. But girls who couldn't afford this nicety merely shortened their skirts slightly and put steel strips in the hems to keep them down. The shorter skirts felt good, and besides men stopped to gape at feminine ankles. Girls liked that!

Meantime, a few daring misses were trying tennis. To play properly it was necessary to remove stays, corsets, and other tight garments. The pious were horrified. One writer recalls, "Ministers exhorted their congregations to eschew this ungraceful, unwomanly, and unrefined game which offended all the canons of womanly dignity and delicacy." But life was much more fun

without corsets, and word got around.

Another step was the rainy-day (or rainy-daisy) skirt, cut off at ankle length for snow and rain. Girls felt mighty strange in them at first, not to say embarrassed. It gave rise to a contemporary joke about a boy who asked his older sister:

"Priscilla, what is a centipede?"

"It's a bug, with nearly as many feet as I thought I had the first time I wore a rainy-day skirt."

"A Man May Work from Sun to Sun, But Woman's Work Is Never Done."

MONDAY
Wash Day
(Clothing and sheets put to soak the night before.)

TUESDAY
Ironing Day
(Irons heated on kitchen stove.)

WEDNESDAY
Sewing and Mending Day
(Piles of socks and stockings to be darned.)

THURSDAY
Rest Day
(Crochet, embroider, knit.)

FRIDAY
Cleaning Day
(Carpets swept by broom, kitchen floors and porches scrubbed.)

SATURDAY
Baking Day
(All bread and cakes made at home.)

SUNDAY
Preparation of Major Meal of Week
(Relatives or company usually invited.)

*Whether riding a bicycle into
the country on weekends, a highly
popular pastime, or dressing to impress, women
were swathed in yards of material.*

♥ Although most American women labored hard at home, there were some who never had to lift a finger. These were the ladies of wealth, with husbands or fathers rich enough to employ servants. In this era, such women could live a long life without ever brewing a cup of tea. And why should they, when housemaids cost $3.50 a week, and cooks, ladies' maids, butlers, and footmen only slightly more. "Ladies were ladies," writes Mrs. Gwen Ravarat in her charming reminiscence of childhood in this storied era. "They did not do things themselves, they told other people what to do and how to do it."

By far the most conspicuous such women were those who comprised society with a capital S. They lived flamboyantly, giving sumptuous balls and dinner parties at which the ample bosoms of dowagers gleamed with priceless jewels. The few ladies who made a lifetime career of being social leaders deemed it hard work. Declared Mrs. Oliver Hazard Perry Belmont, "I know of no other profession, art, or trade that women are working in today as taxing on mental resources as being a leader of society."

It was a period when the poor were poorer and the rich were stupendously wealthy. The fabulous antics of high society were something of an opiate to the masses. Newspapers gave social events front-page treatment. Like peasants peering up at royalty, American housewives forgot their worries by gorging on the reported details of Mrs. Astor's glittering dinner parties, or the wedding of an American heiress to a titled European. Guest lists and menus were printed in full. Articles concluded with an estimate of the cost of the dinner, which usually took place in some gilded spot like the Waldorf-Astoria, Delmonico's, or Sherry's in New York. There was also much malicious gossip of social intrigue to be heard, for a magazine called *Town Topics* printed indiscreet items, engaging in lucrative blackmail on the side. The public was fascinated, awed, and sometimes infuriated by it all.

Undisputed social leader of the era was Mrs. William Backhouse Astor, née Caroline Schermerhorn. Tall and commanding, she appeared at social functions "borne down by a terrible weight of precious stones." Mrs. Astor's husband was totally uninterested in society and took no part in that side of her life. However, the stresses and strains of social leadership put her in need of a co-conspirator, friend, and major domo, all rolled up in one. For this she picked a prissy fellow named Ward McAllister. It was Ward who first called New York society "the Four Hundred." Requested by a newspaperman to estimate the number of society's blue bloods, McAllister replied that Mrs. Astor's ballroom held four hundred people and that only

Being a leader of society was a taxing role. Mrs. George Gould never ranked with Mrs. Astor, but she obviously had the necessary vivacity and charm, as well as the wardrobe.

38

those invited to her annual balls could be considered high society. From then on the phrase Four Hundred was established.

Ward McAllister stood at Mrs. Astor's elbow through several sharp challenges to her jeweled eminence. One came from the Vanderbilt family, which blasted its way into the Four Hundred by building fabulous Fifth Avenue mansions. The first of these, on the corner of Fifty-second Street, cost $3,000,000 and duplicated a French chateau of the fifteenth century. At first Mrs. Astor was determined not to attend the fancy dress ball that unveiled this new Vanderbilt domain. Yet, like the rest of the world, she was dying to view the interior. So she went to the ball and from then on the Vanderbilts were in.

Mrs. Astor next engaged in bitter strug-gle with her nephew William Waldorf Astor. He wanted his wife to be *the* Mrs. Astor. The two families lived in adjoining Fifth Avenue mansions, between Thirty-third and Thirty-fourth Streets. Willie Waldorf lost out, but spitefully got even by selling his mansion to make way for a hotel to be called the Waldorf. This forced Mrs. Astor to sell hers for a hotel named the Astoria. The two were joined together, and the rest is hotel history.

In New York, Boston, Chicago, San Francisco, and such out-of-city enclaves as Newport and Tuxedo Park, society rose to Neronian heights. While ordinary folk struggled, the wealthy capered.

The pattern for the capering was set by the Bradley Martin ball of 1896. This was conceived by Mrs. Bradley Martin when

Mansions of the rich had the magnificence of European palaces. From left: The Crocker mansion in San Francisco; Vanderbilt house on New York's Fifth Avenue. Interiors were as sumptuous as taste allowed.

she learned that the world around her was going through a bad financial depression. She immediately decided to help the national economy by giving a ball. The money spent, she fondly believed, would trickle down to the masses and perhaps end the depression; it was a fancy edition of the old make-work fallacy of economics. Proudly, Mrs. Bradley Martin announced plans to spend $250,000 for the pleasure of twelve hundred socialites costumed to simulate a ball at Versailles in the reign of Louis XV. Newspapers and ministers railed at her, but she gamely carried on.

The mood of New Yorkers was ugly on the night of the ball, and it was feared that an anarchist might toss a bomb. City police mingled with crowds outside, while Pinkerton detectives screened arrivals. In-

side the Waldorf, Mrs. Martin, seated on a throne, received her guests. She seemed only slightly disconcerted when one guest appeared at her Versailles in a suit of armor and a couple came as Pocahontas and an Indian chief. Guests danced until 6:30 A.M. and consumed sixty-one cases of champagne, to make what newspapers called "a delirium of wealth and an idyll of luxury and magnificence." But criticism of the Bradley Martins continued and they huffily departed to dwell in England.

Extravagance continued. In Boston, Mrs. Jack Gardner built a fifty-five-room Venetian palazzo. She threw her first party in the dead of winter, and astounded guests found themselves in an indoor tropical paradise echoing with nightingale song. The same Mrs. Gardner burned all her ball dresses at the end of each social season.

In San Francisco, horse-lover Francis J. Carolan gave a stable party at which guests dressed in equestrian fashion. Newport, Rhode Island, saw the first American auto race, with gentlemen driving imported runabouts over a grassy course. In Saratoga, E. Berry Wall, King of the Dudes, appeared in forty different costumes in the course of a single day.

Ward McAllister died, and Mrs. Astor dredged up Harry Lehr, blond, pudgy, imaginative, effeminate. "I make a career of being popular," this one confessed modestly. Under him high society achieved new extravagance and insensitivity to the people. Mrs. Astor, now in her seventies, appeared somewhat mummified in her dazzling jewels. Harry Lehr coolly abandoned her to become the pampered darling of her rival, Mrs. Stuyvesant Fish. Brash, restless, ever-bored, Mrs. Fish delighted in being rude and once greeted a roomful of guests by saying, "Well, here you all are, older faces and younger clothes." Mrs. Fish, like Lehr, believed people "want to be entertained, to be made to laugh—they will overlook almost anything as long as you amuse them." Lehr and his lady gave dinner parties at which people dressed as dolls and conversed in baby talk. At one, the much-touted guest of honor turned out to be a monkey. At another, white mice were pinned as favors on screaming ladies. Sometimes a musical-comedy chorus entertained after dinner, and once it was a

William Balfour Ker's drawing, "From the Depths," showed poor rising up against ostentatious and extravagant social life of the wealthy, caused a sensation in 1904.

circus with baby elephants. But the high moment of the evening always came when Harry Lehr appeared in a gown to do his celebrated female impersonation.

Parties were only part of the era's display of wealth. Mansions were far more visible to the public eye. Led by the Vanderbilts, who took possession of Fifth Avenue from Fifty-second to Fifty-ninth Streets, the rich built replicas of royal French palaces, or imported them brick by brick. Homes that cost millions to build cost other millions to furnish. Architects combed Europe for art treasures, furniture, and tapestries worthy of their clients. Millionaires bought art masterpieces like postcards, with sugar baron Henry O. Havemeyer hanging seven Rembrandts in a single room. On upper Fifth Avenue, Henry Clay Frick, associate

42

of steel magnate Andrew Carnegie, built a mansion for himself and his art collection. (It is one of the few still standing.) Ownership of art brought out a poetic streak in Frick. Scanning the financial page once, he said, "Railroads are the Rembrandts of investment."

Those who lived in Fifth Avenue mansions rode in private railroad cars, sailed the ocean in handsome steam yachts. J. P. Morgan owned the mighty yacht *Corsair*, and it was a distinction to be invited aboard. "You can do business with anybody," Morgan believed, "but you can only sail with gentlemen." Morgan also gave the final word on yachts. Queried by a *nouveau* millionaire about the matter of yacht cost and upkeep, J. P. gave the classic reply, "If you have to think what it costs to maintain a yacht, you can't afford one."

The wild extravagance rampaged on. In the midst of an investigation of the high profits of insurance companies, elegant young James Hazen Hyde, who had just inherited a top post in one of them, gave a ball at Sherry's. The great architect Stanford White transformed the ballroom into a replica of the Hall of Mirrors at Versailles, with rose petals on the floor and thousands of orchids adorning walls. The tragedienne Gabrielle Rejane was imported from France to render a few lines from Racine. One of the young extra men at the ball was a Harvard student named Franklin Delano Roosevelt. The ball cost $200,-000, and Hyde's arrogance drove the city into conniptions. Like the Bradley Martins

he had to leave the country.

Society-watching had a field day whenever an American heiress married a titled foreigner. The nation agonized with seventeen-year-old Consuelo Vanderbilt, who so obviously did not wish to marry the middle-aged Duke of Marlborough. Yet mother knew best and the girl droopingly went through the ceremony, to commence a notably unhappy marriage. Newspaper readers were equally fascinated as financier Jay Gould pushed his daughter Anna into the arms of Boni de Castellane, a French count. When Fay Goelet married the Duke of Roxburghe in 1904, a newspaper snapped that a Duchess was being "manufactured." But wide disapproval failed to prevent a wild mob from attending the Goelet wedding, which was described in the New York *Press*:

> The ceremony was simplicity itself, but the scene without and within the church where the wedding took place was one of the most amazing ever witnessed in the city of New York. Thousands of women, impelled by curiosity and forgetful of gentleness or of ordinary delicacy, pushed, hauled, surged, and fought to get into the church; to get close to the carriage of the frightened bride; to carry off souvenirs; to touch the bridal robes; and to do a hundred and one other things, creating such an uproar and confusion that a platoon of police, armed with nightsticks, was actually compelled to charge upon them, and, in many instances, to use force . . . They fought, scratched, and screeched like a parcel of wildcats disputing a quarry.

43

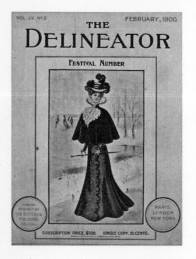

44

*Serene face, hourglass figure, and
elaborate plumage of the turn-of-the-century
woman were celebrated in important
magazines and early ads.*

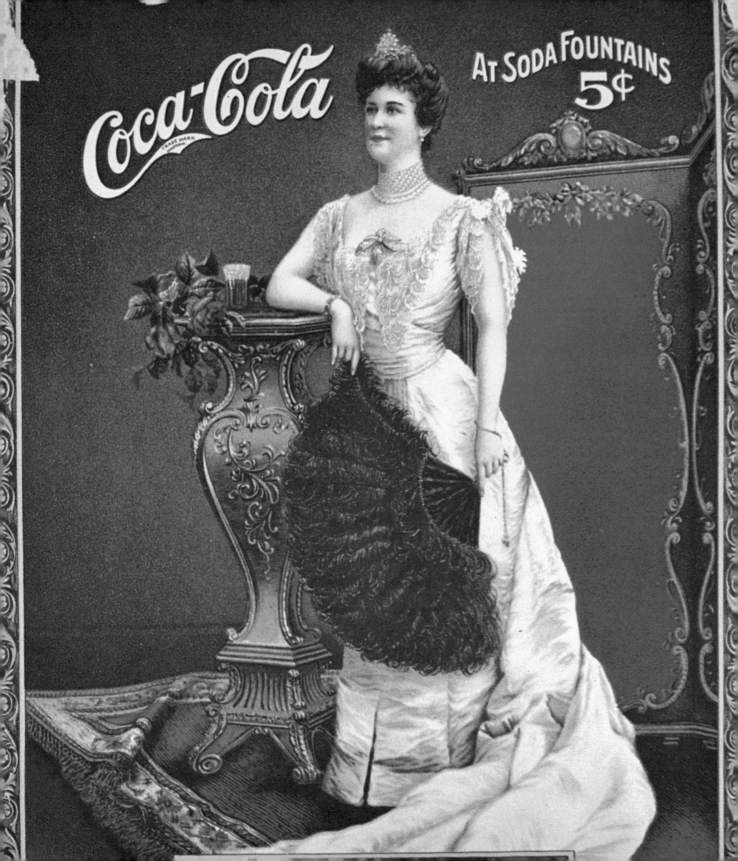

The Roar of the Crowd

♥ In those halcyon days, baseball and football were just beginning to assume the forms familiar to us today. Until then, football had been a static, unimaginative game. Brawn, not brains, counted. Football employed few end runs, fewer forward passes. Instead, hefty players plunged endlessly through the center of the opposing line. Result: A game of constant, mountainous pile-ups, with players shoving, pushing, pulling, grunting. Yardage gains were small; only five yards were needed for a first down.

Football was a sport played almost exclusively by Ivy League teams of the East. Dominant among them were Harvard, Yale, and Princeton, known far and wide as the Big Three. Ivy League colleges supposedly educated wellborn young men to be gentlemen in the finest sense of the word. Yet football was in grave danger of being outlawed because the fine young sportsmen played too roughly. In the twenty-two man pile-ups, there took place much hidden slugging, kneeing, gouging, and foul play for which the apt contemporary word was muckerism.

In 1905 alone, eighteen young football players were killed, an incredible number considering how few teams played the game. One hundred and fifty more boys were seriously injured. Such an uproar arose from the public that President Theodore Roosevelt—ever the advocate of clean, strenuous sport—called the Big Three coaches to the White House. Banging fist on table, Teddy roared that football must adopt more humane rules, give more authority to referees, place more reliance on an open, less dangerous game which used the forward pass. The chastened coaches retired to chart the game we know.

Baseball, too, was having headaches. But first let's take a moment to look at the mellow side of old-time baseball. It was the national pastime. Practically every male in the country played, or had played, the game. Nearly every town had its local ball club. So did factories, banks, social clubs, hiking and beer-guzzling societies. Baseball was truly the game of the people, with families spending picnic afternoons at the local diamond. "Take Me Out to the Ball Game" was more than a song title. It was the cross-country urge.

But this, of course, was amateur or semi-pro ball. In professional baseball you found headaches similar to football's. Pro ball had only one major league, the National. As played in this National League, baseball was rough and ugly. The man held responsible for most of this ugliness was a member of the top-ranking Baltimore Orioles named John McGraw. This is hard to believe, because McGraw stands hallowed in baseball history as the manager of the New York Giants in their later, pennant-winning prime.

Peering from mask is Umpire Jack Sheridan of newly founded American League. Heavyweight Jim Jeffries retired undefeated in 1905. Football, before forward pass was invented, was bone-crunching melee.

46

But the record spells it out. John Mc-Graw was one of the meanest players ever to aim a flying spike. Not only was he vicious, but his personality curdled the entire sport. Short, articulate, cocky, Mc-Graw seemed able to fast-talk himself out of all punishment for dirty playing. It embittered other players, pulled the whole league down.

Came 1900, and Byron Bancroft "Ban" Johnson, a onetime West Coast sports-writer, announced plans for an American League. "Clean baseball and plenty of 25¢ seats," he promised. One thing which gave a black eye to baseball was the raw ob-scenities the players yelled at one another. Johnson dealt with this when he said, "I want to see more ladies at ball games and I don't want them to hear things at ball parks they don't hear at home."

The National League rose in fury at the idea of a well-scrubbed rival. But Ban Johnson was wily and pugnacious. He fought in court for his American League. He almost lost once, then crashed through. At this the fun began. In those days, ball-players got salaries ranging from $1,000 to $5,000 a year. A few bucks made a big difference and the American League began offering raises of $50 a year. Napoleon Lajoie, called the Adonis of the game, was the first to jump leagues. Others followed, among them manager Connie Mack, who took his full Philadelphia team with him. Even John McGraw played briefly in the American League before joining the New York Nationals, or Giants, as manager.

Baseball cards often came in cigarette packages in first decade of century. They had a primitive, hand-tinted look, but memorialized a fabulous array of great players.

Ban Johnson's improved American League did not immediately succeed in eradicating baseball's image as an ugly sport. The man who really performed the trick of making the national pastime re-spectable was a player. His name was Christy Mathewson and he was as clean-cut as a Gibson man. He pitched for the Giants and was, oddly enough, a close friend of the terrible-tempered McGraw.

Matty was a gentleman. He was a Buck-nell graduate and stood practically alone as a college man in baseball. Out of many job opportunities, he had picked baseball as a career. People just couldn't believe it. Christy had promised his mother never to play ball on Sunday, and never did. He brought respectability to the game, and ladies as well. "Let's go out to the Polo Grounds and watch the young collegian play," pompadoured girls whispered to doting dates. It was another way of saying, "Take Me Out to the Ball Game."

Who were other top players in Christy's beginning years? Well, you had the hand-some slugger Nap Lajoie, Cy Young, Honus Wagner, young Ty Cobb, Mordecai "Three Finger" Brown, and fabled Iron Man Joe McGinnity, the Giant underhander who could pitch both games of a doubleheader. The Chicago Cubs won pennants because of the super-infield of Tinker, Evers, and Chance, a trio peerless at double plays. Off the diamond these three young men—the oldest was twenty-two—didn't have much use for one another. But on the diamond they functioned like triplets.

49

If Christy Mathewson brought class to baseball, the World Series brought new thrills to the game. The initial Series was played in 1903, between the Boston Americans, known as the Pilgrims or Puritans, and the Pittsburgh Nationals, called the Pirates because one of their player deals had been branded "a damned act of piracy."

Today this Series would look weird. For one thing, the fans cheered strikeouts louder than home runs. Still, there was much excitement, with spitballs, knuckle balls, and flying spikes. Five out of nine

games won the Series. Pirate pitcher Deacon Phillippe successfully pitched three of the first four games, but after the third victory so many fans shook his hand that it swelled up and ended him for the Series. Boston then took the next four games to win. In the 1905 Series, Christy Mathewson was king. "Big Six" pitched three shutouts (and Joe McGinnity a fourth) as the Giants defeated Connie Mack's Philadelphia Athletics.

It was a particularly memorable era in boxing. The heavyweight titans were at it toe-to-toe. In 1899, James J. Jeffries,

Auto racing was the most exciting spectator sport of the times. Vanderbilt Cup races on Long Island provided most thrills, but had to be abandoned because of unruly crowds.

a San Francisco boy, knocked out gangling, thirty-seven-year-old champion "Fighting Bob" Fitzsimmons.

Jeffries was a champ who liked to fight. Over the next four years he beat Fitzsimmons again, ex-champion "Gentleman Jim" Corbett twice, Tom Sharkey once, Jack Munroe once. By 1904, he had defeated everyone, with no new contenders in sight. So in 1905 Jeffries retired, after bestowing the heavyweight title on Marvin Hart, a champion so dull that the world has almost forgotten him. In retirement, Jeffries ate himself to a massive three hundred and twenty-seven pounds.

Auto racing was a new sport—and never again, really, has it been so colorful.

Racing in cars came to public attention in 1904, when William K. Vanderbilt, Jr., offered a splendid gold cup to the winner of a race of nearly three hundred miles over Long Island roads. Vanderbilt was a sportsman in the best tradition. With money to burn, he craved excitement. In these early days of the auto, he was also in a position to declare that the real purpose of his Vanderbilt Cup was to stimulate scientific development of the automobile.

For his track, Vanderbilt chose mid-island roads like Jericho Turnpike, near (but not through) the aristocratic estates owned by his friends and himself. A stern warning was issued to people who lived along these roads: "Children unattended should be kept off, chain your dogs and lock up your fowl." The natives bristled with fury, threatening to greet the racers with pitchforks and barricades. Then it became apparent that racing enthusiasts were willing to pay $5 merely to sit on porches as the cars pounded by. They would also pay $1 for a sandwich and 25¢ for coffee. Opposition faded.

Some thirty thousand people turned out at dawn on October 8, 1904. Most of them had no idea what an auto race was like. Watchers went wild as the cars roared by, engines banging and shooting sparks, be-goggled drivers crouching like demons. There had been nothing like it since the chariot races of Nero's time, a reporter wrote.

There were five Mercedes' in the race, together with other foreign makes. American contenders drove stripped-down touring cars. Two drivers were killed. Others crashed or skidded into trees. Winner was a ninety-horsepower Panhard driven by America's George Heath, who covered the 284.4 miles in six hours, fifty-six seconds. As the second car crossed the finish line, the crowd surged into the road and the race had to be called off.

For the second Vanderbilt Cup Race in 1905, a crowd estimated at one hundred thousand turned out. Again it was unruly, with people standing on the course itself until scattered by cries of "Car coming!"

American hopes were pinned on a Bridgeport-built Locomobile, driven by Joe Tracy. A French Darracq won, with a Panhard second. Joe Tracy finished third, but few complained. There had been just too much excitement.

Earthquake and fire devastated San Francisco in 1906. Troops sent to aid stricken city pause for chow at campsite in front of ruined Hall of Justice on Kearny Street.

1900 1905
♥
1905 1910
1910 1915
1915 1920
1920 1925
1925 1930
1930 1935
1935 1942

Three Weeks

♥ From the vantage point of our own time, the differences between the years 1900 and 1905 seem small indeed. Women's attire, for one thing, looks much the same. Despite bicycling, tennis, and rainy-daisy styles, skirts still fell to the ankle or below. "The proper skirt length is just showing the tip of the shoe," fashion decreed.

But if women failed to take it off at the bottom, they put it on at the top. Pompadours were higher, with mountains of hair held in shape by an army of hidden hairpins. Often a hat was perched atop the pompadour, held in precarious place by a battery of hatpins. On the hat itself might be feathers or even stuffed birds. With such a hat finally anchored on her head, a lady was understandably reluctant to take it off. This made things hard on the nation's theatergoers in the days before movies, radio, and TV. "Madame, would you mind removing your hat," was a plaintive cliché of the day.

Men's clothes continued drab, with only a few of the rich daring to sport striped shirts, multihued vests, or bright cravats. To the average man colored shirts, two-tone shoes, and snap-brim hats were delights of the future. Photos of sporting events showed unrelieved masses of derbies in winter and straw hats in summer. Few, if any, American males were bold enough to appear hatless out-of-doors. It just wasn't done.

No, the 1905 world seemed much like the world of 1900.

But look closer. Actually, there's a tantalizing change taking place. True, it's in the American mind rather than in the American appearance. But in the five years following the turn of the century, the nation has set foot on the road leading from the Age of Sentiment to the Age of Sophistication. Some even thought it the road to Sin. Stormed Carry Nation, determined hatchet swinger and despoiler of corner saloons, "The times are lewd, besotted, and licentious!" The righteous—many of them still around—agreed with her.

No matter how you looked at it, a change was beginning in the American mentality. People were less naïve, more aware of the peculiar depths in human nature, less prone to accept surface judgments. There was a growing understanding of human foibles, the nature of folly.

Yes, a little fresh air was seeping into American life. Darwin's theory of evolution had already caused many people to question the old fundamentalist views of religion. And now there was a sudden vogue for poet Edward Fitzgerald's translation of the *Rubaiyat of Omar Khayyam*, which bespoke a rich Oriental philosophy.

The foreign playwrights Henrik Ibsen and George Bernard Shaw also caused a stir. Ibsen, especially, wrote shocking plays and for this got his American reward by being called "the nasty Norwegian." His plays probed beneath the surface of characters, exposing tormented types driven by desperation into unconventional acts. Ibsen even dared write dramas with unhappy endings. When Minnie Maddern Fiske, as Nora, slammed the final door in *A Doll's House,* the first American audiences remained seated, despite a furious blinking of house lights. They were simply awaiting Nora's repentant return to provide the traditional happy ending.

After Ibsen came Shaw. The year 1905-6 in the American theater was called "the Shaw season." No less than five plays by the red-bearded Irishman were presented on Broadway: *Caesar and Cleopatra, Man and Superman, John Bull's Other Island, Mrs. Warren's Profession,* and *Cashel Byron's Profession,* with Gentleman Jim Corbett playing the pugilist hero. The "immoral" *Mrs. Warren's Profession* was closed by police the night after it opened. But the others played on, then toured as far west as San Francisco. En route a critic saluted Shaw for his "sardonic reversal of accepted ways of thinking, his mocking impiety toward cherished traditions and reverences, his violent attacks upon familiar conventionalities."

♥

Literature, too, had drawn a bead on the Age of Sentiment. In 1907, American best sellers were *Alice-for-Short* by William De Morgan, *New Chronicles of Rebecca* by

Author Elinor Glyn was as spectacular as her best-selling novel, Three Weeks. *This spurred pleasantly shocking conjectures that book's torrid pages were autobiographical.*

Kate Douglas Wiggin, *The Beloved Vaga-bond* by W. J. Locke, and *Wheel of Life* by Ellen Glasgow. Then, from England, came a novel which shook the United States and the world. It was *Three Weeks* by an exotic looking siren of forty-three. The lady's name? Elinor Glyn.

To read *Three Weeks* today is to laugh heartily at the unbelievable naïveté of a past generation. Yet the novel remains a milestone on the long march to sophistica-tion. Mrs. Glyn's defenders declare that in *Three Weeks* she writes of Love, not Sex. If this is true, she writes with a sensuous-ness that inevitably invokes Sex. Much is left to the imagination in *Three Weeks*. But at the same time, no one can possibly doubt what takes place in the scented scenes so discreetly omitted.

Three Weeks tells the tale of Paul Ver-dayne, a young English gentleman whose haughty family objects to his love for the parson's daughter who has nursed him after a hunting accident. Much annoyed, Paul takes a tour of Europe, finding most of the Continent "beastly rot." His dark moods brighten when, at an inn in Lu-cerne, he spies a dazzling femme fatale. Paul quickly learns that she is the queen of a small Balkan country. From then on, he calls her "Queen."

Queen also has noticed Paul and one afternoon beckons from her window, whis-pering, "Come, Paul." He finds her apart-ment choked with flowers—roses, tube-roses, lilies of the valley. The lights are seductively low and Queen lolls langorous-ly on a tiger skin. From this skin—how it shocked and delighted the reading public! —she teases Paul about his youth and innocence. Then her mood changes.

Suddenly she sprang up, one of those fine move-ments of hers full of catlike grace.

"Paul," she said, "listen," and she spoke rather fast. "You are so young, so young—and I shall hurt you—probably. Won't you go now while there is yet time? Anywhere away from me."

She put her hand on his arm and looked up into his eyes. And there were tears in hers. And now he saw they were grey.

He was moved as never yet in all his life.

"I will not!" he said. "I may be young, but tonight I know—I want to live! And I will chance the hurt because I know that only you can teach me—just how—"

Then his voice broke and he bent down and covered her hand with kisses.

No more than this happens the first time, but at their next meeting milady is once again full of whims. From the tiger skin, she forbids *him* to tease *her*. It is more than poor Paul can bear.

"You mustn't be teased. My God! It is you who are maddening me!" he cried, his voice hoarse with emotion. "Do you think I am inanimate like that tiger there? I am not, *I tell you!" and he seized her in his arms, raining kisses upon her which, whatever they lacked in subtlety, made up for in their passion and strength. "Some day some man will kill you, I suppose, but I shall be your lover—first!"*

The lady gasped. She looked up at him in be-wildered surprise, as a child might do who sets light to a whole box of matches in play. What a

naughty, naughty toy to burn so quickly for such a little strike!

But Paul's young strong arms held her close, she could not struggle or move. Then she laughed a laugh of pure glad joy.

"Beautiful, savage Paul," she whispered. "Do you love me? Tell me that."

"Love you!" he said. "Good God! Love you! Madly, and you know it, darling Queen."

"Then," said the lady in a voice in which all the caresses of the world seemed melted, "then, sweet Paul, I shall teach you many things, and among them I shall teach you how—to—LIVE."

This great love could not be consummated within the confines of a commercial Swiss inn. So the two row across the lake to the shelter of a more intimate spot. Indoors, Queen feels—

a madness of tender caressing seizing her. She purred as a tiger might have done, while she undulated like a snake. She touched him with her fingertips, she kissed his throat, his wrists, the palms of his hands, his eyelids, his hair. Strange subtle kisses, unlike the kisses of women. And often, between her purrings she murmured love words in some fierce language of her own, brushing his ears and his eyes with her lips the while. . . .

Three Weeks *continued to titillate audiences throughout the Twenties. This 1924 film version starred Aileen Pringle and Conrad Nagel—and tiger skin.*

"Oh! darling," cried Paul. "I worship, I adore you—you are just my life, my darling one, my Queen!"

"Sweet Paul!" she whispered, "oh! so good, so good is love, keep me loving you, my beautiful one—keep my desire long to be your Queen."

And after this they melted into one another's arms, and cooed and kissed, and they were foolish and incoherent, as lovers always are and have been from the beginning of time.

The spirit of two natures vibrating as One.

♥

Oh! the divine joy of that night!

"Paul," she said, "out of the whole world tonight, there are only you and I who matter, sweetheart. Is it not so? Remember, Paul," she whispered when, passion maddening him, he clasped her violently in his arms—"remember—whatever happens—whatever comes—for now, tonight, there is no other reason in all of this but just—I love you—I love you, Paul!"

"My Queen, my Queen!" said Paul, his voice hoarse in his throat.

And the wind played in softest zephyrs, and the stars blazed in the sky, mirroring themselves in the blue lake below.

Such was their wedding night.

Oh! glorious youth! and still more glorious love!

In England, *Three Weeks* exploded like a bombshell. "An exceedingly difficult work to know how to review," a baffled critic wrote, adding, "Not for *jeunes filles*." Not young boys either, for Eton and other schools promptly banned it. Yet the book sold so rapidly that stores were unable to keep it in stock. In the United States re-

57

viewers recoiled in horror, with only Mark Twain daring to offer praise. In England a catchy rhyme asked:

> Would you like to sin
> with Elinor Glyn
> on a tiger skin?
>
> Or would you prefer
> to err
> with her
> on some other fur?

America responded with these verses, which appeared in *Life:*

> *"Have you read it?" "Have you read it?"*
> *They hummed it in my ear.*
> *And everybody said it*
> *With a most suggestive leer.*
>
> *Then I read it. Yes, I read it.*
> *As my blushes have confessed.*
> *And I'm proud of dear old England—*
> *She had the book suppressed.*

Meantime, where was Mrs. Glyn?

She was in the United States, one of the first foreign novelists to visit these shores for the express purpose of promoting a book. Though the role was new for her, the lady knew exactly how to behave. Stepping off the *Lusitania,* she was attired head to foot in slinky purple. Velvet coat and dress, toque, and chiffon wrap-around veil were all the same deep color. In her trunk, newspapers reported, were sixty pairs of shoes especially designed for her tiny feet.

As a highborn English lady, Mrs. Glyn was annoyed by the personal questions New York reporters hurled at her as she wended her way to the newly opened Plaza Hotel. "Is *Three Weeks* your own story?" they were bold enough to ask. Mrs. Glyn returned a soft answer. "Oh, no," she purred. "It is the sheerest romance." The lady was the celebrity of the year and as such was entertained by Mrs. Frederick Vanderbilt, who put on $50,000 worth of jewels to welcome her. From brash Mrs. Stuyvesant Fish, Mrs. Glyn got a quotable quote: "They say in Europe that all American women are virtuous. Do you wonder? Look at American men!"

Mrs. Glyn next began a combination sightseeing-promotion tour of the United States. Stopping at Niagara Falls, she took copious notes on the behavior of honeymoon couples. In the big cities she was lionized by high society, but she also insisted on visiting such remote spots as the Nevada mining town of Rawhide where she sought out pithy characters like Death Valley Scotty. "I am helping to spread the ideals and the atmosphere of romance and glamour into the humblest homes," she told the press.

In each locality the best-selling author made a personal sampling of the sensation caused by *Three Weeks.* San Francisco, she discovered, had been more shocked by it than any other American city. But shocked or not, the ladies of San Francisco and everywhere else besieged the writer, asking probing questions about Love, Romance, and even Sex.

They were learning about life from Elinor.

The Great White Way

♥ If literature did much to pave America's path to sophistication, the stage did even more. At this moment the American theater was at its all-time peak of popularity. With the movies an infant, radio a whisper, and TV a Jules Verne vision, the drama (plus musical comedy and vaudeville) held an entertainment-hungry population in the palm of its hand. No one could call the theater of 1905-10 a fabulous invalid. It was just plain fabulous! "It was a great theater to be young in," drama critic Walter Pritchard Eaton recalled years later. Then he sighed and added, "In fact, it was a great world to be young in."

On New York's Great White Way it was common to have four or five brand new shows opening on a single night. And Broadway was only the beginning. Plays successful there invariably went on to tour the country. Almost a thousand legitimate theaters—large, small, in-between—sprawled from coast to coast. They were grouped together under the general heading "the road," and touring companies with great stars appeared in almost all of them.

Theater-wise, the hinterlands were every bit as knowing as Broadway. Indeed, the cross-country theater was such a thriving industry that it had its own trust—a much-hated syndicate which controlled the best theaters in every large show town. Touring attractions were forced to book through the central syndicate office in New York, at top fees, to get the best showcase in a road town.

This robust theater operated on several levels. At the summit were stars like Maude Adams, John Drew, Richard Mansfield, and Minnie Maddern Fiske (the only star who dared fight the mighty syndicate). Usually such stars played in harmless vehicles tailored to fit their talents. After 1905 there appeared a group of young American playwrights who followed Ibsen and Shaw in believing that, instead of pulling ideas out of the air, it was possible to write about the trials and temptations of real people. These young playwrights objected violently to the play written to suit the talents of a particular star. To them the play, not the player, was the thing.

First among them was a young Harvard student named Edward Sheldon, who in 1907 wrote *Salvation Nell*, a play about a Hell's Kitchen evildoer redeemed by his wife, who was a Salvation Army lassie. Nowadays *Salvation Nell* is as silly to read as *Three Weeks*, though not so fancy. Yet for the first time on an American stage tough characters were portrayed realistically. The locale of *Salvation Nell* is Sid McGovern's rough-tough saloon at Tenth Avenue and Forty-eighth Street. It was the gathering place of down-and-outers, drunkards, and whores. To find such types portrayed as human beings was a shocking experience for the opening-night audience. Next morning a critic called *Salvation Nell,* "The most daring play New York has ever seen. It not only dramatizes the Salvation Army, but it serves up Hell's Kitchen piping hot."

In another area of realism stood *The Lion and the Mouse,* by Charles Klein. Here the main character was patterned after one of the country's fabulously rich industrial magnates — "an unscrupulous, self-satisfied, cold-blooded man of money who allows nothing, not even his own honor, not even a man's life, to stand between himself and his own financial success." Up to now the American theater had dealt with homespun people, or with lifted-pinkie society types. When it dealt with famous people, it glamorized them, as with General Phil Sheridan in *Shenandoah.* To have a recognizable type portrayed unsympathetically was a jolt.

But the most violent chafing was in the sacred field of morality. Anxious to picture a world they knew, playwrights wanted to show more than a chaste, final-curtain kiss. What of the turmoil surrounding love, and its emotional offshoots? Yet public, police, and newspapers stood ready to protest any play branded immoral by the righteous.

Mrs. Warren's Profession was shut by the police after one night. So it remained for a play called *Sapho* to strike a first blow for moral emancipation in drama. An adaptation by Clyde Fitch of the best-selling Alphonse Daudet novel, it told of Fanny Le Grand, a swinging chick who habitually treated men like dirt. But suddenly Fanny finds herself wildly in love with a hunk of masculinity named Jean. The first shock in the play comes as Jean tries to toss Fanny out. She falls at his feet, moaning, "I'll blacken your shoes, if only you'll let me stay!" Until now, girls who abased themselves on the stage did so to beg honest favors or protect their purity. Yet here was a grown woman writhing in the throes of fleshly passion!

It was only the beginning. A few scenes later Fanny and Jean indulged in a wrestling-match love scene. Then Fanny, played by Olga Nethersole, was hefted up in the arms of her brutal lover. Slowly, he carried her up a flight of stairs to the door of a bedroom. The two paused, then disappeared inside, at which the stage lights blacked out. Next the stage began to glow with morning light, while mechanical birds twittered in the wings. It was dawn. The bedroom door opened stealthily and Jean stole guiltily down the stairs.

The audience gave a gasp. Some people rose angrily to stalk from the theater. Others sat stupefied. Word of the shocking play spread rapidly and in the morning police roused Olga Nethersole from sleep and took her to the station house. In dark-haired Olga (or in Abe Hummel, her wily lawyer) the cause of stage freedom found a fiery advocate. She demanded a jury trial. In daylight, in a courtroom, the whole business seemed a little ridiculous and the jury acquitted her. Sexy *Sapho* reopened with crowds storming the box office.

Following *Salvation Nell* and *Sapho* there was a pause while native playwrights

61

Top: *Caruso and Geraldine Farrar at
the Met, Frances Starr in* The Easiest Way.
Bottom: *John Drew and Mary Boland in Somerset Maugham's*
Smith, *Minnie Maddern Fiske as Ibsen's Nora.*

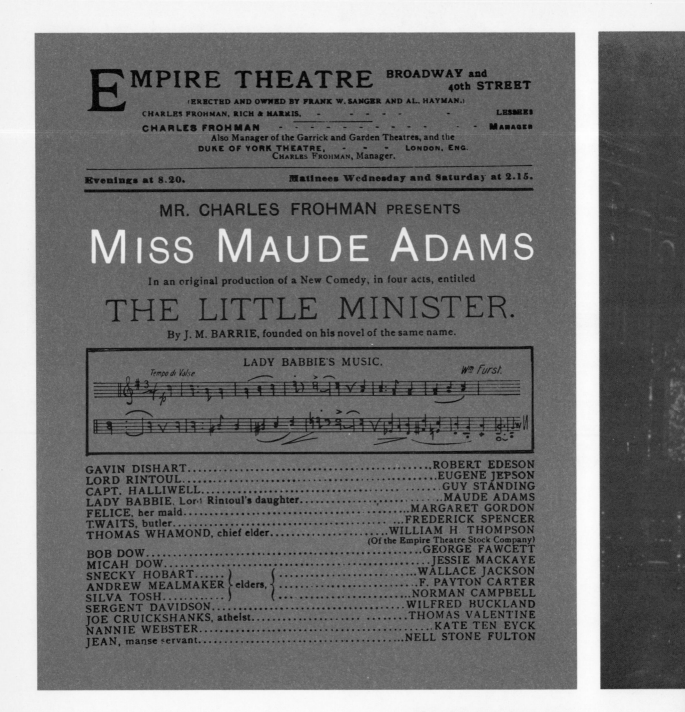

The incomparable Maude Adams
as Lady Babbie, with Margaret Gordon
as her maid Felice, in scene from
The Little Minister.

discovered an aptitude for terse, fast-moving crime melodrama. Authors like Paul Armstrong, Wilson Mizner, and Bayard Veiller wrote about crooks and crimes. Two of them were *Alias Jimmy Valentine* and *Within the Law*. They introduced a new type of stage dialogue which used contemporary slang rather than the stilted sentiments of the past. A speech from a crime play called *The Chorus Lady* not only uses contemporary slang, but shows that temptation has always been present on Broadway. In the play, a pure young chorine declares:

"If a girl's good, she's good anywhere. But, say, if you're scrimping along on twenty per and the girl next to you in your dressin' room comes to the show-shop every night in a benzine wagon in ermine capes and diamonds big as oysters, it ain't religion so much as a firm grip on home and mother that makes you sit tight and keep handin' out the frozen mit an' the icy eye to the man behind the bankroll."

In playwright Eugene Walter another vital figure appeared. Walter was a broad-shouldered, hard-drinking newspaperman who had labored in city rooms from coast to coast. A lusty, pungent barroom talker, he was persuaded to turn his talents to writing plays. The result was *Paid in Full*, about an embezzler who offers his wife's fair body to his employer in an attempt to escape prosecution.

The Easiest Way, Walter's next, was even more of a blockbuster. It tells of a sweet-looking Broadway chorine and bit actress named Laura Murdock who allows herself to be kept by a wealthy older man.

Laura is sympathetically described as doing this out of weakness rather than loose morals. Then she falls in love with an upstanding young man and leaves her protector. But the young man goes off to make his fortune and Laura falls back to the easy way of comfortable sin. When her true love returns, he finds her weakness exposed. Both men leave her in disgust, at which she utters two of the most famous lines in American drama. Calling her maid, she says:

"Doll me up, Annie."
"You goin' out, Miss Laura?"
"Yes, I'm going to Rector's to make a hit, and to hell with the rest!"

Morning-after critics branded *The Easiest Way* "indecent," "vile," "corrupt," "lascivious." One summed up: "An evening of good acting and bad morals." Of course, it was a hit.

The rousing success of rough, tough Eugene Walter offered a particular challenge to Clyde Fitch, whose *Sapho* had been the first big dramatic shocker on Broadway. Aged forty-four, Fitch had been a playwright for over twenty years. His output was prodigious: thirty-six originals, twenty-six adaptations from French and German, five dramatizations of popular novels, among them *Sapho*. Once he had five plays running simultaneously, two of which opened on the same enchanted evening.

In a pre-tax era, Fitch averaged a neat $250,000 a year and lived in fine style. A fastidious and colorful dresser, he was a pioneer in wearing bright colors and un-

In Sapho, *Olga Nethersole was carried upstairs by her leading man. Then the bedroom door closed. It was the most shocking seduction the stage had ever seen.*

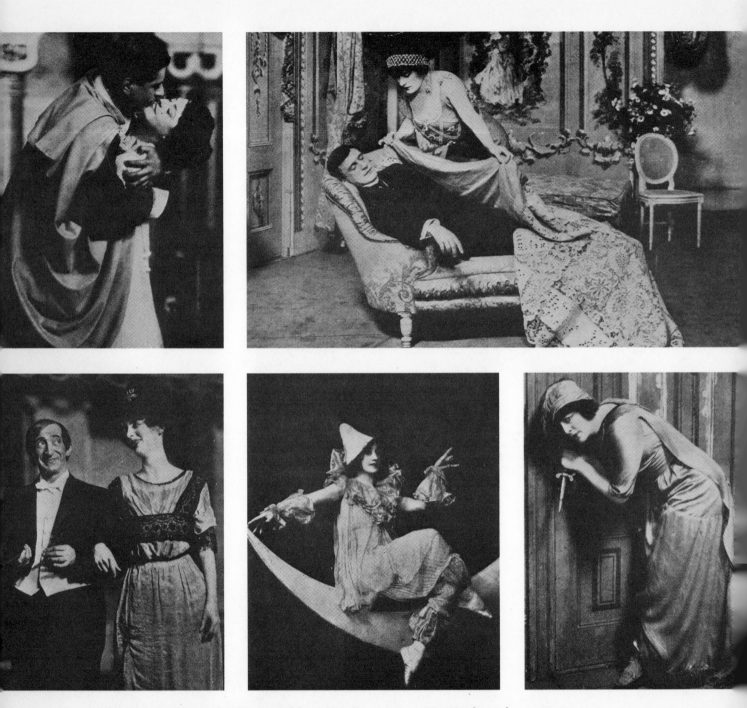

Top: Louise Gunning and Robert Warwick in The Balkan Princess, *Kitty Gordon and John McCloskey in* Alma, Where Do You Live? *Bottom: Lillian Lee and Lew Fields in* The Hen Pecks, *Bessie McCoy in* Ziegfeld Frolic, *Valeska Suratt in* The Red Rose. *Opposite: Playwright Clyde Fitch.*

matched coat and trousers. Some critics disparaged his skill as a playwright, calling him a superb technician who wrote plays without beating hearts. "He embroiders his plays," one complained. Others thought his work feminine (later on the word might be "bitchy"). As an author, Fitch was often dismissed as "a male milliner." As a man about town, he was labeled "a butterfly who lives an exquisite existence."

Yet Fitch was enormously proud of his ability. He decided to write a truly realistic drama, a he-man job even rougher than Gene Walter might do. Called *The City,* it would have a tense second-act curtain. One character, told that he had unwittingly married his sister, would shout, "That's a goddam lie!" Never had the awful oath "goddam" echoed from the walls of a New York theater. Fitch determined to use it.

Fitch worked fast and finished *The City* in record time. With the play scheduled for fall production, he sailed in the summer of 1909 for a vacation in Europe. Motoring through the French countryside, he was stricken by an attack of acute appendicitis. A local doctor operated. Next day Broadway staggered at the news. Clyde Fitch was dead.

Nonetheless, *The City* opened on schedule. Fitch always directed his own plays and his presence seemed to hover over rehearsals. It was the same on opening night, the weirdest premiere in Broadway history. A mixture of horror at the forbidden "goddam," excitement over the yeasty play, sadness at the popular play-wright's death—all these combined to push the audience into mass hysteria. Between the acts, strangers in evening dress argued heatedly with one another, while others stood in the aisles senselessly waving hats and handkerchiefs. A few fainted, among them the critic of the New York *Sun.*

After the final curtain, the actors responded to nineteen curtain calls. Suddenly the stage was momentarily left empty. An eerie hush fell over the audience, as a strange mass hallucination caused many of those present to believe they saw the ghost of Clyde Fitch walk slowly to the footlights and bend low in an appreciative bow. Pandemonium broke loose, with hysterical cries of "I saw him! I saw him!" filling the air.

There has never been an opening night like it. Next morning, critics declared that male-milliner Fitch had succeeded in writing his rugged, realistic, he-man play. "It seems tame to say the play is strong, for its strongest scene is tremendous," one wrote. "The play is strong as a raging bull."

Meet Me at Rector's

♥ Americans, increasingly eager to find fresh sources of that magic thing called glamour, were discovering that it was fun to read about the glittering, lighthearted doings of a new group, known as sporting society or midnight-supper society. Its members were young and far from stuffy. A particularly flamboyant example was "Diamond Jim" Brady, who wore clusters of jewels on his ties, his lapels, his vests, and his pudgy fingers. Some accused Jim of bad taste, calling him "an overdressed belch." But Jim, a super-salesman of railroad supplies, was shrewd enough to see the huge advantages in personal publicity. Businessmen, proud to know such a bejeweled celebrity, pressed on him an annual million dollars in orders.

The hub of sporting society was Rector's, on Times Square. Called Broadway's Cathedral of Froth, Supreme Court of Triviality, Bourse of Gossip, and Clearing House of Rumor, there has never been another restaurant like it. Said its genial owner Charles Rector, "I found Broadway a little lane of ham and eggs in 1899 and left it a full-blown avenue of lobsters, champagne, and morning-afters." Again he quipped, "When Broadway sought to sleep, I turned night into daze."

Celebrities made a midnight habit of gathering under Rector's roof. Primarily, Rector's was a place for actors to dine after a night's labor, but the thespians were joined by a motley array of playboys, Wall Street plungers, prize fighters, opera singers, jockeys, gamblers, playwrights, song writers, explorers, journalists, statesmen, impresarios, and polo players. O. Henry might sit at one table, Richard Harding Davis at another. Rector's was favored by socialites E. Berry Wall and Freddie Gebhard (who married a Florodora Girl); actors Raymond Hitchcock, Eddie Foy, De Wolf Hopper, Willie Collier, Nat Goodwin; song writers Victor Herbert, Paul Dresser, Reginald De Koven; prize fighters Jim Corbett and John L. Sullivan; authors George Ade, Rex Beach, Rupert Hughes, Robert W. Chambers, Booth Tarkington. Accompanying some of these figures might be famous actresses like Sarah Bernhardt, Lily Langtry, or Ethel Barrymore.

But most Rector's regulars had as companions pretty girls newly encountered at stage doors, or picked up in hotel lobbies. A joke of the period deals with two of these Broadway butterflies: one tells the other, "I got a pearl out of an oyster at Rector's." The other replies, "That's nothing, I got a diamond necklace out of a lobster."

For everyone at Rector's the high point of an evening, the moment during which all talk ceased, came with the arrival of one of the great beauties of the era. And there were so many! Lillian Russell—a little hefty perhaps, but glowing in the aura of a

Theater and sporting folk and famous beauties thronged to the hub of midnight-supper society— Rector's on Times Square. Griffin over door was Rector trademark.

woman who knows herself a great beauty. Anna Held—of the naughty eyes and the hourglass figure with its eighteen-inch waist. Frankie Bailey—possessor of the most perfect legs on the American stage. (Her symmetrical gams were so famous that women's legs were not called legs, but Frankie Baileys.)

Rector's had all this, and yet was willing to go to all sorts of trouble to offer more besides. Indeed, one of its efforts to satisfy a glittering patron shows really Machiavel-

lian ingenuity. This episode opened one day when George Rector, then a law student at Cornell, received a telegram from his father Charles, the restaurant's founder. "Come home at once," it ordered. Hastening to New York George found himself closeted with his father and Diamond Jim Brady. That day Jim wore a vest with diamond buttons the size of fifty-cent pieces; on his tie was a diamond horseshoe pin almost as big as the real thing; in his buttonhole was a boutonniere of clustered diamonds. But his face was sober and serious. Charles Rector's was, too.

Diamond Jim had just returned from Europe. In Paris he had gone to the famed Restaurant Marguery. There for the first time he tasted filet of sole Marguery, with its world-famous sauce. Jim had taken a piece of bread in two bejeweled fingers and sopped the sauce up from his plate. It had been the supreme gustatory moment of his life. He had gone to the Marguery every night of his Paris stay. Now he just had to enjoy the same glorious repast in New York.

Yet the ingredients of sauce Marguery were guarded like a state secret. Nowhere in the world was the recipe written down. It lived only in the minds of the master chefs of the Marguery. But Diamond Jim had a plan. Young George Rector was told to forget the study of law and go to Paris. There he must infiltrate the Marguery kitchen, discover the secret of filet of sole Marguery. It would take time, but it must be done. "I received instructions," he re-

"Diamond Jim" Brady was Rector's best customer. He usually dined prodigiously and with beauteous actress Lillian Russell (opposite).

70

called later, "to return either with the sauce Marguery or in it."

No international spy ever worked harder. George knew he was too inexperienced to be hired in so exalted a place as the Marguery. So he went first to the Café de Paris, where he was taken on as apprentice cook. In the Café de Paris kitchen, after he mastered the art of crabmeat Mornay, he was moved into the dining room as bus boy, then apprentice waiter.

Armed with this experience, he applied at the Marguery to be taken on as apprentice chef. For nearly two years, fifteen hours a day, he was drilled by the seven master chefs who presided over the kitchen. Finally, Rector decided that the secret of making filet of sole Marguery was graven on his mind and he sailed home.

Awaiting him on the pier were his father, Diamond Jim, and Rector's gypsy orchestra. Jim's face was a study. He had waited for two long years and his appetite burst all bounds. "Have you got it?" he demanded. Then he ordered, "Hurry up! Get into the kitchen and begin."

That night at Rector's, James Buchanan Brady presided at the head of an impressive table. In those days no woman was considered a judge of good food, so Jim had invited only male gourmets to sample the famous sauce. With him sat Marshall Field, Adolphus Busch, Victor Herbert, John Philip Sousa, Dan Reed, the tin-plate king, author Alfred Henry Lewis, and Sam Shubert, the young theatrical producer.

The first plate of filet of sole Marguery

ever prepared in the U.S.A. was reverently placed before Diamond Jim. A beatific expression wafted over his jowly countenance as he tasted. "It's so good I could eat it on a Turkish towel," he rumbled.

George Rector, the study of law forgotten, settled happily into the family business. Years later he stated that filet of sole Marguery à la Diamond Jim, together with crabmeat Mornay, had brought Rector's at least a million dollars in business.

Sauce Marguery

Here, in Rector's own words, is sauce Marguery as learned in Paris and prepared for a busy evening at Rector's:

First, you must use none but imported sole from the English Channel, which must be shipped over alive in tanks. Cut the fillet with a very sharp knife. There are four fillets to a fish. Take the rest of the fish and put them into a big boiler with plenty of leeks, onions, carrots, turnips, lettuce, romaine, parsley, and similar vegetables. The whole mass is reduced by boiling from eight to twelve hours. This leaves a very small quantity of a jellylike substance, which is the essence of the fish. If properly prepared, only a handful of jelly will be obtained from two hundred fish.

In another pan we place the yolks of four dozen eggs. Work a gallon of melted butter into this, stopping every ten minutes to pour in a pint of dry, white wine of good Bordeaux quality. Add from time to time a spoonful of the essence of fish. This is stirred in and cooked in a double boiler in the same way you would make a Hollandaise sauce.

Strain the sauce through a very fine sieve. Season with a dash of cayenne and salt. At no time in the preparation of the sauce should it be allowed to come to a boil.

Now we take the fillets, which should be kept on ice to retain freshness until the sauce is ready. Place them in a pan with just sufficient water to float them a little. About half an inch of water should be sufficient to cover them. After they boil for ten or fifteen minutes remove and place on a silver platter. Garnish the dish on one end with a small shrimp and at the other with imported mussels from northern France.

The colorful restaurant featured gypsy music, but New Year's Eve celebrations were enlivened by girl who popped out of a clock at midnight, to amusement of an elegant crowd.

Pour a liberal amount of sauce over the whole platter. Sprinkle with chopped parsley and place on the grill for the purpose of allowing it to simmer to a golden brown. Then serve.

From *Rector's Naughty 90's Cook Book,* by Alexander Kirkland, here is filet of sole Marguery updated to today's tastes and pocketbooks:

Fillet **two flounders**. Place bones, skin, heads in stewpan. Add **1 pound inexpensive fish** cleaned and cut into small pieces, **½ cup thinly sliced young carrots** and **1 small chopped leek, 3 sprigs of parsley, 10 whole peppercorns, 1 small bay leaf, 1 sprig of thyme, 1½ quarts cold water.** Bring to boiling point very slowly and simmer until liquid is reduced to 1 pint, then strain through fine cheesecloth. Place fillets in buttered baking pan and pour over them **1 cup fish stock.** Season with sprinkling of **salt** and **pepper,** place in moderate oven (325° F.) 15-20 minutes. Carefully lift fillets from pan and arrange on hot ovenproof serving platter. Garnish with **1 dozen poached oysters** and **1 dozen boiled shrimps,** shelled and cleaned. Pour remaining fish stock into baking pan in which fillets were poached and simmer gently until quantity is reduced to 3 or 4 tablespoons, no more. Strain into top part of double boiler and add **4 tablespoons dry white wine, ¼ pound butter.** Cook over hot water, stirring until butter is melted. (Very little water in lower part of double boiler, just enough to make a gentle steam.) Add **4 egg yolks,** well beaten. Stir constantly until sauce is consistency of medium cream sauce. Pour creamy sauce over fish fillets, oysters, and shrimps, and place under broiler flame until nicely glazed or lightly browned. Allow 1 fillet per serving.

Flickering Flicks

♥ Movies were called flickering flicks, galloping tintypes, and a host of other condescending names. "Cheap shows for cheap people" is the way one Broadway big shot dismissed them. And indeed, in those days, they were hardly a challenge to the supremacy of the powerful and popular American theater.

Movies were produced by a group of small companies and shown in empty stores and deserted buildings across the land. At first, they were seen only in penny arcades. You dropped a coin into a slot, peered into a viewer, and turned a crank. What you saw might be instructive ("Surf at Dover," "Beavers at Play,") or naughty ("What the Bootblack Saw," or "How Bridget Served the Salad Undressed.")

Then came movies projected on screens. Sometimes the screen was no more than a bedsheet, but people sat and watched with total fascination. Firms such as Biograph, Essanay, Vitagraph, and Kalem each averaged two films a week. One day was spent shooting outdoors, one indoors. The films looked like scenes from plays, with actors walking into view from off range. Characters were photographed at full length, always the same distance from the camera. The man of the moment was Edwin S. Porter, who had advanced the film medium from "Beavers at Play" to such exciting epics as *The Great American Train Robbery* and *The Life of an American Fireman.*

The tiny film industry was so prosperous that it, too, had a trust. Called General Film, its figurehead president was Thomas Alva Edison, inventor of the motion picture. General Film had a tight grip on the industry, yet, as always, a few men fought back. Prominent among the battlers were Carl Laemmle and William Fox. Like other trusts, General Film was arrogant. Afraid popularity would make actors demand wages higher than $5 a day, it refused to allow cast-listings telling who played what part in their films. With no names to go by, early filmgoers were forced to call their favorites the Biograph Girl, the Little Girl with the Golden Curls, or the Country Boy with the Nice Face.

Such was the film scene in 1907. Pictures were little more than episodes. The public then began to notice that Biograph pictures were improving. Instead of episodes, they began telling a story—something sensationally new in the galloping tintypes. Because of the trust's stifling rule about credits, movie-goers had no idea who was responsible for this innovation. But insiders knew that an unsuccessful stage actor named David Wark Griffith had been given a chance to try his hand directing movies.

Griffith was thirty-two years old. His Kentucky father had been a colonel in the Confederate army and David Wark behaved as if he were himself a Southern aristocrat. He also considered himself a

Two episodes from The Great American Train Robbery, *first film to tell a story—of sorts. It was directed by Edwin S. Porter and gave an early intimation of movies' potential.*

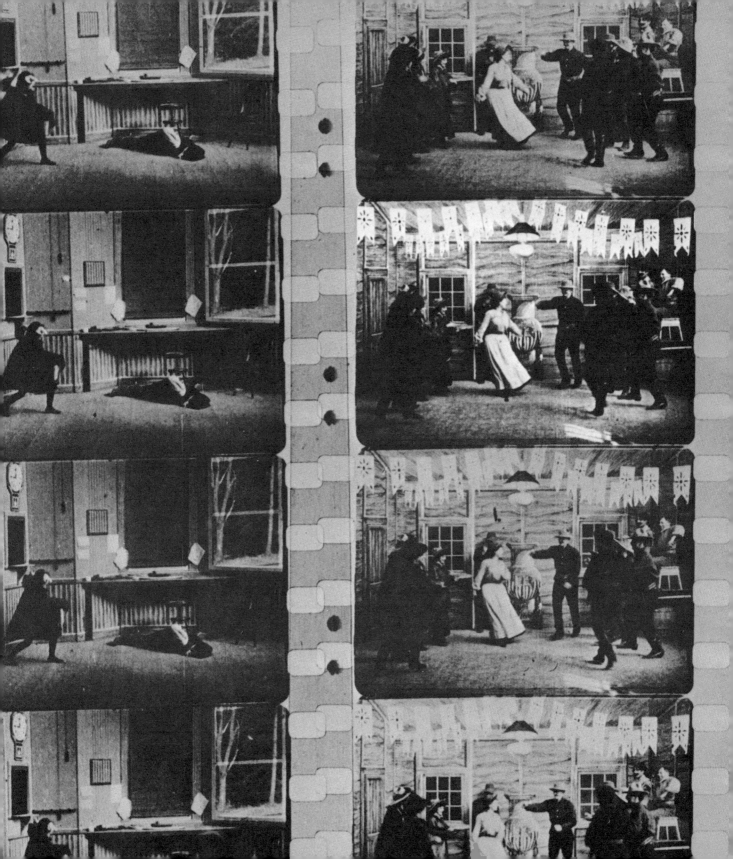

*Pioneer director D. W. Griffith (with megaphone)
and ace cameraman Billy Bitzer on set.
Child actor at left is Ben Alexander, who grew up
to be a star of TV's "Dragnet" series.
Petite figure, heart-melting smile,
and golden ringlets turned a little Canadian
girl named Gladys Smith into Mary
Pickford, America's Sweetheart. Broncho Billy
Anderson was first of a long and
distinguished line of cowboy stars. Slides
(left) conveyed pertinent messages from theater
management to audiences.*

great writer, which no one else did. His tremendous conceit, however, gave him self-confidence in the moving-picture medium. Further, he was smart enough to listen to words of wisdom from his veteran cameraman, Billy Bitzer, who had been filming movies since 1896. "Four eyes are better than two," D.W. said of Bitzer's help.

Perhaps because he thought of himself as an author, Griffith saw films in story terms. He also believed in moving the camera around. Instead of photographing his actors full length, he moved the camera close to show the expressions on faces. Despite his gentlemanly Southern manners, Griffith could be as temperamental as his actors and kept his sets in constant turmoil. But he knew how to make a film express ideas and arouse emotion. The movie public, given a sudden chance to be selective, began to look for the "Biograph Picture." The next step was for Griffith to step forth and make films like *Birth of a Nation* and *Intolerance* on his own.

Another change occurred when Carl Laemmle lured the Biograph Girl into his employ. Her name was Florence Lawrence,

and Laemmle promised to give her billing. Broadway actors who made extra money by doubling in movies—among them John and Lionel Barrymore—didn't know whether to be glad or sad about the trend toward billing. They didn't particularly want the world to know about their work in this lowly medium, yet at the same time they wanted the professional credit.

Biograph found a successor to Florence in the Little Girl with the Golden Curls—Mary Pickford. At sixteen she was a child actress who had worked too hard to have gotten much fun out of life. When she began acting in films some of her old theater friends missed her. One was actor-director William C. De Mille, who wrote producer David Belasco:

Do you remember that little girl, Mary Pickford, who played Betty in The Warrens of Virginia? *I met her a few weeks ago and the poor kid is actually thinking of taking up moving pictures seriously. She says she can make a fairly good living at it, but it does seem a shame. After all she can't be more than sixteen or seventeen and I remember what faith you had in her future; that appealing personality of hers would go a long way in the theater, and now she's throwing her whole career in the ash-can and burying herself in a cheap form of amusement which hasn't a single point that I can see to recommend it. There will never be any real money in those galloping tintypes and certainly no one can expect them to develop into anything which could, by the wildest stretch of imagination, be called art.*

I pleaded with her not to waste her professional life and the opportunity the stage gives her to be known to thousands of people, but she's a rather stubborn little thing for such a youngster . . .

T. R.

♥ The greatest entertainer in the country was Theodore Roosevelt, the man in the White House. While he was President (1901-1909) there was never a dull moment. Energetic, ebullient, radiating optimism, Teddy was the son of a solidly aristocratic New York family. Surviving a sickly youth, he graduated from Harvard, won election to the State Assembly, ran unsuccessfully for Mayor of New York, served as U.S. Civil Service Commissioner, as New York Police Commissioner, as Assistant Secretary of the Navy, as a dashing Rough Rider colonel, as Governor of New York, and as Vice President under William McKinley. At the age of forty he became the nation's youngest President ever, when McKinley was assassinated by the demented Leon Czolgosz.

Even in the cold light of history, Teddy Roosevelt remains the most important figure of his era. Though some have found his boyish utterances and bumptious actions hard to take, Teddy shaped and developed the nation as have few Presidents. For one thing, he believed that the Chief Executive was the country's big wheel. Where previous Presidents had functioned slowly, allowing shifting forces to move them, Teddy believed in moving first, banging heads together when necessary.

Roosevelt also humanized government and personalized the presidency. Before Teddy, most Presidents of the United States had been colorless. "It is a solemn thing to be President," Grover Cleveland thought, and his behavior in office bore him out. There was nothing solemn about Teddy. The man was loud, vivid color. The White House "dee-lighted" him, to use one of his favorite words. The presidency was "bully," to use another. Teddy often acted like a wild man, but his actions perfectly fitted the brash American mood.

Teddy's influence on the national life was extensive. The grown-up boy liked to box, swim, hunt, hike, play tennis, and read books. With his fondness for the strenuous life, cowboy hats, and pithy utterances, he blasted the American male out of his drab mold of conformity.

Roosevelt's solid accomplishments as President are many. He was the first national leader to view America as a world power and he talked turkey with the German Kaiser, the Russian Czar, and other world plenipotentiaries. He sent the American fleet around the world, thereby serving notice on other countries that the United States was a power to reckon with. He invited Booker T. Washington to the White House, the first President to give recognition to a distinguished Negro. It made a national ruckus and produced ugly cartoons in Southern papers, but a grinning Theodore gleefully rode out the storm. He also has come down in history as the great trust buster. He didn't actually bust trusts;

At seventeen, Teddy was overcoming childhood ills. Mature TR with his active family at Sagamore Hill, the Long Island home they all loved. Tree-climbing Quentin is at far right in group picture.

78

bankers and industrialists and "malefactors of great wealth" found his bark rather worse than his bite. But he did manage to curb them, and he was the first President who even tried.

Nor was Teddy the only Roosevelt to brighten the national life. His family did, too. Teddy had six children, the three younger ones boys who might have been created by the mischievous pen of Booth Tarkington. The pranks of the Roosevelt boys—called the "White House Gang"— kept the country chuckling, and in so doing knit it closer together.

The Gang looked on Washington as a big playground. They rode the city's trolleys, making faces at passers-by. One day they found themselves grimacing at Teddy, who made faces right back. They blew out streetlights after lamplighters lit them. They smuggled a pony into the White House. They hurtled down bannisters into the center of diplomatic gatherings.

Even more important was Alice Roosevelt, Teddy's oldest daughter. She was seventeen when the family entered the White House, where she soon made her debut. Lucky Alice led such a lively life that she was dubbed Princess Alice. Every bit as vigorous as her father, she drove her own foreign runabout and rode horseback astride, as only men were supposed to. Even before her father was President, Alice smoked cigarettes, blowing the smoke up a chimney at Sagamore Hill, the family's Long Island home. She also loved publicity, which nice girls were supposed to

80

Roosevelt and his Rough Riders atop San Juan Hill. Their victory was small-scale, but Teddy's courage and high spirits were captivating. He emerged from war as the most famous man in the world.

shun. Young Alice was forthright, independent, a trifle defiant, and impatient with women's secondary position in the world. She thought herself as good as any man and considered women's confining clothing a nuisance. As Princess of the White House, popular Alice did as much or more for the emancipation of women than the grim-lipped legions of determined suffragettes who were forming at the time.

The Theodore Roosevelts were the first aristocrats to inhabit the White House since the days of John Quincy Adams. But aristocrats or not, they behaved just like the family next door.

In 1908 the entire country lay under the sobering knowledge that Teddy and his family would soon depart the White House. Four years before, on the night of his landslide election, Theodore had issued a statement vowing not to run again in 1908. (His first term, of course, only completed McKinley's.) This was the sort of trigger-happy utterance Teddy's wife and advisors worked hard to prevent. Why say it at all? But in Teddy's mind, to run again would be seeking a third term. Since no other President had ever done so, it was wrong. Despite strong pressure, Roosevelt held to his word.

A figure as powerful as Teddy could pick his own heir to the office of President. Roosevelt passed over Charles Evans Hughes, whom he called "the bearded lady." Instead he picked three-hundred-pound William Howard Taft, his Secretary of War. By hindsight it was a

mistake, but at the time Teddy was pleased with his choice. Taft was a hard worker who also liked to take a snooze, his bulk cradled in a comfortable chair. There is a possibility that torrential Teddy liked Taft because the two men were such opposites. Teddy, never quiet, probably admired and envied the slow-moving man who knew how to take it easy. He also believed Taft to be a progressive Republican in his own image, although Taft was actually a conservative.

Teddy persuaded the somewhat reluctant Secretary to run, then proceeded to campaign harder than the candidate himself. Taft won, defeating the perennial candidate, William Jennings Bryan.

Now a curious question arose: What would Teddy do? He was only fifty years old, a dynamo of a man in the prime of life, with a background of unparalleled political experience. Yet to all intents and purposes he was unemployed. He could run for the Senate, become president of a college. Both seemed beneath him. The man of explosive energy and superior mentality could think only of a safari in Africa.

He sailed after Taft's inauguration. On the dock a band played "There'll Be a Hot Time in the Old Town Tonight," his long-time campaign song. By his side stood son Kermit. Guns and jungle equipment were packed away, along with ten extra pairs of his pince-nez eyeglasses. The turbulent Roosevelt era seemed to have ended. No man in his right mind thought Teddy would ever run for the presidency again.

In 1908, Teddy had finished what he considered his second term as President. Departing the political scene, he grinned his well-known grin. But did he mean it?

In the Air

♥ According to the record books, the Wright brothers first flew under power in 1903. Therefore, this should stand as the biggest year of their lives. But look again. Their big year was really 1908.

They were an odd pair, the two Wright brothers of Dayton, Ohio. Though a four-year age difference lay between them, they were kindred souls, more like twins than brothers—more like twins than most twins.

Wilbur, the elder, and Orville often started to say the same thing at the same time, or burst into identical snatches of song. More than anything they enjoyed each other's company. They talked together a lot, in voices that sounded alike, carrying on what have been called "long, friendly arguments." With other people, the two were quiet, chary with words. As a famous man, Wilbur was once taken to task for his public silences. "I don't want to emulate the parrot, the bird that talks most and flies least," he explained.

In addition to enjoying each other's company, the two sparked one another intellectually. They thrashed out problems together—"thrashed them to pieces," one friend thought. It has been said that only two such minds, thinking alike, could ever have solved the mystery of flight. It's past

proving now, for the Wrights—two men acting as one—did the job.

Sons of an Ohio bishop, the Wright brothers both left high school at age seventeen. From 1889 to 1895 they published a newspaper, seeming to be more interested in tinkering with the presses than in news beats. When the invention of the safety brake triggered a nationwide bicycle craze, the boys followed their innate mechanical bent to become bike makers. One day they read about European attempts at flight. The two minds instantly flared with determination to become the first men to fly.

At first they tried gliders, and these efforts at Kitty Hawk, North Carolina, have been called "feeble hopping on crutches of wind." In 1903, the Wrights (Wilbur was thirty-seven, Orville thirty-three) re-turned to Kitty Hawk with a self-made motor and propellers attached to big clumsy wings. On December 17, Orville (it was his turn that day) climbed into the plane, which was catapulted into the air. The motor chugged and the crate shot ahead 120 feet in twelve seconds. A few hours later it covered 852 feet in fifty-nine seconds. In Orville's matter-of-fact words, this was "the first time a machine carrying a man, lifted by its own power into the air in full flight, sailed forward without reduction of speed."

A Virginia newspaperman heard the story and persuaded his paper to headline it. Few others mentioned it. There was a reason, however. Only seven days before, a highly publicized attempt at flight by Dr. Samuel Langley of the Smithsonian

Man sprouted wings when Orville Wright, prone at center, flew this plane at Kitty Hawk with brother Wilbur looking on.

Institution had ignominiously failed. The Government had given Dr. Langley $50,000 to undertake his venture. With his failure, anyone attempting to fly was branded a phony. This blanket indictment included the Wrights, who now claimed to have succeeded. "If God wanted us to fly, He'd have given us wings," people said.

Matters went on like this for five years. The Wrights, patiently talking out problems, set up shop outside Dayton. In 1904 and 1905, they made 150 flights, one of them twenty-four miles long. Each year they did better, but no one seemed to care. A few locals gathered to watch. That was

all. The Wrights themselves, lacking personal glamour, made no efforts at publicity. True, they wanted recognition. But they also feared their secrets might be stolen. They had taken out a basic patent in 1903, but now they were making new discoveries and wanted control of the patents.

There was also the question of what to do with the planes they built. Rich men were not likely to buy them. The Wrights hoped the Government would want planes for military purposes, but the War Department, still smarting over the expensive Langley experiment, had no such plan.

Oddly enough, it was the French who

Glenn Curtiss, once a motorcycle speedster, was the Wrights' rival. In 1908, he flew plane he called "June Bug" (above). Henri Farman's complicated biplane (right) had more wings than any bird.

turned world attention to the Wrights. Learning of the flights in Ohio, they dispatched an observer to the United States. He watched a flight, then found a dirt farmer who had grown so accustomed to having the boys wing overhead that he no longer looked up from his corn shucking. The Frenchman returned to report, "I was immeasurably astounded." The French invited the Wrights to France.

Almost at once, the American Government sprang to life. The War Department announced an open competition for a $25,000 contract to build a plane that would go forty miles per hour, carry two passengers, and fly for at least an hour. Other inventors filed plans, but the Wrights were the only ones who had planes. Trial flights in the competition were set for the late summer of 1908. The importunate French demanded a Wright brothers exhibition at the same time.

With two important flights scheduled for the same moment, the brothers took the unprecedented step of separating. Orville went with a plane to Fort Myer, Virginia, while Wilbur transported another to France. Wilbur was a deliberate chap who, like the later Lindbergh, flew only when conditions were perfect. The French grew

impatient as days rolled by without a spectacular exhibition. But Wilbur waited, patiently tinkering. At Fort Myer, Orville flew for over an hour, fulfilling the Government requirements so well that he won the $25,000 contract, plus a $5,000 bonus. With this Wilbur took to the air in France. He flew for an hour and a half, after which a French syndicate gave him $100,000 for European rights to Wright planes. He was lionized by Paris, but the thrill departed with news that Orville had been badly hurt in a crash at Fort Myer. His passenger, Lt. Thomas Selfridge, was killed. Orville recovered slowly.

Triumphs on both sides of the Atlantic caught the public imagination and at last the Wright boys were heroes. On December 31, 1908, Wilbur saluted the finish of a great year by staying in the air two hours and twenty minutes.

Fame never altered the calm nature of the Wrights, but it changed their lives. An American Wright company was capitalized at $1,000,000 and from then on the brothers did more managing, less flying. They trained pilots, worked at improving motors. There were also a multitude of legal battles over patents. Then, in 1912, Wilbur Wright, a man with the world truly at his feet, died of typhoid fever. Orville lived quietly on until 1948.

The Wrights may have been the first American fliers, but there were other pioneers in the history of American aviation. One was Glenn Curtiss, the Wrights' main rival and a mechanical genius who began with bicycles and engines. Curtiss differed from the Wrights in that he loved speed and had been a motorcycle racer. As the Wrights never entered flying races, the field was left to Curtiss. He won the Scientific American Cup so often that it was given to him to keep. He also won $10,000 for making the first flight from Albany to New York.

Curtiss was no wild-eyed daredevil. He built his own planes (the Wright brothers promptly sued him) and experimented with motors. Like the Wrights he flew less as his business responsibilities increased. It was he who made the flat area around Mineola, Long Island, an aviation center.

In 1909, there were perhaps six civilian pilots in the United States. Twelve months later there were nearly forty, and with them the exhibition era dawned. Daredevil pilots, trained in Wright and Curtiss schools, toured the country doing stunts before big crowds. Most of these barnstormers eventually were killed, which made the exhibitions morbidly fascinating. Thrill-hungry crowds demanded stunts and more stunts from such birdmen as Lincoln Beachey, Art Smith, Rutherford Page, Bud Mars, and Roy Knabenshue. At the end of his flights, barnstormer "Sure Shot" Kearney paused to shout at crowds, "You can go home now. I'm still alive!" Shortly, he too was dead.

"They died to amuse the mob" is an epitaph given to those early stunt fliers. But they did a lot to publicize aviation and to win public acceptance for it.

Wilbur (top, left) and Orville abandoned flying to build nation's first airplane factory (left) at Dayton, Ohio. They also worked to improve motors and train pilots.

In My Merry Oldsmobile

♥ A mere ten years elapsed between the first American automobile ride and the first flight in an airplane. But by 1908 a whole century of progress seemed to separate the two events. Planes still were rarities. Cars were commonplace. Their progress had been swift. The first American auto show, held in New York in 1900, was a curiously assorted collection of oddities. Two-thirds of the cars exhibited were electrics (battery powered) or steamers (steam-engine driven), and all of them showed the influence of the pioneer inventors and manufacturers of Europe—Daimler, Benz, Panhard, Renault, Delahaye, and Peugeot—who really made the auto possible. The first popular American car was the Curved Dash Olds, produced in 1901 by Ransom E. Olds. It was gas driven and cost $650. In his first year Ransom Olds sold 425 cars. In 1904, he sold nearly four thousand.

Now, in 1908, the auto had become an accepted sight on nearly every main street in the land. Doctors used them, so did clergymen. A few businessmen drove to work. Others used the family car to take mother and the kids on Sunday outings. The automobile was still a male animal, for it had to be cranked and only the strong masculine arm could do it. But Americans had accepted the auto. People wanted cars. The number already on the road proved it.

To satisfy the demand a multitude of manufacturers sprang up—men like the Duryea brothers, Olds, Haynes, the Appersons, Maxim, and Ford. Some of the autos they turned out have lived on as hallowed names, others have dropped into oblivion: Cadillac, Pierce, Buick, Moline, Star, Haynes, Studebaker, Reo, Winton, Packard, Locomobile, Stearns, Case, Maxwell, Auburn. The number and variety of car makers posed a major problem to the industry. Writes Lloyd Morris: "Despite its prodigious and rapid development, the automobile industry, broadly viewed, remained violently unstable—an affair of boom or bust; a plunger's paradise in which new companies arose and collapsed with alarming frequency."

It's difficult to believe, but conservative Wall Street bankers looked askance at the motor car, seeing no hope for it on the American scene. Auto shares were not listed on the New York Stock Exchange. Manufacturers got their financial backing from private individuals. Some of these backers were genuinely wealthy; others were make-a-fast-buck frauds. Still others were eccentric or bossy. It all added up to near chaos in the industry and to many financial failures. Automobile motors were improving—indeed, many experts call the motor developed between 1908 and 1914 as good as the ones produced today. But a bewildered public had trouble discovering which were the good cars.

Curved Dash Olds (used here as movie prop) was the first American car model to catch on with public. Manufacturer Ransom Olds sold 425 in 1900, some 4,000 in 1904.

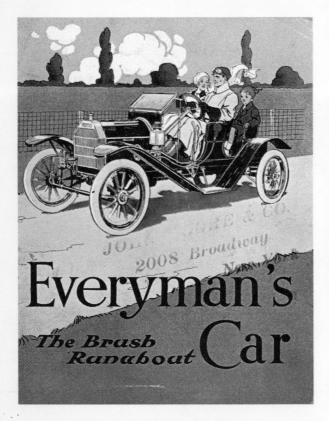

Everyman's Car
The Brash Runabout

WILL HE RISK IT?

Detroit was slowly becoming the center of the industry, though cars were still built in Hartford, Springfield, Kokomo, and Cleveland. In each place, the manufacture of parts was farmed out to local foundries and machine shops. When finished, they were hauled by wagon to the plant or factory, often no more than a shack where men and boys assembled the parts into motor cars. In Detroit, the Dodge brothers were the best makers of auto parts. Henry Ford scored a major victory when he lured them away from Ransom Olds.

It was haphazard, full of splitting headaches, and Ford had as many as anyone in the game. In 1904, when he set up his own auto shop, incorporating as the Ford Motor Company, he was a man of forty-one who had tinkered none too successfully— or profitably—in the employ of others. His father was pressing him to return to a sensible life on the family farm, offering a parcel of land as an enticement. But Henry was adamant. He was determined to build a sturdy car for general use, what he called the "universal car."

It was a time of wonderful cars—large, eccentric, often uncomfortable, but bold and handsome in design, honest in execution, and exhilarating to drive. All we needed was roads.

The popular image of lanky Henry working single-mindedly toward the perfection of his engine is misleading. Much of his precious time had to be spent raising money, after which he alienated backers by inbred cussedness. Though acclaimed a genius, Ford got important mechanical assists from a side-kick with the unlikely name of Childe Harold Wills. A visitor to the Ford factory of the time recalls hunks of cars propped carelessly against walls. It did not seem they could ever be assembled into autos that would run.

Nor was Ford as relentless as pictured in his pursuit of the universal car. Between incorporation in 1904 and the introduction of the fabulously successful Model T four years later, he turned out four other models. Once he allowed himself to be deflected into a luxury car costing $2,800. It was a dismal failure and Henry returned to pondering his universal car.

The Model T, priced at $850, was unveiled on October 1, 1908. Soon after this, Ford, for various reasons, was on the verge of selling out, but with much haggling over terms, the deal fell through. Next, Ford made a decision almost as great as his development of the Model T. In 1909, he abruptly issued orders to freeze the Model T. There would be no more drastic changes, no different models. The Ford plant would make only one car, and it would be the Model T. His 1912 model sold for $600, the '24 for $290. If a universal car could be made at all, Henry Ford had made it.

Taking the family out for a Sunday drive was hazardous, but many did it. Doctors and clergymen bought early cars, giving the industry a boost. Farmers made hardy Model T Ford a success.

More dramatic is the concurrent saga of William Crapo Durant, who founded General Motors. Durant was one of the great American promoters. He had enormous vision, fierce personal drive, and a hypnotic gift of gab. The one thing he lacked was judgment. Sad to relate, Billy Durant was a man who didn't know when to stop.

The basis of Durant's meteoric success was a car built in 1903 by David Dunbar Buick. This had been abandoned when the Buick company failed, but Durant learned of it. He tested a leftover Buick model, found it good, and began a whirlwind operation at Flint, Michigan. Soon he had the world's largest auto plant, turning out five different Buick models.

As a rapid, ever-expanding manufacturer, he feared a shutdown that would halt production. He dreamed of owning a chain of suppliers and processors with every single operation leading to final assembly of a car. This amounted to that contemporary anathema, a vertical trust, but Durant achieved his goal. He was also dissatisfied with making one type of car. He wanted to aim at rich, poor, in-between.

By 1908, he was making Cadillac, Buick, Oldsmobile, and Oakland cars. In addition, he controlled twenty subsidiary companies. In one year he grabbed twenty per cent of the nation's automobile production and earned a $9,000,000 profit.

A wiser man might have stopped to consolidate, but not Billy Durant. He tore on. Within two years his business had increased by two thirds, but profits were

Luxurious Welch tourer, restored to perfection by enthusiast Ralph Stein, is survivor of 1907. By second decade, Sunday traffic through America's parks was paralyzing.

down. Why? Because Durant spent millions buying inventions that did not work out. Other mistakes in judgment cut into his prospering empire and soon he stood hat in hand on the threshold of Wall Street. He needed only a few paltry millions to keep GM going, but bankers sneered at him. To them the auto was still the horseless buggy, the futureless devil-wagon. Finally two big banks agreed to help, but their terms were stiff. For one thing, Billy Durant had to fire himself. A few years later he won GM back, but only briefly. He lost it again, and his momentum as well.

This high-echelon finance was of gripping interest to the industry, but the public cared only about more and better cars. So the really dramatic story of 1910—the year Durant lost GM—was furnished by a spark of electricity. There had been hopeful talk of self-starters, since the hazards of cranking a car were great. Men broke wrists, arms, and even killed themselves turning the cranks of stubborn cars. Other inventors had worked on self-starters operated by compressed air, springs, or acetylene gas. Young Charles F. Kettering claimed he could do it by electricity—and he could.

His instant reward was an order for four thousand starters for Cadillacs. His invention was of lasting importance, an added shot in the arm to an industry already booming. Not the least of its effects was to put women behind the wheel.

97

"By the Light..."

♥ *They All Sang!* That's the title of a book about American music at this time. And it was true. Up to the second decade of the twentieth century, America sang its songs. After that, it danced to them. But through 1910 you had the warm pattern of families clustering around parlor pianos to harmonize the old songs. On street corners there were barber shop quartets, in vaudeville were sweet-voiced tenors, or girls like Nora Bayes, Eva Tanguay, Trixie Friganza, Sophie Tucker—no one ever put over songs like those gals! Parties and church socials became close-harmony songfests. Gay groups carrying picnic baskets rode trolleys to the end of the line, then gathered around roaring fires to strum banjos and sing "By the Light of the Silvery Moon."

Songs of the era were written to be sung —and memorized. This meant they had to tell a story. Usually it was a sad one about an aching, breaking heart, with long verses setting the stage for a chorus. Other songs were lively, like "Down Where the Wurzburger Flows" or "Has Anybody Here Seen Kelly, K-E-Double-L-Y?" They all stemmed from Tin Pan Alley, a compact district between New York's Fifth and Sixth Avenues at Twenty-eighth Street, where most of the music publishers were located. Here pianos pounded day and night; the tinny sound of it gave the place its name.

The Alley's leading composers from 1890 to 1910 were Charles K. Harris, Paul Dresser, and Harry Von Tilzer—a trio as potent in music as Tinker, Evers, and Chance in baseball. Harris wrote America's first great song hit, "After the Ball" (Many's the heart that is aching/If you could read them all/Many the hopes that have vanished/After the ball). Composed in the Nineties, it retained year-after-year popularity. Even the big John Philip Sousa Band thumped it out.

In those days song hits seldom made a composer rich. (The publisher got the dough.) Harris kept writing songs, some

Songwriters were dreaming up some of America's all-time favorite tunes. And once a popular performer had put a song over, everyone bought the sheet music.

98

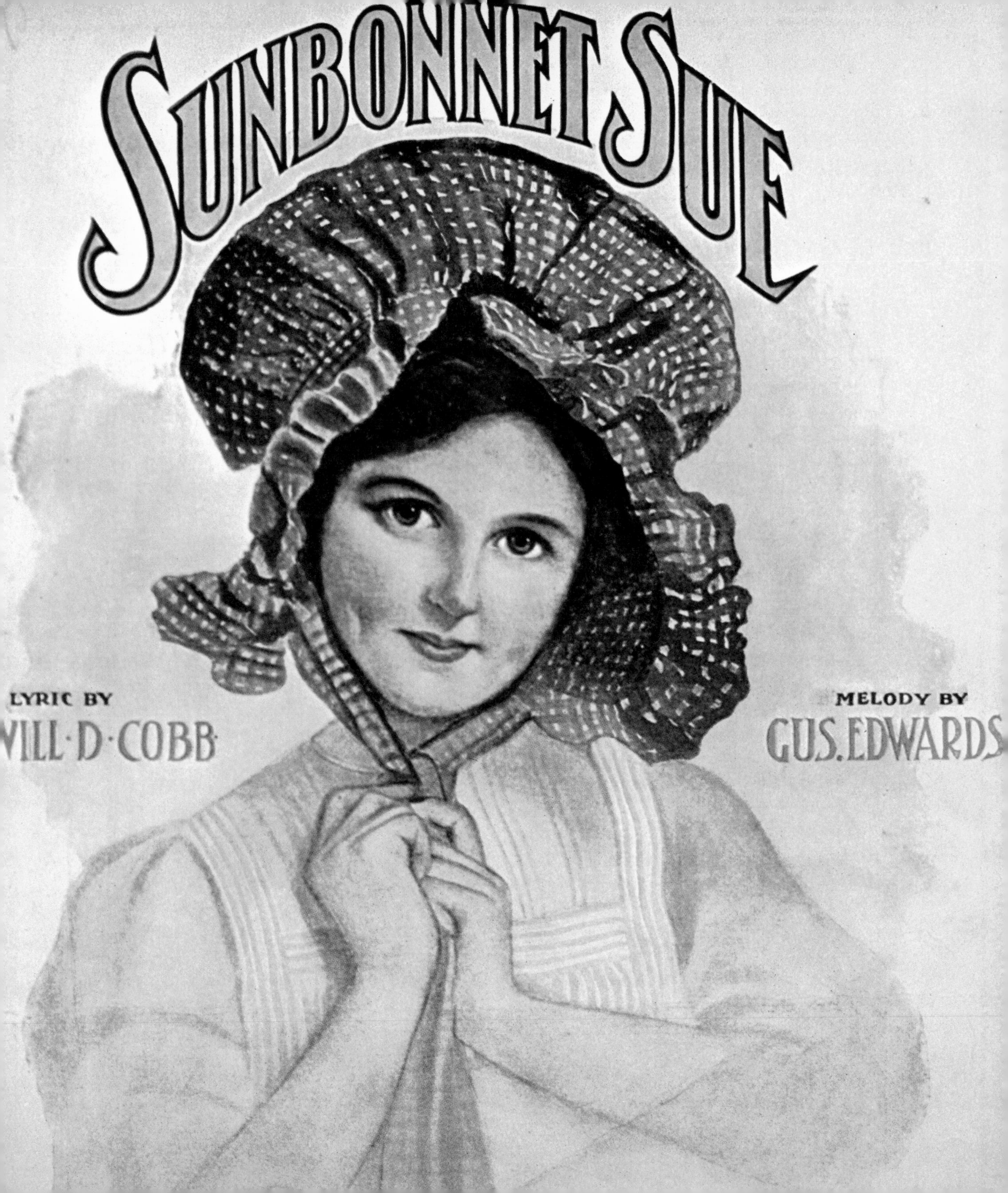
SUNBONNET SUE
LYRIC BY
WILL D COBB
MELODY BY
GUS. EDWARDS

hits, others flops. He scored again with "Break the News to Mother" and "Hello Central, Give Me Heaven" (For my Mommy's there). The clever fellow parodied his own type of song in "Heaven Will Protect the Working Girl," sung by Marie Dressler in the show *Tillie's Nightmare.*

Harris was undisputed king when big, bluff Paul Dresser first strolled down Tin Pan Alley. From Indiana (his brother was novelist Theodore Dreiser), Paul's first success was "On the Banks of the Wabash." Later he wrote "Just Tell Them That You Saw Me," plus other heart-throbbers. Dresser prospered well enough to form his own music publishing company. At the same time, he was an easy-come, easy-go spender who couldn't stay solvent. By 1907 he was flat broke. Fair-weather pals ducked him and Tin Pan Alley heard the chilly whisper, "Paul's washed up." He had just completed "My Gal Sal," but lacked the money to promote it to success, or so he thought. He got the song printed and distributed, then went to bed to die of a broken heart. After his death, "My Gal Sal" took the country by storm. It was his greatest hit.

Harry Von Tilzer was amazingly prolific. He wrote three thousand songs—he liked to say—before his first hit. This was "Only a Bird in a Gilded Cage," and he went on to do "Wait Till the Sun Shines, Nellie," and a host of others.

For more gilded tastes came the fresh new operetta music of Victor Herbert. Born in Ireland, musically educated in Germany, Herbert was a rare person—a fat man always in a hurry. He worked fast, moved fast, talked fast, relaxed only over night-time steins of his beloved Pilsener beer. He wrote several operettas before 1904, among them *Babes in Toyland.* In that year, he crashed through with *Mlle. Modiste,* a surpassing success. In it, Fritzi Scheff sang "Kiss Me Again." He followed with *The Red Mill* (1906) and *Naughty Marietta* (1910). But he never got complete satisfaction from his work. "I'm a good tunesmith, but six months after I'm dead no one will remember my name," he often said. He really believed it.

A Broadway celebrity of another type was George M. Cohan, who had been writing songs since the age of sixteen. Now a quintuple-threat man on Broadway, he was author, composer, lyricist, dancer, and leading man in the famous Cohan musical comedies. Georgie's music, like his shows, was fast, staccato, unabashedly sentimental. Sweethearts, mothers, the Red, White and Blue, all got tribute in his words-of-one-syllable lyrics. He wrote "So Long, Mary," "Forty-five Minutes from Broadway," "You're a Grand Old Flag," "Give My Regards to Broadway," and many others. He paved the way for the swift-paced musical shows of the Roaring Twenties.

Except for Victor Herbert, all this was popular stuff. Many Americans of conservative stripe looked down on it, preferring Enrico Caruso, Ernestine Schumann-Heink, Amelita Galli-Curci, John McCormack, and other musical longhairs. Yet there was a middle ground where admirers of both classical and popular met in happy harmony. Here are found the three best-known songs of a song-conscious era. They were "The Rosary," "O Promise Me," and "The End of a Perfect Day." Each was a "sincere" song which plunged arrow-straight into the heart and stirred up the nobler emotions. "The Rosary" had merit; its music was by the well-known Ethelbert Nevin, its words by poet William Cameron Rogers. "O Promise Me," plucked from Reginald De Koven's successful *Robin Hood*, is still warbled at weddings.

"The End of a Perfect Day"—most popular of the super-popular trio—has a strange history. It was written in 1910 by a hard-luck lady named Carrie Jacobs Bond. Wife of a doctor at a time when medical men had difficulty earning money, Carrie wrote songs to augment the family income. When her husband died, leaving her with a child to support, she was driven to the only occupations open to impoverished widows. She painted china, took in boarders, made dresses, sang in church choirs. With the help of friends she scraped up enough money to publish (from her own parlor) seven songs, among them "I Love You Truly" and "Just A-wearying For You."

It was an uphill battle and Mrs. Bond took sick as a result. Sent to California to recuperate, she went with friends on a day-long trip to the top of Mount Rubidoux, near Riverside. At the trip's end, the Widow Bond sat down and spontaneously dashed off the words, then the music, of "The End of a Perfect Day." Shortly it was America's favorite, second in all-time sales to "Home Sweet Home." It sold over five million copies, plus countless records and piano rolls. Among its early admirers were State Senator and Mrs. Warren G. Harding of Ohio. Never did this average couple lose their taste for the song.

As if this musical abundance were not enough, there was also the new ragtime jazz—or jass, as it originally was spelled. It originated with American Negroes, who first sang spirituals, then blues, and now played jazz. Much has been written about New Orleans as the cradle of American jazz. The bawdy houses of Storyville and the funeral processions of respected Negroes get credit for the birth of the blues and the jazz tempo. But the story of New York—where jazz led to the fox trot rather than to Dixieland—is less well known and just as important.

Jazz in New York highlights an entertainment phenomenon of the time. This was the work of a group of Negro entertainers so talented that they were able to succeed despite the formidable color barrier of the day.

In vaudeville, Bert Williams and George Walker cakewalked to "Has Anybody Seen Miss Dora?" "Bon Bon Buddy, the Chocolate Drop," "You're In the Right Church But the Wrong Pew." To drawling Bert Williams alone belonged the song "Nobody" (I ain't never done nothin' to Nobody/and I ain't never got nothin' from Nobody/no time).

In musical comedy, Bob Cole and the Florida-born brothers J. Rosamond and James Weldon Johnson wrote more than two hundred songs for Broadway shows. Their best was "Under the Bamboo Tree," a clever transposition of the great spiritual "Nobody Knows the Trouble I've Seen." When "Under the Bamboo Tree" was slipped into a Broadway show the audience rose to clap, stomp, and sing along.

Williams and Walker, Cole and the Johnsons—they played before white people, or wrote Negro songs with whites in mind. But at Broadway and Thirty-ninth Street, the heart of the seamy Tenderloin, was a hangout patronized by Negro entertainers. Run by Baron Wilkins, it was little more than an all-night saloon, but the ragtime piano never ceased. In time, white people heard about Baron Wilkins' place and a few dared pay a visit. Then a society hostess heard about the new ragtime piano and hired a Negro pianist to play at parties. Others followed her. James Weldon Johnson, one of the ragtime pianists, later remembered, "The ragtime music came near spoiling the party. As soon as I began, the conversation suddenly stopped. It was a pleasure to me to watch the expressions of astonishment and delight that grew on the faces of everybody. Several women left the table and asked what kind of music I was playing. . . . They watched my fingers." (Indeed, Johnson himself bore watching, for this talented man went on to become an author, professor, diplomat, and founder of the N.A.A.C.P.)

New York produced the nation's popular music in Tin Pan Alley, on West 28th Street. In 1914, it looked like this. "My Gal Sal" was Paul Dresser's great, posthumous hit.

The Negro entertainers lived in one spot, the Marshall Hotel, on Fifty-third Street. Next door, musicians established the Clef Club, a place to practice and await jobs. On Sunday nights the Marshall Hotel dining room was turned into a cabaret for all-Negro entertainment. As word got around, white entertainers and song writers were begging to get in. It's said one was a beginner named Berlin, from New York's Lower East Side.

In charge of the Marshall Sunday nights and the Clef Club was a now almost-forgotten fellow named James Reese Europe. A big man, Jim not only had rare rhythm, but the organizing talent necessary to be a band leader. Another asset was a wife who was a hairdresser popular with Fifth Avenue social leaders. As she set hair, Mrs. Europe urged her ladies to hire Jim's orchestra for dances. No such hostess had nerve enough to hire only a Negro orchestra, but they allowed Jim to alternate with the white orchestras playing sedate waltzes, tangos, one-steps. People at the parties went wild over Jim Europe's music and tried desperately to one- and two-step to it. But the one-step and two-step weren't quite right for dancing to jazz.

Soon Jim Europe had enough prestige to proclaim his men Europe's Society Orchestra. He trained several orchestras so that different Jim Europe bands could play on the same night. Newspapers quoted him: "Ragtime may be Negro music, but it is American Negro music, more alive than other American music." Jim also hired

Carnegie Hall for a jazz concert, a tradition carried on by Paul Whiteman, Benny Goodman, and other greats. "He established jazz on Broadway," Joe Laurie wrote.

People of all ages were hearing jazz for the first time in 1910. And they were shocked by the "barbaric harmonies, the audacious resolutions, often consisting of an abrupt jump from one key to another, the intricate rhythms in which the accents fall in the most unexpected places but in which the beat was never lost."

Don't get the idea that Jim Europe played jazz as we know it today. His was syncopation—ragtime, cakewalk, with jazz overtones. Mandolins, guitars, banjos, and an instrument called the bandolin all but drowned out trumpets, trombones, bass.

Yet there was a beat to the new music, a beat that made people hop up and dance. Soon they would figure out the right steps to use.

♥

Tin Pan Alley was awash with composers and would-be composers in the days when "they all sang." Thousands of songs were published annually. Most are now forgotten, but when a song of this era was good, it was very, very good. Nearly all the songs we sing in sentimental moments today come from the teeming old Alley on Twenty-eighth Street. Take a look at just a few titles:

Broadway traffic (at 46th Street) was less dense in 1909, but it was already a great white way. Tunes of the times included list at right.

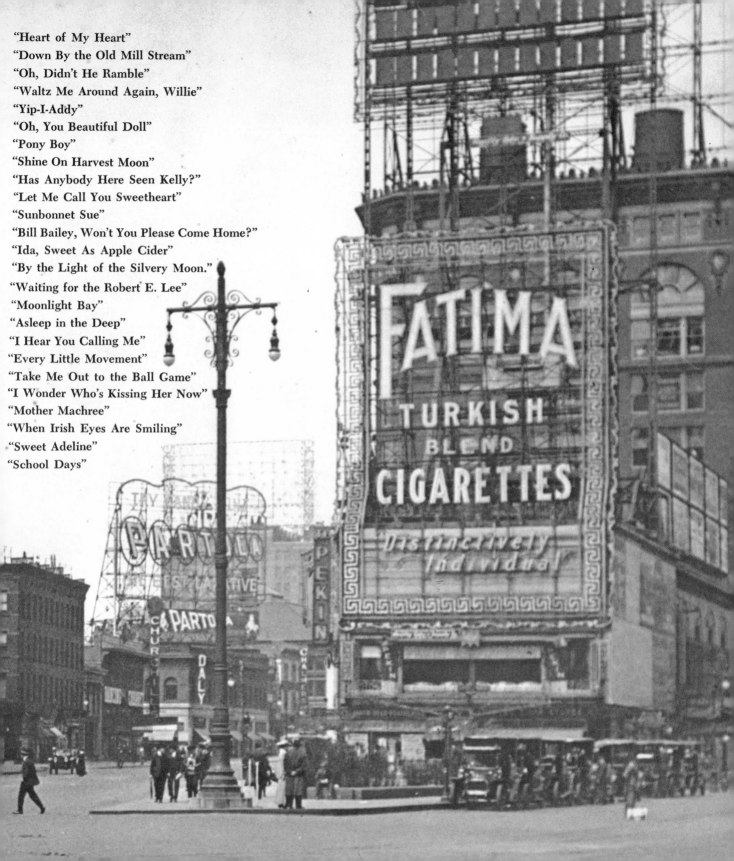

"Heart of My Heart"

"Down By the Old Mill Stream"

"Oh, Didn't He Ramble"

"Waltz Me Around Again, Willie"

"Yip-I-Addy"

"Oh, You Beautiful Doll"

"Pony Boy"

"Shine On Harvest Moon"

"Has Anybody Here Seen Kelly?"

"Let Me Call You Sweetheart"

"Sunbonnet Sue"

"Bill Bailey, Won't You Please Come Home?"

"Ida, Sweet As Apple Cider"

"By the Light of the Silvery Moon."

"Waiting for the Robert E. Lee"

"Moonlight Bay"

"Asleep in the Deep"

"I Hear You Calling Me"

"Every Little Movement"

"Take Me Out to the Ball Game"

"I Wonder Who's Kissing Her Now"

"Mother Machree"

"When Irish Eyes Are Smiling"

"Sweet Adeline"

"School Days"

New York's immigrants clustered in tenements on lower East Side.

1900 1905
1905 1910
♥
1915 **1920**
1920 1925
1925 1930
1930 1935
1935 1942

1910 1915

♥ Historians say so: The years between 1910 and 1915 were the pleasantest this country has ever known. The years seem to have had a Peter Pan quality, a fact which made them no less pleasant. "There was an incredible innocence and security," Elmer Davis once recalled. "It was a time of peace, wherein we trusted." An editorial in *Collier's* predicted that fifty years in the future the world would look back and call 1905 to 1915 the most progressive era in the nation's history.

108   A number of factors had brought the country so close to being a paradise. America was growing, its people prospering. Theater, books, education, all reflected a fine new freedom. "Man had been freed from his fear of hell," is the way one writer put it. There was so much to know, so much to learn. It was called the "Why?" era, because everyone asked so many questions.

It was—in a funny way—a period when everyone was rich. Not in money, exactly; in other ways. The new wealth encompassed hope, energy, and access to a full life. It was freedom to buy—a car, for instance. "*Things* were in the saddle," social historian Mark Sullivan wrote. For the first time in history mass production placed the average man in a position to own things formerly available only to the

rich. Wealth was becoming diffused. Up to now it had been tightly controlled.

Ours was a nation in a hurry, but it was a good kind of hurry. "To stay where you are in this country, you must keep moving," a wit remarked. People knew the world could be a better place and wanted it that way as rapidly as possible. There was an aggressive drive toward this better world. Wrote the distinguished diplomat Walter Hines Page: "Our activities go well, such as road building, school improvement, sanitation, helpful concern for the unfortunate and the growth of our interest in one another."

Our interest in one another. It was this last that brought uniqueness to the era. People were not only demanding things for themselves, but for others as well. Never before or since has a nation manifested so much heart. "It was like the awakening conscience of a fifteen-year-old boy," a writer has said. This was the period during which philanthropists, led by tough old Andrew Carnegie, began endowing libraries and other useful institutions.

City folk looked around, saw slum squalor, and agitated for improvement in tenement living. Country folk fought against cruelty to animals. Neighbor thought about neighbor, performed acts of next-door kindness. Groups worked for the abolition of child labor, or tried to exterminate the horsefly and other carriers of disease. War was waged on white slavery and on men who expectorated. "Gentlemen will not, others *must* not, spit on the floor," newly posted signs read.

Yet there was an ambivalence in American life. People were trying to live by the Golden Rule, abide by the eternal verities. But at the same time they felt the conflict of new against old. Trying to live by the old ways, they couldn't help but admire the new.

Old methods of work were first to go. As early as 1910, the phrases "scientific management" and "time study" rang through the land. A man named Frederick Taylor—who remembers him today?—became the country's first efficiency expert. He reorganized industries, even told hod carriers how to pick up bricks more efficiently. Taylor's theories meant the end of the old individuality of the working class, but the public was for him. Scientific management really triumphed in 1912 when Grand Central Station was constructed in New York. Excavation, rock drilling, erection of steel and stone—all went on with trains moving in and out. People marveled.

The approving phrase "go-getter" was coined for the extra ambitious. Men and boys signed up for self-improvement correspondence courses. People began to take pride in intellectual pursuits and there was talk of highbrows and lowbrows. By definition, a highbrow said *eye-ther,* a lowbrow *ee-ther.* Or the highbrow asked, "Do you know ping-pong?" And the lowbrow answered, "No, who wrote it?"

Even old theories of love were questioned. It's a forgotten fact that Dr. Sigmund Freud visited the United States in 1909, giving a series of lectures at Clark College in Worcester, Massachusetts. Word got around that Freud deemed the sex urge the basis of human personality and the root of all human problems. His name promptly became anathema to right-thinking folk. Yet a few creative minds saw his point and authors began writing books and plays with Freudian motivations. In this subliminal fashion the country began absorbing Freud.

Change, change, more change! It was everywhere. Women began to smoke in public, the ladies of society first. "I don't believe in bragging, but I know three ladies who smoke cigarettes," a social climber was quoted as saying. A few brave girls—college graduates, no doubt—dared question the word "obey" in the marriage ceremony. Divorce was newly tolerated.

You'd never believe it from looking at pictures, but women were shedding a few layers of clothing. On the outside, they still seemed to be swathed in blankets. But, underneath, shifts, petticoats, and even corsets were disappearing.

Men began wearing wrist watches, which had been around for years but had been considered effete. Then rugged Richard Harding Davis put one on and liked it. Thus redeemed, the wrist watch for males was here to stay.

♥ In 1912, Teddy Roosevelt was back in the spotlight. What was he doing there? He was running for the presidency—something he had vowed never to do again.

How did it happen? Back in 1910, home from his African safari, Teddy became disenchanted with William Howard Taft. Actually, Taft hadn't done badly as President. But the fat Chief Executive tried to be himself, rather than tread in Theodore's footsteps. It made Teddy's blood boil and he developed a man-sized hatred. In 1912 he was determined to grab the Republican presidential nomination from Taft.

But things didn't work out that way. Delegates to the Republican convention in Chicago may have wanted Teddy, but the bosses liked the pliable Taft. So Taft got the nomination, though Teddy made an impassioned speech which warned, "We stand at Armageddon." A rejected Teddy was immediately nominated by the Progressive party, headed by Robert M. LaFollette, the liberal Senator from Wisconsin. Roosevelt was still an enormously popular man. He liked to boast about feeling as strong as a bull moose, and usually he did. He said it now, and the Progressives became known as the Bull Moose party.

Meantime, the Democrats had picked Woodrow Wilson, former President of Princeton University and Governor of New Jersey. Of himself Wilson once said, "I am a vague, conjectural personality, more made up of opinions and academic prepossessions than of human traits and red corpuscles."

An outsider couldn't have described the man better. But the point is that Wilson was a liberal and an idealist, which exactly fitted these splendid new times. Rampaging Teddy, as a progressive Republican, had identically fitted his own period. Now the two champions were arrayed against each other, with Taft an uncomfortable third in the ring. Alert citizens realized that Teddy very likely would split the Republican vote and thereby allow Wilson to win. Teddy himself must have known it, but in his burning hatred the important thing was to boot Taft out of the White House.

So the famous campaign of 1912 began. Wilson kept his speeches on a high, idealistic plane. Bumbling Taft wore a look of injured innocence. Teddy provided the color. He was uncomfortable on the radical Progressive platform, but he fought hard. Just before a speech in Milwaukee, a would-be assassin shot him in the chest. Teddy didn't know whether the wound was serious, but declared, "I will make this speech or die! It is one thing or the other. I have a message to deliver and will deliver it as long as there is life in my body!" After speaking for nearly an hour, he went to a hospital, lay in bed for a week.

As expected, Teddy split the Republican party. Wilson, the professor-idealist, was President of the United States.

In 1912, Roosevelt ran a three-way race for President against Wilson (top) and Taft. His entry split the Republican effort and gave Wilson a narrow victory.

♥ With mass production came mass advertising. It had to—there were so many new products, so many consumers to be reached. Of course, advertising was no novelty in America. Only its sudden magnitude and persuasive pitch were new. American business had been halfheartedly advertising—patent medicines for the most part—since the 1860's, when J. Walter Thompson and N. W. Ayer started business. By 1900, the country boasted some fifteen ad agencies, though agency is hardly the word. "Brokers" is better, since these outfits merely took an ad from a company, then dickered with a magazine or newspaper for good position and a discount. They neither wrote ads nor rewrote them. Just placed them. "Advertise Judiciously" was the credo of one agency, and the whole business was as low-keyed as that.

Then one fireball of a man came along and revolutionized advertising. You've heard of him—Albert Lasker.

Texas born, Lasker was young when he got a job with the Chicago advertising firm of Lord & Thomas. A day or two on the job sold him on the importance of advertising. He insisted on writing ads himself, meticulously describing the clients' products in clear prose. They impressed people so much that at age twenty-three he was earning $52,000 a year, an almost unheard-of salary for a young man of the time. Still, he felt frustrated. He knew that advertising had not yet achieved its full potential. When you came right down to it, what *was* advertising?

Lasker asked a lot of people that question and word of his interest got around. One day an office boy handed him a note. "I am in the saloon downstairs," it read, "and I can tell you what advertising is." Lasker high-tailed down and found John E. Kennedy, an obscure copywriter. Kennedy lifted his glass and intoned, "Advertising is salesmanship in print."

To Lasker it was like glimpsing the Holy Grail. That was it! A copywriter should not be satisfied just to describe; he must sell, sell, sell. Instead of writing straight copy, he must angle the copy. Lasker hired Kennedy and set to work.

So modern advertising was born. Another dawn came when an unsung genius at J. Walter Thompson coined a new slogan for Woodbury Soap : "A Skin You Love to Touch." This, the industry believed, introduced sex into advertising. The ad business was on the road to profits of untold billions of dollars.

It also brought much zip to American life, with ads promoting catchy slogans and top artists drawing peachy girls or lovely landscapes as backgrounds. In fact, nothing can beat these old ads for nostalgia. Just look once again at those stately Packards and Pierce Arrows! Or read those vintage slogans: "Ask the Man Who Owns One,"

"Keep That Schoolgirl Complexion."

There were so many opportunities for advertising! The citrus industry of California, for instance, was having great trouble selling its oranges. It consulted the dynamic Lasker. He conceived a campaign to make the nation squeeze and drink orange juice, something only a few health-faddists had ever done. Did he succeed in selling California's oranges? You know he did.

Despite the big early advertisers—Hart Schaffner & Marx, Arrow Collars, American Tobacco, Ivory Soap ("It Floats"), Heinz baked beans, Smith Brothers cough drops— it was automobiles that dominated advertising. And why not? Automobiles were a luxury, making splashy, persuasive advertising a necessity. They were relatively high-priced, so that a manufacturer could allocate $100 in advertising for every $1,000 car sold. Only a few people, really, owned cars. The trick was to pressure the public into buying your make.

Naturally, the boom in advertising changed American newspapers and magazines. Up to now these had stumbled along on circulation income, the small change people paid for their copies. Now a stupendous increase in advertising money poured into their coffers. Publishers began taking care not to offend advertisers and there was far less journalistic crusading as a result. In magazines, the short story became the office favorite, since it could be larded through pages of ads. Competition for large circulations brought popular authors unprecedented sums for their work.

In the early advertising business, the big thing was a catchy slogan. The air was full of them: "Time to Retire" (Fisk tires), "Watch the Fords Go By," "Poor Beer vs. Pure Beer" (Schlitz), "Try Our Rivals Too" (Van Camp soups), "His Master's Voice" (Victrola).

The year 1914 brought an event that immeasurably increased both mass production and mass advertising. Responsible for it was Henry Ford. Henry was no great social thinker. He probably never read a book on economics in his life. But for a manufacturer of autos, he had a lot of horse sense. Henry's brainstorm involved labor, a market that manufacturers and advertisers had never taken into consideration. Employers and sellers of goods saw labor only as mass of nonpotential customers. Ford took another view. If paid better wages, he reasoned, labor could become the country's greatest consumer.

Ford himself could hire all the labor he needed at $2 a day. But suddenly he began paying $5 a day. It raised a nationwide howl and turned Henry Ford into a world figure. Capitalists called him a Socialist, a worse tag than Communist in those days. Socialists hastily disavowed him. Henry stood pat. He couldn't explain what he was doing, or why. He only knew it was right. A man getting five bucks a day would spend more than a man who got two. He would buy more, and in the end everyone would be better off. It was as simple as that!

Next to the Heart of
Candy Lovers
are

WHITMAN'S

Chocolates and Confections

The Perfection
of
Confections

ASK FOR THEM ANYWHERE

WHITMAN'S Instantaneous Chocolate
Made instantly with boiling milk.

STEPHEN F. WHITMAN & SON
1316 Chestnut Street
Philadelphia

A skin you love to touch

Why it is so rare

A skin you love to touch is rarely found, because so few people understand the skin and its needs.

Begin now to take *your* skin seriously.

You can make it what you would love to have it by using the following treatment *regularly*.

Make this treatment a daily habit

Just before retiring, work up a warm water lather of Woodbury's Facial Soap and rub it into the skin gently until the skin is softened, the pores opened and the face feels fresh and clean. Rinse in cooler water, then apply cold water—the colder the better—for a full minute. Whenever possible, rub your face for a few minutes with a piece of ice. Always dry the skin thoroughly.

Write today for Samples

For 4c. we will send a sample cake. For 10c., samples of Woodbury's Facial Soap, Facial Cream and Powder. For 5c., copy of the Woodbury Book and samples of the Woodbury Preparations. Address The Andrew Jergens Co., Dept 7-E, Spring Grove Ave., Cincinnati, O. In Canada, address the Andrew Jergens Co. Ltd., Dept. 7-E Perth, Ontario.

Woodbury's Facial Soap

For sale by dealers everywhere throughout the United States and Canada.

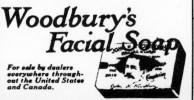

Good morning!
Have you used
Pears' Soap?

Advertising, once content to describe products, now undertook to sell them. "A skin you love to touch" was a milestone. It introduced sex-appeal as a buying motive.

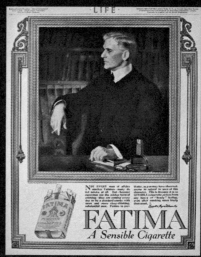

♥ BIFF! BAM! ZOWIE! BANG! POW! GOTT IN HIMMEL! S'MATTER POP? In those days comic strips were funny, or tried to be. People referred to them as "funny papers" or "the funnies." On Sunday mornings many a merry battle took place over who got to read the funnies first.

The early comics were aimed at grown-ups, since kids seldom bought papers. But old and young liked the funny papers.

The artists who drew them tried to put a chuckle in each strip, or tickle the funny bone with a wry comment on human quirks. It was done in many ways—by straight humor, mad stuff, or slapstick. Then, after the first twenty years, comics proceeded into an era which produced such fine talents as Fontaine Fox ("Toonerville Trolley"), Clare Briggs ("When a Feller Needs a Friend"), Sidney Smith ("Andy Gump"), and more realistic, less loony strips like "Harold Teen," "Gasoline Alley," and "Little Orphan Annie." Some of the old comics kept right on, drawn by new artists when the originator died. But with age and competition they became a little less inspired. "When comedy went out, with the literal and suspenseful taking over, the great days of comics ended," one expert believes.

If nothing else, these old comics were robust, for the majority were the work of men who had been sports cartoonists. It furnished a kind of male madness to the new medium.

116

Bright color also assisted the comics, at least in the big comic sections of the Sunday papers. Fact is, color led the comics into their own. Back in 1895, a newfangled primary color printing press was bought by the New York *World*. To test it, a bright glob of loud yellow was added to the Kid, a character in R. F. Outcault's pioneering strip, "Hogan's Alley." Overnight, the moderately successful "Hogan's Alley" became a sensation. Everyone talked about the "Yellow Kid," as he was quickly dubbed. Competition between the *World* and the New York *Journal* for ownership of the strip brought the name "Yellow Journalism" to the whole newspaper era.

The Yellow Kid—gap-toothed, flap-eared, always in a nightgown—also had things to say. The balloon had not yet been invented as a medium for comic-strip words, so Outcault lettered the Yellow Kid's talk on his tinted nightgown. The Kid's first auto ride was down a thoroughfare called Uneasy Street. The bright yellow demon said, "Gee, dis beats de carpet, which is hard to beat."

In time, Outcault abandoned the Yellow Kid for a politer Buster Brown and his talking dog, Tige. "His kids had an impudent look to them," a critic has written of Outcault. By now, his success had pulled others into the comic field. Most of these early strips are forgotten today, but a few will remain forever in the minds of the middle-aged-and-more.

"Desperate Desmond," one of several strips drawn by Harry Hershfield, was first adventure-and-suspense comic to appear in daily installments.

There was "Happy Hooligan," drawn by F. Opper. Happy was a homely, amiable moron, his head adorned by a silly tin can. Happy was the eternal butt of life's cruel jokes. Opper also created "And Her Name Was Maud." Maud was a mule who ended each strip with a well-aimed kick of the hind legs. He also drew "Alphonse and Gaston," that polite duo who enriched the language with the undying expression, "After you, my dear Alphonse."

Slapstick arrived with Hans *und* Fritz, the "Katzenjammer Kids." Drawn by Rudolph Dirks, they inhabited a universe where reality seldom impinged. Katzenjammer, literally "the yowling of cats," is the German word for hangover. The kids were inspired adult-baiters who spent their time playing fiendish tricks on Mama and the Captain. Mama remained philosophical about her terrible offspring. "Kindness mit kidlets is der pinochle of life," the hefty lady believed.

Like all top strips, beginning with the Yellow Kid, the Katzenjammers brought the world new slang. Probably its best remembered was the word "nix," from the German "nichts," or "nothing." "Brains you got nix," one kid snarls at the other.

But there was a bedrock of solid respectability to the Katzenjammers. Returning from one of his many voyages, the Captain is greeted by Mama, "Yoo-hoo, Dollink, back to der home sweet home! Giffs flop chacks for breakfast." Touched by these warm words, the Captain decides, "Ven all iss done and said, dere ain't no dod-

rotted place like home."

The Katzenjammer Kids were the first to talk in drawn balloons. Their heavily accented dialogue also pointed up the racial temper of the times. The nationalities making up the American melting pot were still conspicuous. To many, their old-country characteristics were funny. So the Katzenjammers caricatured the German-Americans; Happy Hooligan, and Jiggs and Maggie, the Irish; Alphonse and Gaston, the French; Abie the Agent, the Jews.

Until 1907, the funnies usually appeared on Sunday. Then Bud Fisher, a San Francisco artist, dreamed up Augustus Mutt, a harried horseplayer. He introduced Mutt to a character christened Jeff (for Jeffries, in honor of ex-heavyweight champion Jim). Fisher was willing to draw Mutt and Jeff seven days a week, the first artist to do so. Soon he was making almost $5,000 a week.

Mutt and Jeff were the first with biff-bam-zowie humor, getting laughs by physical violence. Jiggs and Maggie, late-1913 arrivals, began the husband-wife cycle in "Bringing Up Father." Maggie with her rolling pin endlessly tried to keep Jiggs from enjoying a man-type existence with his friend Dinty Moore. Maggie was also a dreadful parody of a wife. Hideously ugly, she had pretensions to high style. Maggie was any husband's horror.

There were strips and more strips. "Foxy Grandpa," "Percy and Ferdie" (the Hall Room Boys), "Little Jimmy," "Hawkshaw the Detective." Harry Hershfield, creator

"Little Nemo in Slumberland" was perthaps the high point of cartoon artistry. Creator Winsor McCay's brilliant and fanciful panels have become museum pieces.

Mutt and Jeff

Foolish Questions

The Yellow Kid

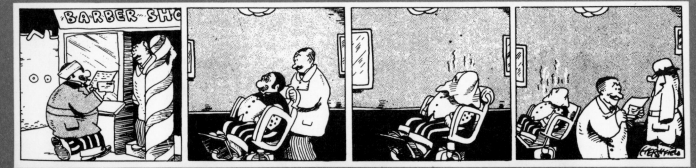

Abie the Agent

of "Abie the Agent," also did "Desperate Desmond," first of the day-to-day suspense stories. Later he did "Ish Kabibble." Rube Goldberg, a cartoonist much cherished by fellow craftsmen, began with "Foolish Questions," proceeded to "Boob McNutt," then to zany inventions. In Rube's original "Foolish Questions," a man topples off a skyscraper. "Are you hurt?" a passerby asks. "No," the man says, "I jump off this building every day to limber up for my business."

The artist TAD (T. A. Dorgan) used to say, "My stuff is for the gents, the squaws don't like me." His was a weird world. Perhaps his best work was "Tad's Favorite Indoor Sports," such as "Watching the boss as he listens to the wife on the telephone." Tad's drawings were jammed with characters, all uttering statements of inspired irrelevance. "No matter how young a prune may be, he's always fulla wrinkles," one may be telling another. Or, off in a corner, "She was only a postman's daughter, but she knew how to handle the males." It was TAD who created the nonsense expression, "For cryin' out loud." He also coined the slang expressions "hot dog," "bum's rush," "tank town," "dumb Dora," "cat's pajamas," and "baloney."

The strip that came closest to real art, however, was "Krazy Kat," drawn by West Coast artist George Herriman. The history of comics rings with tributes to Krazy. "Maddest and merriest of them all, but also art," says one book. Another: "A peak of humor and fantasy."

Batter Mutt (top) preceded Jeff in Bud Fisher's cartoon. "Foolish Questions" was an early Rube Goldberg notion. Outcault's Yellow Kid was first comic-strip character. Abie the Agent was Hershfield inspiration.

Krazy Kat lived in a world divorced from reality. In this topsy-turvy universe, the dog (Offisa Bull Pupp) loved the cat (Krazy) who loved Ignatz the mouse. Ignatz cared for no one. All he ever wanted to do was hurl a brick and "krease Krazy's bean."

Herriman loved the desert, and his Krazy Kat background was a strange wasteland interrupted by odd shapes. His dialogue was fascinating, for Herriman had a touch of the poet. "And this another romance tells," he wrote in one strip. It's a warm day and Krazy feels blue—"My, but there's nothing to do but get lonesome now-a-hot-days."

The artist was also a man of limitless inspiration with phonetic spelling. Says Krazy: "Fancy those foolish fingers fashioning a fabric. Ah, the futile foof and fuff of it—a waste of warp, a wanton wear of weft, and woof, Foowy!"

The world of Krazy Kat, with Ignatz dominant, was full of other krazy karackters. There were, among others, Kristopher Kamel, Joe Bark, Mock Duck, Don Kiyote, Walter Cephus Austridge, Krazy Katbird, Osker Wildcat, Alec Kat.

In this loony atmosphere, Krazy asks Ignatz:

"See those two hice?"
"Hice?"
"Sure, hice."
"What's hice in American?"
"Listen, Ignatz, one house, but two hice, sees do?"
"O. I. C. now, You mean two houses."
"Idyik, Would say two mouses, Ignatz?"

121

Five Big Acts

♥ The luckiest man in show business, people used to say, was not the star with a devoted following. Nor the producer with a Broadway hit and other companies touring on the road. Nor the prolific playwright, who in days of puff-ball income tax might take home $3,000 to $4,000 a week. Nor even the idolized Hollywood film star.

No, the lucky man was the owner of a chain of vaudeville theaters. Or only one theater. This fellow did little more than sit back and reap large rewards. True, he had to furnish theater, stagehands, orchestra, and salaries. But the performers themselves contributed the rest—wardrobe, sketches, musical arrangements, and (presumably) talent. When one small Midwest impresario died leaving $7,000,000, no one was particularly surprised.

This was the Golden Age of Vaudeville! Famous as clean, family-type entertainment, vaudeville traditionally offered something for everyone. Daddy could take his wife and entire brood to a show, serene in the knowledge that each would find delights in the program's mélange of songs, dances, funny sayings, acrobats, animals, contortionists, illusionists, tightrope walkers, sketches, quartets, tenors, comedians.

There has never been another art like vaude, as it was lightly called. Across the U.S.A. stretched its two thousand thriving theaters. Big cities had the anchor theaters of such flourishing chains as Keith-Albee,

Orpheum, Poli, Pantages, Proctor, Martin Beck. These were the proud homes of the two-shows-a-day, aristocratic showcases of the art. Around them, like a gigantic pinwheel, revolved the other theaters, offering three shows a day, or four, five, even six. At each level the public was offered a wide variety of acts, with bills changing in midweek to offer another grand assortment.

Indeed, there were so many gradations to vaudeville that, when promised a contract, one entertainer inquired, "What is it —small time, medium small-time, big small-time, little big-time, medium big-time, or BIG TIME?"

The Golden Age! A vaudeville bill traditionally opened with a dumb act: animals, acrobats, jugglers. Next, a single act: ventriloquist, monologist, boy-girl dance team, or song-and-dance man slapping out rhythm with the old soft shoe.

After this a magician or illusionist, a comedy team with fast patter, or a sister act. Then an elaborate act like Singer's Midgets or Karno's "Night at an English Music Hall," featuring Charlie Chaplin. With each step toward the top of the bill, quality (not to mention salary) increased. At the top perched the star act. The Star! By hard work, he, she, or it (sometimes the star act was a sketch, stunt, or tableau) had usually worked up from the bottom of the bill. In the classic phrase, the star act spent fifty years polishing twelve minutes. By the time the twelve minutes reached

Admissions were cheap in Golden Age of Vaudeville. For as little as ten cents, gallery-goers could see live performers in a variety of headline acts.

Eva Tanguay (right, as Salome) was noted for ebullience.
Below: Ziegfeld's 1918 Follies had W. C. Fields, Will Rogers, Lillian
Lorraine, Eddie Cantor and Harry Kelly as stars.

the top of the bill, they were superb. Vaudeville headliners could sweep out and take instant command of an audience better than performers in any medium.

Star acts! The headliner might be Eddie Leonard, singing "Ida, Sweet As Apple Cider," "Roll Them Roly Poly Eyes," or "Playmates"; Vesta Victoria, doing "Waiting at the Church"; Pat Rooney, rapping out his famous clog dance to "She's the Daughter of Rosie O'Grady."

Or Harry Houdini, the first dumb act to reach vaudeville's top rung. Houdini was a magician and escape artist who let himself be snapped into handcuffs, strapped into strait jackets, and buried alive. Each time, he extricated himself in minutes.

Or Annette Kellermann, beautiful high diver, winning world fame by appearing in a one-piece bathing suit. Home base for Annette was the Hippodrome in New York, where in an immortal smash finale the entire chorus of dancing girls calmly disappeared under water.

Great acts invited competition, and Miss Kellerman's was Enoch, the Fish Man. He too dived and swam in a glass tank. Underwater he placed a pail over his head (thus

*Glamorous Dolly Sisters and young Sophie Tucker,
first of the Red-Hot Mamas. Sir Harry Lauder, one of the
all-time great acts, joked and sang in Scots brogue.*

assuring himself some oxygen), and sang an audible song. After that, he played an underwater trombone solo.

A headline act might be Smith and Dale's immortal Dr. Kronkheit, or the hilarious skit "Billy's Tombstone," done on the circuit for years by Mr. and Mrs. Sidney Drew (uncle and aunt to the Barrymores). "Fun in a Gym" was another popular act, while others had such names as "Flinder's Flats," "Pest House," and "Tell Them What I Did to 'Philadelphia Jack' O'Brien." The Lunatic Bakers were a

dumb act in which the mute bakers dashed insanely in and out of ovens. The twelve Speed Mechanics assembled a Ford in two minutes. Wills, West and McGinty, one of the great acts, were the Comedy Builders.

There were many, many more: The Empire City Quartette, first to sing a *bum-bum-bum* counterpoint; Cissie Loftus, with her skillful impersonations; Elsie Janis, Everybody's Sweetheart, singing, dancing, impersonating; Leo Carrillo, telling Chinese dialect stories (believe it or not!); Moran and Mack, the Two Black Crows; Van and

THE FOUR VANNIS
Tightrope act

LA NAPIERKOWSKA
Pantomimist and cooch dancer

OTTO GYGI
Violinist

TAYLOR HOLMES
Monologue

THE ETERNAL WALTZ
Thirty-person spectacular

ED WYNN
The Perfect Fool, assisted by two straight men

Magicians, card men, hypnotists. Houdini, Thurston, Keller, Blackstone, hundreds more.

Animal acts—a million of 'em: Rhinelander's Pigs, Gillette's Dogs and Monkeys, Fink's Mules, May Barkley's Bulldog Music Hall. The list was endless.

In a class by himself was Julian Eltinge, female impersonator supreme. For thirty years Eltinge averaged $3,000 a week, built a Broadway theater which bore his name. Year after year, audiences flocked to see him. Why? Declares vaudeville authority Joe Laurie, "His make-up, wardrobe, dancing, artistic ability, and songs were never offensive. His act was true art."

Family acts: Eddie Foy and the Seven Little Foys ("If we lived in Flatbush, it would be a city"); The Three Keatons, with Buster tossed around as the Human Mop; Hyams and McIntyre, with beautiful daughter Leila; Keno and Green, with

Schenck; Duffy and Sweeney; Clark and McCullough, whose Clark became the immortal Bobby; Montgomery and Stone; Willie and Eugene Howard; the Four Marx Brothers; Cantor and Lee, the Cantor being Eddie; Wynn and Russon, with Wynn eventually graduating into Ed Wynn, the Perfect Fool.

The Palace Theater, at Broadway and Forty-seventh Street, New York, opened in 1913, and rapidly became the pinnacle of vaudeville success. The first bill to play at the Palace ran as follows:

smart-kid Mitzi; those brats of Gus Edwards' School Days—Walter Winchell, George Jessel, Georgie Price.

Sister acts: the dazzling Dolly Sisters, clever Duncan Sisters, glamorous Courtney Sisters.

Single women: Greatest of all, Nora Bayes with her poignant rendition of "Shine On Harvest Moon." An old-timer recalls, "Nora was heart, all heart, her act was full of heart. She sold songs, where others just sang them." This girl's voice was a husky contralto, throbbing with personality. She strode up and down a stage, putting over songs, clowning, swinging her hips, pausing center stage (mellow spotlight) for a sentimental recitative. Our Nora also was a lady. She walked out of a

Four Men & Two Women: Magician Harry Houdini (with livestock) also was noted escape artist; Will Rogers twirled rope and spun wisecracks; Ed Wynn was a delightful fool; Trixie Friganza (in bonnet) and Blossom Seeley (with blossoms) were vaudeville stars. Charmer opposite is Julian Eltinge, premier female impersonator.

Follies when Flo Ziegfeld told her to wear tights.

Nora's main rival was energetic Eva Tanguay, who sang "I Don't Care." The girls today still sing it, but not the way peppy Eva did. Trixie Friganza, Irene Franklin, May Irwin, Fay Templeton were other top single women. Then along came a kid from Hartford. Born Sophie Abruza, she changed her name to Tucker after marrying a gent named Tuck. She became the last of the Red-Hot Mamas. Then she was the first.

Single men were never as glamorous as single women. Why, Nora, Trixie, Eva, and Sophie would pay $5,000 for one sequined show-gown, but single men had it much easier. A single man simply strolled out on stage clad in a business suit and told stories. No props, no overhead. Just talent. When people complimented blackface comedian Frank Tinney on his low-overhead act, he remonstrated that he had to spend a fortune on burnt cork. "You see, I use only champagne corks," he explained.

Single men: Walter C. Kelly, the Virginia Judge (today's Princess of Monaco is his niece); Will Rogers, a cowboy rope twirler, who rose to world fame; Fred Allen, billed as the World's Worst Juggler, who also drawled his way to the top. You couldn't keep those jugglers down—W. C. Fields, the world's greatest (really), turned into the funniest comedian of them all. Jimmy Savo also began as a juggler—"Juggles Anything from a Feather to an Auto."

Hilarious Charles "Chic" Sale introduced the word "wisecrack" to the language. Also "wise guy." His monologue, "The Specialist," was devoted to construction and care of outhouses.

Joe Cook, Frank Fay, Julius Tannen. The list goes on. But never forget the greatest single act of them all—Sir Harry Lauder, a name well-nigh forgotten today. He was king. The little Scotsman was past master of the magical art of seeming to be the happiest person in any theater. Sir Harry did it by conspiratorial winks, cozy chuckles, you-know-how-it-is shrugs. With his rakish tam-o'-shanter, Scotch kilts, and gnarled walking stick, he sang burry songs like "Roamin' in the Gloamin'," "A Wee Doch an' Dorris." He told stories on his Scotch neighbors, himself, and his "wee wifey." Meanwhile, his phonograph records swept the country. The man was peerless. People *had* to see Harry Lauder.

The Golden Age of Vaudeville! It turned first to silver, then to brass, as movies and radio slowly strangled it to death. Midway, in desperation, vaudeville turned smutty, lost its family trade. Today it's the Lost Art of Vaudeville.

The acts, monologues especially, represented years of careful editing. The laughs were retained, the un-laughs discarded, so that nearly every line clicked. Some of the monologues sound corny today—perhaps even did then—but if delivered by expert monologists they probably still would be good for laughs.

Jim Thornton (he wrote the song "My Sweetheart's the Man in the Moon") had a surefire monologue in which he told of a visit to a barbershop:

"The barber put a hot towel on my face and scalded me alive. When I asked him why he put such a hot towel on my face, he explained that it was too hot to hold in his bare hands. Then a little boy about five years of age climbed on a soap box and started to shave me. He began to cut my face into jigsaw puzzles. When I objected to a boy shaving me, his father told me it was the lad's birthday and we had to let him do anything he wanted to on his birthday. All this time a dog was running around the chair howling and barking. When I asked the man why the dog was running around the chair, he told me that the dog had got a piece of ear that morning and wouldn't go away until he got another. . . ."

The humorous battle between the dumbbell and the wise guy was a vaudeville standard. One act closed with a song, "The Dumbbell Is the Wise Guy After All," and this sums up all the fast, practiced patter. Usually the straight man was the wise guy, the comedian the not-so-dumb one.

Straight Man: *I think you're stupid. In fact, I'm so sure you're stupid, I'm going to give you a test.*

Comic: *A test for stupidity?*

Straight Man: *Yes. Now a teacher has twelve pupils and only eleven apples.*

Comic: *She has twelve pupils and only eleven apples?*

Straight Man: *That's right. Now she wants to give each pupil an equal share of the apples. How does she do it?*

Comic: *She makes applesauce.*

Then, as now, comedians depended heavily on childhood and family for laughs.

Charley Case rambled along: "When I was a kid, my family lived next door to the county jail. Not because my mother was sentimental, but because she wanted to be just as close to father as she could get. . . . My father was a very brave man because he used to hunt lions. One day he caught up to a lion, but he didn't shoot it. Not because he lost his nerve, but because he was afraid it might be a neighbor's lion."

Nat Wills, possessor of a stentorian voice, used to bawl out fake news announcements:

"Twentieth Century Limited, four hours late. Reason—it struck a cow. Erie Express, on time. Reason—unknown."

More than families, wives were the prop of a fast-talking comedian's act:

"My wife won't tell her right age. Last week was the anniversary of her birthday; she was twenty-six for the twelfth time. No wonder everybody says she holds her age well. But there's one person she couldn't fool; that's the census taker. She has to tell him her right age or go to jail. But my wife got the best of him all right. She asked him did the Hill sisters who live next door give their age? And he said, 'They certainly did.' And she said, 'Well, I'm just as old as they are!' and the census taker wrote down that my wife was as old as the Hills.

"My wife is a frail little creature. She weighs three hundred pounds. That's two pounds less than a horse. I'll never forget the day of our wedding. No, siree. The minister looked her over and then said to me, "This don't look like an even match. You are giving away too much weight." Then he pronounces us man and wives. Yes, siree, my wife comes from good stock. Her father is a fine old German: his name is Shamus O'Brien. He said his daughter was too good for me. I didn't know what he meant until I had my first scrap with her. Then I found out he was right. Yes, siree."

131

Sinking of the Titanic

On the night of April 14, 1912, the unthinkable happened. The White Star Lines' *Titanic* sank on her maiden voyage. This was the ship the world had waited for. She was huge, fast, reputedly unsinkable. Sailing from Southampton, word was that she would reach New York in record time. But south of Newfoundland an iceberg ripped the great hull open, and in a short time the *Titanic* disappeared bow first into the icy sea. More than 1,500 people perished with her, among them some of society's most glittering names.

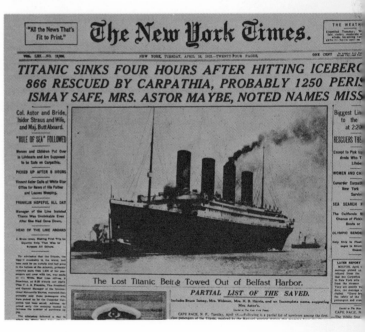

Opposite: Titanic *on ways before launching. Drawing (top) of disaster from survivors' accounts. Times (above) gave story banner headlines. Silent crowd (middle) awaits news. Bottom: Two who survived.*

♥ June 28, 1914. What was it like on this historic Sunday? On the day an archduke was assassinated at Sarajevo, in far-off Serbia, the day that wrote finis to a way of life? What were things like in the United States of America?

Life was a mixture of the old and the new. The automobile was in, but horses were not yet out. Livery stables advertised: "Carriages and outfits for weddings and socials." The prospering Cadillac company was even promoting a new model with the slogan, "Pulls Like a Team of Horses." The corset was also doomed, but didn't seem to know it. Taking advantage of the upsurge in magazine advertising, together with the willingness of famous artists to do commercial ads, corset companies paid big money to picture ladies attired in chic foundation garments. One advertised, "The Bon Ton Corset, Makes You Look and Feel Younger."

A year before, in 1913, the first mild income tax had gone into effect, and it was something of a distinction to be in a bracket high enough to make a payment.

Also occurring in 1913, and just as lasting in its effects, was the Postimpressionist Art Show, held in April at the Sixty-ninth Regiment Armory in New York, and forever after called the Armory Show. Organizers of this pioneering art show were a group of robust native painters determined to banish "The Angelus" and

"The Storm" from the living rooms of American homes, and to drive Charles Dana Gibson and Maxfield Parrish from their eminence as the country's most representative artists.

To help in this, they imported the works of French moderns like Picasso, Brancusi, Matisse. In all, some sixteen hundred paintings and sculptures filled the barren armory. There were cubists, expressionists, neoimpressionists, postimpressionists, Fauvists—artists of every modern school.

Rarely, if ever, has an art show caused such a violent public reaction. The main reason for the uproar was Marcel Duchamp's "Nude Descending a Staircase." People gaped at it. Nude—you call that a nude! Why, a real nude was "September Morn." This was no more than a mass of jagged lines. Even art critics were baffled by "Nude Descending a Staircase." One said it might better be called "Explosion in a Shingle Factory."

People couldn't believe what they read about the Armory Show in the newspapers and went in droves to see for themselves. "The first, and possibly the last, exhibition of paintings which everybody attended," Carl Van Vechten called it. Paintings by the rugged Americans were overlooked while crowds gaped at cubists and expressionists. Teddy Roosevelt called the artists "lunatics," but newspapers happily printed front-page interviews with painters

Militant suffragettes parading in Columbus, Ohio, heralded changing spirit of the country. Women everywhere were clamoring for greater freedom, particularly the right to vote.

134

BUFFALO BILL'S WILD WEST

"THE MAZE"

THE MOST ANI...QUESTRIAN SPECTACLE EVER SEEN. A GORGEOUS MOVING PICTURE IN WHICH OVER 300 HEROIC HORSEMEN PARTICIPATE

and spectators. A crowd of reporters dared artist Walter Pach to point out the nude in "Nude Descending a Staircase." "Where is the moon in the 'Moonlight Sonata'?" he answered.

The Armory Show toured cross-country, jolting American minds out of a rut of conventionality. There were a few real shockers in the show, like Brancusi's sculpture "The Kiss" and the Matisse nudes. More important was the fact that a group of grown-up artists had begun painting in a new way and seemed to believe fervently in what they did. Another missile had been hurled at the old standards.

Little things, too, were changing the quality of American life. The safety razor had arrived for men, silk stockings for women. City dwellers were beginning to live in apartment houses. The language was being enriched by many new words because of the automobile and airplane, although slang, as always, provided the real vigor in our speech. New slang words were *flossy, classy,* and *peachy.* Up to the minute expressions were *Beat it! Sure! It's a cinch! Get your goat.*

"Buffalo Bill" Cody, a fine relic of the past, continued to tour with his famous Wild West Show. The record does not tell

Duchamp's "Nude Descending A Staircase,"
sensation of 1913 Armory Show, was meant to blast
favorites like "The Storm" (left) and
"September Morn" (top) off parlor walls. Timeless
poster art, like Buffalo Bill, survived.

what he thought of the competition of William S. Hart and other cowboy movie stars. Congress had just established Mother's Day on the second Sunday of May, but no one had yet mentioned a Father's Day.

South of the border, General Venustian Carranza, Mexico's top man, was locked in bitter battle with the rebel leader Pancho Villa, and there was much talk of American intervention to make sure the right man won. But who was the right man?

In America, voting males had won the right to elect U. S. Senators, which previously had been done in state legislatures. This made women clamor louder for the right to vote. Already, the suffragettes had won out in ten states, and it only whetted their appetite. Indeed, a group of militant females had just marched on Washington, where the speaker of the House, Champ Clark, had astonishingly predicted that women would vote in the national election of 1916 or 1920.

There was controversy whether movie houses should be open on Sunday. Many people thought not, but most movie theaters stayed open anyway. In Des Moines, sixty-five movie houses attracted Sunday business and it is notable that admission prices were 5¢ and 10¢. Some of these theaters were featuring the *Perils of Pauline*, starring Pearl White.

But if movies were sinful on Sunday, how about baseball? The national pastime listed professional games seven days a week. The fight against Sunday baseball was led by Billy Sunday who only recently had pitched for the Chicago White Sox. Billy had turned hell-fire evangelist, bellowing that the world needed "muscular Christianity, strong-arm religion."

For all his posturings, Billy Sunday was no fool. He was an opponent of demon rum, and recent developments in the prohibition field brought him comfort. Until 1914, prohibition groups in America seemed to be working against one another, with the Anti-Saloon League (all male) looking contemptuously at the Women's Christian Temperance Union. Then the Anti-Saloon League realized that the WCTU roster included many women of great wealth, all too willing to shell out money to battle the scourge of liquor. The men of the Anti-Saloon League made coy overtures to the WCTU. Soon the two organizations were together, amply supported by WCTU funds. One of their first acts was to hire a big-shot Washington lobbyist, together with a series of expert, cross-country press agents.

Prohibition forces did have a point in the unhappy fact that so many working men made stops at corner saloons on payday. On getting home to wives and children, the men were all too often drunk, disorderly—and broke.

But, in urging a dry America, prohibitionists promised more than clearing up an ugly mess. According to the Drys, the U.S.A. would be a blue heaven if prohibition became law. Billy Sunday shouted, "Slums will be only a memory. We will turn our prisons into factories and our jails

138

Mexican revolutionist Pancho Villa (on horseback) was considered a menace to U.S. Bible-brandishing Billy Sunday had turned from pro baseball to evangelism, preached prohibition with fervor.

Carry Nation was fearless and spectacular prohibitionist who broke up saloons with her hatchet.

into storehouses and corncribs. Men will walk upright, women will smile, children will laugh. Hell will forever be for rent."

The forces of prohibition made a lot of noise, but Drys seemed such an assortment of oddballs that few citizens took them seriously. When Secretary of the Navy Josephus Daniels (his Assistant Secretary was handsome young Franklin D. Roosevelt) banned the use of alcohol in the Navy, the country erupted in ridicule, mockery, indignation. No other event of 1914 was so widely lampooned. "Naval vessels," joked the *Wall Street Journal*, "will now have no port side."

There were no home radios in 1914, no news flashes of important events. So no one knew, as the pleasant Sunday hours passed, of the incident at Sarajevo, Serbia. Here a group of young patriots awaited the arrival of Archduke Francis Ferdinand, heir to the Austrian throne. The boys planned to assassinate the Archduke, but they were disorganized, jittery, and lacking in discipline. Their attempt turned into a tragicomedy of errors as the auto bearing the Archduke and his wife proceeded through the streets of the town.

But suddenly the official car made a wrong turn. As it braked to swing around, it came abreast of Gavrilo Princip, a would-be assassin. Princip was thunderstruck, but in a reflex action he lifted his gun and fired two shots into the royal car. One hit the Archduke in the jugular vein, the other went into his wife's side. Shortly, both were dead.

Next morning Americans opening newspapers in big cities found the assassination headlined on front pages. In small towns, it rated only a stick or two of type. Altogether, the murder seemed to be a one-day sensation destined to vanish forever with the burial of the royal couple and Princip's trial. Instead, it sounded the first note of an awful fandango of European nationalism, bravado, and diplomatic ineptness that led to World War I.

Within thirty days Europe was at war. Then an entire continent reeled as the German generals unleashed an attack across helpless Belgium that nearly reached Paris. Never again would the world be as it was on the morning of Sunday, June 28, 1914.

1900 1905
1905 1910
1910 1915
♥ **1915 1920**
1920 1925
1925 1930
1930 1935
1935 1942

THE WEATHER—RAIN TO-NIGHT, SATURDAY CLEARING.

VOL. XLVIII. NO. 18,018.   NEW YORK, FRIDAY, MAY 7, 1915.—TWENTY-TWO PAGES   PRICE ONE CENT.

LUSITANIA BLOWN UP BY GERMANS; LOSS OF LIFE REPORTED SLIGHT

EXTRA!

The Lusitania, the largest and fastest steamship in passenger service, was torpedoed by a German submarine off the coast of Ireland at two o'clock this afternoon.

An official announcement given out in London this evening says the vessel remained afloat "at least twenty minutes" after the explosion.

A despatch from London, timed twenty minutes to seven o'clock, says it is believed "there was no great loss of life." The passengers numbered 1,253 and the crew about 750. Late this afternoon it was stated that about twenty of the Lusitania's boats were afloat near where the steamship sank and that a Greek steamship, several patrol boats, and two motor fishing boats were standing by the small boats. The patrol boats and the other fishing boats took the smaller craft in tow and started for Kinsale.

The Lusitania was attacked at a point off Old Head of Kinsale. She was then

No Man's Land

♥ The trenches of enemy armies spread across France. The dangerous, cratered ground between them was No Man's Land. It had taken only a month for the war to lose its fierce momentum and degenerate into static trench warfare, although occasionally the fighting rose to full battle stature. Casualties were horrendous. At the Battle of the Somme, sixty thousand men were killed in a day. There were more than a million Allied and enemy losses in the Somme offensive. Total gain for the Allies: seven miles of ground.

Trenches were freezing in winter, muddy the rest of the year. Yet they were a haven when shells burst, machine guns clattered, and cannon thundered. The war remained a stalemate, with Germany conscripting fifteen-year-olds, while its people subsisted on potatoes. Neither side could think of anything but hurling men and more men at impregnable enemy positions. Victory was no longer glamorous, but a matter of deadly attrition. Which side would hold out longer?

America didn't consider herself involved. "The mess in Europe," the war was called. For the most part, Americans were determined to leave Europe alone. Many citizens had only recently arrived in the States, bent on beginning new lives. This was the New World; the Old was forever left behind. American newspapers sent war correspondents to the front and every day printed maps showing the minute fluctua-

tions in the battle lines. But any thought of entering the war was far from the American mind.

As always, you could tell the national mood from Tin Pan Alley songs. On the vaudeville stage—about the only place in a dance-mad world where the words of songs still mattered—Nora Bayes, Empress of the Two-a-Day, sang, "I Didn't Raise My Boy to Be a Soldier." Or, "Don't Take My Darling Boy Away." Audiences cheered approval. In the presidential campaign of 1916, the Democratic theme song was, "Elect Wilson, He Kept Us Out of the War."

From the humblest home up to the White House, with few exceptions, the prevailing mood was "We don't want to get involved." Yet in time we did get deeply involved.

In the early hours of the war, American sympathy was equally divided between the warring sides. German-Americans were a respected minority in the United States; Germany itself had always been far closer to America than France, a remote, immoral nation whose males read *La Vie Parisienne.* But the invasion of Belgium put the first heavy anti-German weight on the scales.

The rape of Belgium brought England into the war, and from then on Americans viewed the conflict as England vs. Germany. In the invasion of Belgium America saw a big bully attacking a harmless little guy, and this stirred sympathy for the un-

143

Torpedoing of Lusitania *by German U-boat did much to push a reluctant America toward war. Despite early newspaper reports (inset) loss of life was great and included many Americans.*

♥During World War I songs poured from the jangling pianos of Tin Pan Alley as never before. Here is an old kit bag of the songs America sang, danced to, and marched to during World War I.

"Keep Your Head Down, Fritzi Boy"
"Sister Susie's Sewing Shirts
    for Soldiers"
"Good-bye Broadway, Hello France"
"Don't Try to Steal the Sweetheart of a Soldier"
"God Save Kaiser Bill!"

"It's a Long Way to Berlin, But
    We'll Get There!"
"We're Going to Hang the Kaiser
    Under the Linden Tree"
"I May Be Gone For a Long, Long Time"
"What Kind of an American Are You?"
"If I Had a Son for Every Star in Old Glory,
    America, I'd Give Them All to You"
"Lorraine, My Beautiful Alsatian Love"
"When the Moon Shines Somewhere in France"
"When the Yanks Come Marching Home"
"Your Lips Are No Man's Land But Mine"
"When You Come Back, And You Will Come
    Back, There's A Whole World
    Waiting for You"
"Bing-Bang-Bing-em on the Rhine"
"Would You Rather Be a Colonel With An
    Eagle on Your Shoulder, or A Private With
    A Chicken on Your Knee?"
"Rose of No Man's Land"

"They're All Out of Step But Jim"
"I Don't Want to Get Well, I'm In Love
    With a Beautiful Nurse"
"How You Gonna Keep Them Down on
    the Farm After They've Seen Paree?"
"Madelon"
"Going Up, Going Up, Like a Rocket
    Gone Insane—Flying in an Aeroplane"
"If He Fights Like He Makes
    Love, Goodbye Germany!"
"Just Like Washington Crossed the Delaware,
    Pershing Will Cross the Rhine"
"When Yankee Doodle Learns to
    Parlez-Vous Français"
"Pack Up Your Troubles in Your Old Kit Bag"
"There's a Long, Long Trail Awinding"
"Good Morning, Mr. Zip-Zip-Zip"
"Where Do We Go From Here, Boys?"
"Keep the Home Fires Burning"
"Till We Meet Again"

"What an Army of Men We'd Have, If
    We Ever Drafted the Girls!"
"Are We Downhearted—No!"
"For Your Boy and My Boy"
"Pick a Little Four-Leaf Clover
    and Send It Over to Me"
"Somewhere in France Is a Lily"
"Oh, Frenchy"
"Bring Back My Soldier Boy to Me"
"My Buddy"
"The Soldier's Rosary"
"The Farther We Get from Tipperary, the
    Closer We Get to Berlin"
"Dear Old Pal O'Mine"
"Bugle Call Rag"
"Mlle. from Armentières, Hinky Dinky,
    Parlez-Vous?"
"You're in the Army Now"
"I'll Pin a Medal on the Girl
    I Left Behind Me"

derdog. Allied propaganda, already fever-ishly at work, ground out stories of brutal German soldiers slicing off the breasts of Belgian women, chopping off hands of sup-plicating children. None of the stories was ever proved, but at the time Americans believed them.

"This is the first press agent's war," said *The New York Times* as early as Septem-ber, 1914. The Allies were skillful in in-fluencing American public opinion, the Germans clumsy. Of the many factors that caused America's eventual entry into World War I, the decisive one appears to have been Germany's ineptness.

In 1915, a U-boat sank the four-stacker *Lusitania,* first liner to be called a floating hotel. Aboard were 1,924 persons, of whom 1,128 drowned as the U-boat crew watched. Dead were many Americans, among them Alfred Gwynne Vanderbilt and theatrical producer Charles Frohman. On the night after the sinking President Wilson spoke in Baltimore, saying, "There is such a thing as a nation being too proud to fight." Yet the New York *Herald* showed a shift in public emotion as it headlined: WHAT A PITY THEODORE ROOSEVELT IS NOT PRESIDENT!

In August, the Russians joined the En-glish and French in opposing the Central Powers led by Germany and Austria. Re-sult: Eastern and Western fronts. At the same time, there was war at sea as Ger-many launched a sinister submarine fleet to fight Britain's control of the seas.

As the devastating war continued, Wil-son tried to thrust himself forward as a peacemaker. Backed by the power and prestige of the United States, he made ef-forts to step in as an Olympian mediator. "Peace without victory," was his cry. His moves irritated both sides. America, not a combatant, wanting to impose a peace—what a brassy, upstart nation! Wilson was taken aback by the reaction, but the elec-tion of 1916, which he barely won, gave him added confidence. He conceived the idea of a postwar League of Peace to which all nations would take their problems.

Yet it was actions, not ideas, that pushed America into the war. "The President does not mean to go to war," observed the shrewd Senator Henry Cabot Lodge, "but I think he is in the grip of events." Following the sinking of the *Lusitania,* Wilson per-suaded the Germans not to fire on unarmed vessels. It was a diplomatic victory which increased his appetite for the peacemaker role. But tragic events rolled inexorably on. In an act of dubious legality, an American secret service agent snatched the briefcase of Germany's propaganda chief in this country. Papers inside disclosed that the Germans were spending $28,000,000 in the United States, some of it for legitimate propaganda, more for espionage and sabo-tage. The public was infuriated. "The loss of the portfolio was like the loss of the Marne," a German stated later.

On February 1, 1917, the Germans cold-ly informed Wilson that unrestricted sub-marine warfare would be resumed. It was a blow both to the President's pride and his utopian plans. He broke diplomatic relations with Germany, ordered merchant ships armed. At the same time, England handed over to America the so-called Zimmerman telegram, which had been intercepted by her agents. In it Berlin instructed its ambassador to offer Mexico a military alliance in the event of American entry into the war. In the event of a German victory, Mexico would "reconquer" her "lost territories" of Texas, New Mexico, and Arizona. It also hinted at a pact with Japan. U.S. relations with Mexico, a country still resentful of the Alamo, were on a precarious basis. Japan, though an ally, had long been suspected of aggressive plans. The thought of a German-Mexican-Japanese axis, with Texas as one prize, was alarming. "The issue shifts," stated the Omaha *World Herald,* "from Germany against Great Britain to Germany against the United States." Before the Zimmerman telegram three-quarters of the American people had opposed the war. After it, the country was gripped by war hysteria.

Although President Wilson spoke of war without hate, hatred and anti-German sentiment now reached a pitch. Theodore Roosevelt helped churn it up, ranting, "The only way to make a Hun friendly is to knock him out." Other patriotic speakers outdid themselves in reviling the Germans. "The Prussian is a moral imbecile," people were told. There was wild talk of a disease called Mania Teutonica. People with German names were hounded, accused of being spies. In Milwaukee, St. Louis, Cincin-nati, and other German-American localities, people lived in terror, fearing German spies would pollute the water supply or blow up bridges. German opera singers were boycotted, even though they had chosen to stay in this country. German classics were yanked out of public libraries —"to prevent the pollution of our people by the letting loose of the German moral sewers." In Hollywood, the motion-picture industry ground out inflammatory movies featuring supposed German atrocities.

Meanwhile, in the theater of war, German subs sank three American merchant ships. It marked the end of "too proud to fight." Theodore Roosevelt was snapping at the President's heels, castigating him as a man who waged peace. Our national pride was outraged. There were new pressures from abroad, where the war was costing the Allies more than $25,000,000 a day. The need for food and ammunition was desperate. England, especially, stood on the verge of starvation. "We are beaten," Britain's cabinet cabled, pleading for food.

It was too much. In 1914, Europe had marched to war overnight, as if going on a holiday. America, anxious to be disassociated from the Old World and to create the New, had taken nearly three years to reach a warlike pitch. But now it was here.

On April 2, 1917, President Wilson addressed a cheering Congress. "The world must be made safe for democracy," he intoned, asking Congress to declare war. Returning to the White House, he put his head in his arms and wept.

147

The Castles

♥ While Europe fought, America danced. In 1915 the dance steps that fit the new jazz beat had finally emerged and seemed to release a spring in the national personality. Gaily leading the dance mania was a truly wonderful couple. Young, handsome, supremely enviable, they were Irene and Vernon Castle—Mr. and Mrs. Castle.

The Castles had evolved with the kind of jazz Irving Berlin boosted to popularity in "Alexander's Ragtime Band." English-born Vernon—tall, limber, nonchalant—had been a dancer-comedian in the Broadway musical hit *Hen Pecks*. Feminine hearts fluttered over the lanky fellow (including that of child-actress Helen Hayes, also in the show). But Vernon broke all the hearts by marrying lovely young Irene Foote, of Westchester society. Vernon's salary in *Hen Pecks* was merely moderate, so he got Irene a bit part in the show, as well.

Switch now to Paris, where the Castles go on a delayed honeymoon after *Hen Pecks* closes. Vernon Castle is the kind of man who spends money with no thought for the morrow, and the two are flat broke. Then a letter arrives from Irene's mother in New Rochelle. It contains no money, but its words can be valued at millions. It tells the desperate young couple that, thanks to show-star Blossom Seeley and the dancers Maurice and Florence Walton, New York has gone wild over toddling to the new jazz. People are doing steps called bunny hug, Texas Tommy, turkey trot, grizzly bear. No matter what the name, you simply grab your partner and toddle around the floor, seesawing arms and shoulders in time with the tricky beat.

Irene and Vernon gaze at each other. Perhaps they can dance out of poverty by introducing the turkey trot to Paris.

The rest, in an amazing way, is history. The young Castles danced in Paris cabarets and the city went wild over them. News of their success reached America; they were called home. On these shores their youthful good looks absolutely suited the dance craze. "We were young, clean, and married," Irene recalls. All America believed there had never been a man as graceful as Vernon Castle. Irene, light as vapor, was ravishing to look upon. The Castles themselves loved every moment of it. "We had a great sense of bubbling joy as we danced," Irene says.

Money poured in. Vernon charged $1 a minute, then $100 an hour, to instruct society dowagers in the lame duck, half-in-half, Castle walk, and jazzed-up versions of the tango, maxixe, and waltz. The couple hired a manager, opened an elegant East Side establishment for tea dances, and a Broadway supper club called Castles in the Air. A host of imitators sprang up, but none could rival the marvelous style

148

Irene and Vernon Castle, young and glamorous, led America into a whirl of dance madness. From it emerged the fox trot. Many women followed Irene in shedding corsets and bobbing hair.

of the Castles. The entire country swung into step behind the glamorous youngsters. The Castles danced to "Too Much Mustard" and "Snooky Ookums" at breakfast dances, luncheon dances, tea dances, dinner dances, supper dances, after-midnight dances. Once they did a jazz tango down the aisle at a fashionable wedding.

The Castles appeared so often in public that the need for new steps and music grew desperate. For aid they called in Jim Europe, still busily promoting his society orchestras. It was an inspiration. Actually, there was little difference in the bunny hug, turkey trot, lame duck, or Castle walk. Sometimes Irene didn't know what dance Vernon was leading her through. But to the delight of the Castles, Jim Europe's syncopated rhythm made each dance seem different.

On Sunday afternoons, Jim and an associate named Ford Dabney journeyed to the Castle home in Manhasset. Here the four rehearsed for the coming week. Vernon, whose balance was superb, liked to move fast, carrying Irene into intricate steps at dazzling speed. Jim kept urging him to slow down, dance more.

One Sunday Jim refused to play anything but slow music, stressing the back or afterbeat heard in the delayed hand clapping to Negro jubilee songs. Trying to match this slowness, Vernon found himself rising up on the beat, holding the step. So the easy, rhythmic fox trot was born, and Castle popularity soared higher.

"Everybody's doin' it, doin' it, doin' it," chortled Irving Berlin's latest tune. The Castles pirouetted happily on the crest of a cross-country wave. They conducted a coast-to-coast Whirlwind Dance Contest, with banners proclaiming THE CASTLES ARE COMING, HOORAY, HOORAY!

It was fun, it was wonderful! American males aped Vernon's glorious nonchalance and impeccable manners. Irene, reigning young princess of the world, discarded corsets and those instruments of torture began to disappear forever. Then she tossed out petticoats and shortened skirts. Most important of all, she bobbed her hair, and girls the country over tried to work up courage to do likewise.

Suddenly everything changed. One night late in 1915, the famed Hippodrome in New York was jammed to capacity, with six hundred extra seats on the stage. The occasion was a farewell to Vernon Castle, who was ending his dance career to return home and join the British Air Corps. The audience clapped and wept as he and Irene (wearing a tilted army overseas cap) danced to the tunes they had made famous. Then Vernon went overseas, where he became a wartime ace. Following this, he was sent to train pilots in Canada and the United States. In Texas, he and a student were coming in for a landing when a plane piloted by another student crashed into them. Nonchalant Vernon Castle was killed.

He and Irene never danced professionally after that farewell night at the Hippodrome. That night matched the 1915 mood —froth on top, tragedy below.

Bohemia

♥ America was indeed growing up. Now it had a Left Bank, just like Paris and other colorful centers of culture.

Most of the American artists in the 1913 Armory Show lived in a picturesque part of New York City called Greenwich Village. Americans studying art abroad had returned to find in this quaint area below Fourteenth Street an almost Parisian atmosphere. There was another reason why they liked the Village. A poet expressed it:

"These, needful of a place to sleep,
Came here because the rents were cheap."

In the Village, painters had quickly been joined by writers, poets, musicians, assorted nonconformists, and others stifled by the cultural drabness of America. The influence of Greenwich Village, an area of only a few picturesque blocks, began to permeate the entire United States. One Villager, asked to define the boundaries of his Bohemia, answered, "There are no boundaries, Greenwich Village is a state of mind!" The state of mind began to spread, as Villagers talked, wrote books, painted, and edited little magazines featuring free verse. By 1917, popular publications like *Collier's, Everybody's,* and *The Saturday Evening Post* had discovered the freethinking Village and gleefully used stories about it. Even the *Ladies' Home Journal* exalted Village life in an article called "The Village In a City."

Villagers, intoxicated by their release from drab conformity, began discussing such dynamite-laden subjects as equal rights for women, arguing not only the right to vote, but also to enjoy premarital sex and even sex-sans-marriage. After this came heady talk of birth control, female dress reform, the right of women to smoke, and the dangerous doctrines of Freud and sexologist Havelock Ellis.

Young people from every state began flocking to Bohemia. Once there, every act of nonconformity—even a girl smoking a cigarette—seemed to strike a blow for universal freedom. Girls whipped off heavy, ten-yard dresses and prim shirtwaists to wear smocks, secured at the neck by a droopy bow. Under the smocks were new-type bloomers—or maybe nothing! On her head the Village girl wore a colorful tam-o'-shanter, on her feet loose sandals. Poet Harry Kemp, a hairy-chested male, won newspaper notoriety by daring to stroll the streets without a hat. Next he appeared without a necktie and with his collar informally open.

Let's not forget it—Chicago, too, had a bit of the Left Bank. Fact is, the Windy City for a time was home to the greatest literary and artistic talents in the country: Carl Sandburg, Edgar Lee Masters, Vachel Lindsay, Sherwood Anderson, Margaret Anderson, Harriet Monroe, George Cram Cook, Maurice Browne, Maxwell Bodenheim, Ben Hecht. But Chicago never could hold its geniuses. A few remained but most lit out for Greenwich Village as fast as possible. One reason was that the Village attracted girls anxious to put on (or take off) smocks and tam-o'-shanters.

New York's Villagers, drunk on ideas and freedom, had little use for intoxicating liquors. They foregathered mainly in tearooms called Polly's, Mad Hatter, Purple Pup, Wigwam, Samovar, Vermilion Hound, Three Steps Down, and The Jumble Shop, the only one remaining today. Across the country young matrons, seeing pictures of murky Village tearooms, began turning off the electricity, lighting candles, and giving parties where guests sat on cushions on the floor to discuss forbidden subjects.

It was brave, bold, exciting! Even New Yorkers were shocked at Greenwich Village, haven of free thought, free verse, and free love.

But the Village also had its serious side. It was best seen in a magazine called *The Masses,* whose editors were the intellectual movers and shakers of the early Village: Max Eastman, Floyd Dell, John Reed, Harry Kemp, Mary Heaton Vorse. *Masses'* artists were the lusty talents responsible for the 1913 Armory Show. Among them were John Sloan, George Bellows, Art Young, Maurice Becker, Glenn Coleman, Robert Minor, Stuart Davis.

As was proper in a liberal, or radical, Village magazine, *The Masses* hated war. Any war. It saw the European conflict as a matter of bloated capitalists luring sheep-like humanity into a struggle which would bring immense profits. The true enemy, in *The Masses'* view, was a huge, amorphous *they* composed of men determined to impede world progress and exploit the common man.

Except for the writing of John Reed, who today lies buried near the Kremlin, *The Masses'* prose now seems mild, though it was considered fiery then. But if *Masses'* text seems tepid, its art ranks with the greatest antiwar propaganda in history. With art as its weapon, *The Masses* fought America's entry in the war with a fury seldom seen in journalism. The most sensational *Masses* drawing of all—it certainly shocked all good folk—pictured Jesus Christ standing before a firing squad composed of soldiers of all nations. Caption: The Deserter.

A favored figure of *Masses'* artists was Death on Horseback. In one sketch, Death cocks a skeletal head to ask, "America, did you call?" In another, he is leering, "Come on in, America. The blood's fine."

And so it went, in illustration, prose, poetry.

Inevitably, *The Masses* ran into trouble. First it was banned from subway newsstands in New York. Next, entire cities banned it, Boston and Philadelphia first. Then colleges tossed it out. Canadian officials burned it at the border. Finally, the United States Government arrested the editors for sedition. Two long trials resulted in hung juries. By then the war was over and *The Masses* long gone.

"The Yanks Are Coming!"

♥ Mobilization began the day war was declared, when George M. Cohan tapped out a ditty with the simple clarity of a bugle call. He added lyrics that matched the tune in one-syllable simplicity and called it "Over There." When Nora Bayes gave the song its first performance, the audience rose wildly to its feet to sing along with her. Soon all America was singing Cohan's war song.

All eyes and ears now turned to the White House. Could scholarly, ascetic Woodrow Wilson rally an entire nation behind him? The President soon put doubts to rest by utilizing one peerless attribute—his wizardry with words. "War to end war," "War without hate," "Peace with honor," "Make the world safe for democracy," were phrases to lift men's hearts.

Wilson's appeal to the intellect was even stronger. From the first he sought to convince the German populace that they were being exploited by the Kaiser, that the world did not consider them responsible for the conflict. How successful he was can be judged by General Ludendorff's statement in defeat: "While her armies were victorious in the field, Germany failed in the battle of the intellects."

But it was the tangibles of muscle, steel, and gun powder that Wilson had to muster in that spring of 1917. It was a staggering task. The army needed nearly a million men under arms at once. How to raise

them? The administration decided to register all American men of draft age—ten million in all—as painlessly as if they were going to the polls. And the registrants came, thanks partly to ballyhoo and patriotic slogans that made them feel like heros. Next came the job of drafting one man out of every ten. This was done by a much-publicized lottery, and again the process was sugared with patriotism. The draftees marched happily off to training camp. "It was like a joyous pilgrimage," a writer said.

But men were not enough. Mobilization called for uniforms, rifles, cannon, ammunition, ships, fuel, and—most of all—the brain power to bring the tools of war into being. It was all done, miraculously, through the combined efforts of the Navy and the War Industries Board, financier Bernard Baruch, Chairman. Top industrialists consented to serve under Baruch for $1 a year.

The terrible shortage of food in Europe was another of Wilson's concerns. One of his finest moves was the appointment of Herbert Hoover as Food Administrator. The idea was to make Americans eat less food and to rush the surplus abroad. From Hoover's office slogans poured forth: "Food Will Win the War," "Use All Leftovers," "Serve Just Enough." Billboards, posters, movie screens, newspaper headlines carried tighten-your-belt messages. Hoover decreed wheatless Mondays and Wednesdays; meatless Tuesdays and Fri-

153

days; porkless Thursdays and Saturdays. The people complied in good humor, and someone made a quip about "meatless, wheatless, eatless days."

Behind America's remarkable war spirit lay what was perhaps Wilson's most brilliant innovation. It was the Committee of Public Information, a giant propaganda organization designed to involve every American in the war effort. As boss of the CPI, Wilson chose an energetic, high-echelon newspaper man named George Creel and started him off with a massive appropriation of $5,000,000. Vowing to give Americans the unvarnished truth, Creel set about his task with the zeal of both salesman and showman. War posters that stirred the blood were painted by Charles Dana Gibson and other of the country's finest artists. Liberty Bond rallies, staged by top stars of the theater, brought in floods of dollars. Monster benefits in big cities lifted crowds to cheering enthusiasm. Broadway stars took their shows right into the training camps and overseas bases of the AEF. Movie stars and movie screens exerted their glamour in the cause of war. Children were urged to pinch enough pennies to buy 25¢ War Saving Stamps—"Lick A Stamp and Lick the Kaiser!"

Not even the enemy was immune from "the world's greatest adventure in advertising." Wilson's speeches, trimmed down and printed in heavy Germanic type, were air-dropped behind the German lines. "We are not the enemies of the German people," said one, "and the German people are not our enemies. We are fighting for their cause

as much as our own."

But as the winter of 1917 passed, those words rang hollow in No Man's Land. General Ludendorff faced the problem of winning the war before American soldiers and supplies arrived in sufficient quantity to assure an Allied victory. It was a desperate moment. In both armies, the best soldiers had long ago been killed. Combat troops now rated no higher than militia. Nonetheless, morale remained good. On both sides, men obeyed orders and died almost unquestioningly for home and country.

On March 21, 1918, the great Ludendorff offensive began. Casualties were fantastic. The Germans took ninety thousand prisoners, creating another behind-the-lines problem. The German armies fought their

way to within fifty miles of Paris and actually bombarded the city.

Marshal Ferdinand Foch, Allied commander in chief, begged General John J. Pershing for American troops to use as replacements. Pershing said no. The American Army would fight only as a unit, he declared. But as Allied losses grew, he released one American division and then another—First Division, Rainbow Division, Yankee Division, the names were household words at home. All told, there were twenty-six American divisions in France, including some from the Marine Corps.

So American soldiers fought at Château-Thierry and Belleau Wood. (One was a Brooklyn youth named Alphonse Capone, who there learned the lethal efficacy of the

Nearly a million draftees marched off to train at hastily erected camps. For many at Camp Upton, N. Y., payday (above) and inspection preceded fighting in France.

machine gun.) It was war at its most elemental—man against man, gun against gun, bayonet against bayonet, grenade against grenade. The only way to advance was to go over the top of the trenches and plunge into No Man's Land. It was noted that the American soldiers were overeager, inclined to storm machine-gun nests head on. "Men fell around me like duck pins," an American officer wrote home.

As the German drive slowed, Marshal Foch grabbed the offensive. On August 8, the British launched an attack at Amiens. It was the beginning of the end, but no one realized it then. German armies still fought hard, though the smell of defeat permeated their lines. German soldiers carefully read the words of President Wilson in leaflets dropped from airplanes.

At last, Pershing had enough troops for his American Army. Eight Yankee divisions were ordered to capture the Saint-Mihiel salient. In Berlin, the Kaiser and the Crown Prince urged German troops to fight harder, hoping for a peace settlement that would let them keep power. Slowly the Allied armies pushed the Germans back. Early in October, the Kaiser weakened, sending a feeler to Washington asking Wilson to take steps for the restoration of peace. Wilson replied with terms the other Allies considered too mild. On the Western Front, the slaughter continued.

The German armies never cracked, but they began to offer less resistance. Then the German navy mutinied. With this, the Kaiser gave up and fled to Holland. Luden-dorff resigned, as crowds in Berlin clamored for a republic. On November 11, 1918 —eleventh month, eleventh day, eleventh hour—emissaries of both sides solemnly affixed signatures to a surrender document.

At last the war was over! Allied casualties came to ten million men. Germany lost as many, or more. American losses were 116,516. An entire generation of men had been wiped from the face of the European continent. But everyone said the world had been made safe for democracy.

America had two armistice days. On November 7, a false report flashed over wires of the United Press and was sent to member papers across the nation. People poured into the streets to sing, march, yell.

The UP story went unconfirmed and slowly the celebration dwindled. But there was no real letdown. People knew the armistice was due, even if men still fought.

News of the real armistice arrived at 3 A.M. on November 11. Lobster-shift newspapermen phoned the news to firehouses and bells clanged. In New York, the lights of the Statue of Liberty switched on.

On the morning of that Monday, the real excitement began. Everywhere, it seemed, there were soldiers and sailors home on leave and they led impromptu parades carrying signs, "No More Beans," "No More Camouflaged Coffee," "No More Monkey Stew," "No more KP."

In big cities, the main avenues were a mass of people, some carrying effigies of the Kaiser which said, "Let him rule in Hell!" In New York, five thousand war

157

America's war posters, done by top contemporary artists, have been called greatest ever. Charles Dana Gibson, of Gibson Girl fame, headed project.

mothers marched up Fifth Avenue. People who had thrilled to the war songs found them nostalgic and heart warming. At the Winter Garden that night, the audience made Al Jolson sing them again and again.

It was grand! It was wonderful! Two million doughboys were coming home to receive America's open-arms welcome. "We ought to let the boys sit in the grandstands, while *we* march past *them*," quipped humorist Will Rogers. His humane suggestion went unheeded. The return of the AEF was a signal for parades, parades, and more parades. Aside from the immediate families, few bothered to think of the dead, the wounded, the gassed.

Looking around, the doughboys found many changes after a year and a half of home-front war. In New York, the first spot to see, it was joyously noted that girls' dresses were shorter, revealing shapely calves and sometimes a kneecap. "The human knee is a joint and not an entertainment," grumped drama critic Percy Hammond, but few agreed with him. One reason for tighter dresses and shorter skirts was the craze for a dance called the "shimmy." In the shimmy, a girl just stood and shook every possible muscle.

Other people were madly fox-trotting to "Ja Da" and "Dardanella," but soldiers with an ear for jazz were free to discover another of its facets. Dixieland, old in New Orleans, new in Chicago, had made its New York debut at Reisenweber's where it was played by Nick La Rocca's Dixie Land Band. According to Mezz Mezzrow

in *Really the Blues,* the Dixie Land Band wasn't much. "They were a really corny outfit, and if they ever had a touch of New Orleans it was frail as a nail and twice as pale. But they were fast and energetic and had a gang of novelty effects the public went mad about." Those who went to hear Dixieland found their emotions stirred, where the fox trot only tickled the toes.

Soaking up the wonders, doughboys slowly moved homeward and into private life. Having fought the war, they were prepared to enjoy the peace. But the sad fact is that most of them didn't. Something had happened to the good old U.S.A. What, exactly, no one ever quite figured out. One pundit has said of this period, that America was the only nation on record to jump from adolescence to decadence without taking the intervening steps. It could be. Where the America of 1910 to 1915 was anxious for a better world, the nation now seemed to be disillusioned. Mark Sullivan called it "an exaltation that had gone sour."

There were reasons. One was the fact that Woodrow Wilson had been a war casualty. On the day of the first German peace overture in October, 1918, Wilson had heaved a mighty sigh and let himself relax. It was, apparently, a psychological mistake. Never again did he pull himself up to the unerring pitch of his war years. Everything he had done then was shrewd and subtle. Now his acts seemed slightly off the beam. The country sensed it.

After the armistice, Wilson announced

plans to travel to Paris to take a personal part in the Peace Conference. He was the first President ever to visit Europe in his official capacity, and it caused a furore. His blunders began before he left, for he ignored the Senate in picking a delegation to accompany him to Paris. He also infuriated Republican Senators by implying that only the Democratic Senators had helped him to win the war.

People were especially uneasy about Wilson's ability to cope with Clemenceau, Lloyd George, and Orlando—the other Allied leaders. He had annoyed them during the war by his efforts as a peacemaker. In addition, these were callous statesmen, far removed from Wilsonian idealism. And they outnumbered him. Wilson, however, had always been stubborn about getting his own way.

So the President took off for Paris at a time when, by staying home, he might have put himself in a far stronger bargaining position. He had thought out and given to the world a Fourteen Point program for future peace. One of the points, a League of Peace, still simmered in his head. The program had given hope to the world, and in Europe Wilson was hailed as a demigod. The President had vowed that not one comma of the Fourteen Points would be changed, but at the peace table the crafty Europeans whittled away at them. Surprisingly, Wilson allowed it. His League of Peace became a League of Nations, and he believed this would eventually right any wrongs of the Peace Treaty.

Wilson worked long hours, insisting on doing everything himself. Then, suddenly, the frail-looking man was struck by a cerebral thrombosis, clumsily diagnosed as an attack of influenza. When he got to his feet again, his mind seemed affected. He suspected the French of trying to poison him. He senselessly moved the furniture about his suite of rooms.

Wilson returned from Paris, his glowing image tarnished. His face looked like a death's head; one eye twitched. Yet he was brimful of messianic zeal for the League. While he dickered in Paris, Republicans had closed ranks to oppose American entry into the League. At first Teddy Roosevelt led the fight. When Teddy died in January, 1919, his place was taken by Senator Henry Cabot Lodge, who shrewdly corralled some Democratic support and warned the country that membership in the League would mean involvement in other European wars.

Wilson looked more dead than alive as he set out on a cross-country speaking tour to rally people to the League. His intense speeches were slowly pulling the country behind him when, in September, he was hit by another thrombosis. He had permitted changes in his Fourteen Points, but from an invalid's bed in the White House he issued orders that not a single one would be tolerated in the League proposal. This time he meant it. Henry Cabot Lodge offered a compromise acceptable to other Democrats, but Wilson refused. Had he agreed, the history of the world might have been different. But the sick man was ada-

When doughboys recrossed the Big Pond,
New York and parade down Fifth Avenue came
first—then home. After that, disillusionment
for many who found their jobs gone.

*Anarchists executed for murder,
Sacco (left) and Vanzetti became famous as
martyrs to postwar hysteria.*

162

mant. American entry in the League went down to defeat.

This increased American disillusionment—as did other matters. Returning soldiers found that there had been much profiteering while they fought and bled overseas. A country that boasted sixteen thousand millionaires before the war now had twenty thousand. There also had been much profiteering below the million-dollar level. Slackers—the name given those who avoided military service—had grabbed the good jobs and held onto them. Women had captured others. Worse, there was a sudden shortage of work as the peak production of the war years ended abruptly. Industry floundered, resulting in two years of depression and five million unemployed.

No one wanted to go back to the old days. Unions began to demand shorter hours, Ford-type pay envelopes, and the open shop. The result was strikes in steel, meat packing, railroads, construction, coal. Whole cities were shut down by strikes.

Industrial leaders fought back hysterically, accusing labor of trying to take over the country as the working class had taken over Russia in the Bolshevik revolution. Indeed, the Bolshevik had supplanted the Hun as America's archenemy. The country lived in terror of Bolshevik bombs and Attorney General A. Mitchell Palmer spearheaded a manic witch-hunt. Outside Boston two men were arrested for murder, largely because they were anarchists who didn't speak English. They were Nicola Sacco and Bartolomeo Vanzetti, and in time they would be world famous.

Returning soldiers had another king-size grievance in prohibition. They felt something had been put over on them while they were overseas. With the country preoccupied by war and a good percentage of the nation's manpower in the armed forces, the Drys had made a titanic effort. Rabid prohibitionists in southern and midwestern states had inundated Congress with anti-alcohol mail and every other kind of righteous propaganda. On May 1, 1919, with demobilization still in progress, Congress passed the Eighteenth Amendment. This was supplemented by the Volstead Act, which the invalid President rallied himself to veto. It was passed, however, over the President's veto.

Soon no one would be able to buy beer, wine, or liquor in the Land of the Free.

1900 1905
1905 1910
1910 1915
1915 1920

♥   **1920 1925**

1925 1930
1930 1935
1935 1942

Roaring Twenties

♥ The Roaring Twenties have come down in history as the decade of sensations—a mélange of monkey trials, tabloid headlines, dance marathons, gangland wars, and transatlantic flights, all tied up in one glorious package.

It's true, of course. Such things happened. Never, sociologists say, has a modern people been so recklessly dedicated to thrills or to keeping itself amused. But another element also made itself felt in the temper of the nation. Cynicism, the logical successor to disillusionment, set in.

It first became apparent at the outset of the decade, when newly published books started changing the public mind. The books were not heavy, uplifting tomes, but novels of the type later known as best sellers. There had been surpassingly successful works of fiction in the past, but usually these had been escapist romances. In the Twenties, fiction and fact combined to make a literature which drastically reshaped national thinking and—it must be admitted—did much to increase the mood of cynicism.

The first author to produce such a novel was Sinclair Lewis. His *Main Street,* published in 1920, told of Carol Kennecott, Midwest housewife, an unhappy, frustrated girl. Why shouldn't sensitive young Carol be unhappy and frustrated? Around her in the town of Gopher Prairie lived types the author (a superb mimic in private life)

caricatured magnificently in words. The local doctor, storekeeper, and undertaker emerged as limited, loud, and boring.

Lewis did it again with *Babbitt,* published in 1922. George Follansbee Babbitt was a leading realtor in the Midwest town of Zenith. Through him Lewis ridiculed the small-town go-getter, the human dynamo, the backslapper, mixer, joiner, greeter, and Rotary Club booster. The word "Babbitt" quickly slipped into the language as a synonym for the pompous middle-class bore. Greeting a friend he had left only a few hours before, George F. Babbitt roars: "How's the old horse thief?"

"All right, I guess," the friend responds. "How're you, you poor shrimp?"

"I'm first rate, you second-hand hunk o' cheese."

With Babbitt and other of his creations, Lewis lampooned the things America had heretofore considered estimable—success in business, pride in the old home town, a brassy personality, pushing salesmanship. His sharp-edged satire brought a new dimension to literature.

It also exposed a topsy-turvy world in which people living in the midst of plenty were beginning to feel cheated and resentful. Greenwich Village, still the tail wagging the dog, pointed this up. Many of its most fiery rebels had left and it was turning into an entertainment area, almost a sucker trap. Young talents arriving in Bo-

Maxfield Parrish painted this cover for Easter, 1923, issue of Life. Aura of fantasy, luminous blues, and dimensional quality are typical of this popular artist's work.

hemia looked around, noted the change, and took the first boat to Paris, where the younger generation became the Lost Generation.

Like the Village, the whole nation was becoming restless, dissatisfied, hectic. It was smart to mock everything that had once seemed sacred.

Not only literature but the law as well stepped in to boost the country's cynicism. The Eighteenth Amendment, given a shiny set of enforcement teeth by the Volstead Act, became the law of the land on January 16, 1920. For a year the nation lived under prohibition, fully believing that the Noble Experiment was workable. Then whispers began. There were shady men, it was said, who had liquor to sell. Bootleggers, they were called, and they delivered gin and whiskey to your back door. The men who brought the liquor across the country's borders, or landed it after midnight on deserted beaches, were known as rumrunners.

More whispers told of big-city basements and small-town stores where bars had been set up. Sometimes the bar was no more than a wooden plank supported by two stools. These were speakeasies. A peephole in the door allowed the proprietor to scrutinize patrons of his surreptitious joint before letting them in. "Joe sent me," became a catchword of the time. Fashionable metropolitan speakeasies even printed membership cards.

If liquor was available—as suddenly it was—Americans felt free to buy it. For as the liquorless months passed, Americans began to lose patience with this curb on their precious freedom. The answer was defiance of the law, assertion of the right to be totally free.

Swift pace of Twenties had symbol in Stutz
Bearcat, car every young buck had to have. Prohibition,
toasted dubiously on eve of enforcement, became
outrageous as agents poured out the good with the bad.

Yet the purchase and consumption of liquor meant breaking the law of the land. This produced feelings of guilt, and here perhaps the Roaring Twenties really began. For guilt tussled with the desire to protest and defy the law. And into this mixed bag of feelings also went the growing mood of cynicism and disillusionment.

Defiance of prohibition became the impulse—or the poison—that drove the entire nation into its wild, jazz-age excesses. There was plenty to drink; every drink was a noble protest against the ignoble experiment. It made the Twenties roar. As if on a perpetual binge, the nation began to think that nothing mattered except making whoopee. It had put handsome Warren G. Harding into the White House on his promise to return the country to what he called "normalcy." But with prohibition gin suddenly available, normalcy seemed

dull. Fun and frolic became the order of the decade. Yet it was the wrong kind of fun and frolic—hysterical, escapist, silly.

The younger generation led the way. For the young, too, were cynical. "We didn't ask to be born," they told fathers and mothers. "You brought us into a crummy world." To get even, young people began doing things young people had never done before.

From F. Scott Fitzgerald's *This Side of Paradise* and his short stories, parents learned that sons and daughters were not only thinking in new patterns, but behaving in new ways. The shocker was the American girl. Boys were expected to sow a few wild oats, especially in a country growing increasingly prosperous. But girls insisted on the right to toss a few oats of their own. For the moment it upset the middle and older generations.

Girls aspired to curveless silhouette of
John Held Jr.'s peppy flapper. Lyric poetry of Edna
St. Vincent Millay celebrated free existence.

From Greenwich Village came poetic inspiration. "My candle burns at both ends," strummed Edna St. Vincent Millay. On college campuses, and everywhere else, the young hungrily perused the magazine *College Humor,* with its bittersweet stories by Katherine Brush and its daring ones by Lynn and Lois Montross.

Such stories told parents that the family car was being used by sons and daughters for nocturnal petting parties. Scott Fitzgerald's novels told more. Said one Fitzgerald heroine, "None of the Victorian mothers—and most of the mothers were Victorian—had any idea how casually their daughters were kissing." Another Fitzgerald girl confessed, "I've kissed dozens of men, and I suppose I'll kiss dozens more."

Promiscuous kissing suddenly was no longer enough for the thrill-mad young.

169

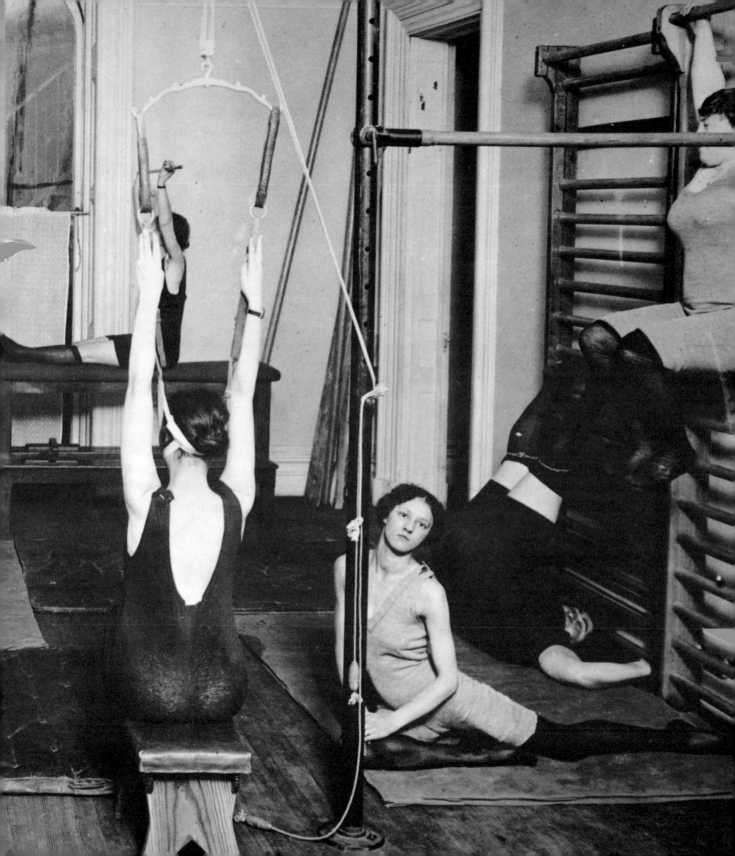

The hip flask became an indispensable adjunct of the petting party. Jokes that dealt with the modern girl's readiness to pet now pictured her passing out from too much prohibition gin.

Out of somewhere came the perfect word to describe this madcap girl of the Twenties. It was "flapper." The flapper was something to see. Her skirts stopped at the kneecap. Stockings were rolled below these same knees, allowing males frequent glimpses of bare thigh. Short skirts and stockings rolled below the knees! Preachers thundered: "Low-cut gowns, the rolled hose, and short skirts, born of the Devil and his angels, are carrying present and future generations to chaos and destruction." A few states tried to legislate short skirts out of existence by passing laws against the "sale of any garment which unduly displays or accentuates the lines of the female figure."

The flapper's dress, made of the thinnest material possible, looked no larger than a handkerchief. Underneath she wore only scanties—"briefs" or "teddies," they were called. "Brevity is the soul of lingerie," quipped literary flapper Dorothy Parker.

If a mother told her daughter to wear a foundation garment to a dance, she was pertly told that boys didn't like to touch such things while dancing. And the dancing! Couples seemed glued together, cheek to cheek, pelvis to pelvis, fox-trotting to "Stumbling," "Why Did I Kiss That Girl?", "Sheik of Araby," or "Whispering." One preacher branded the dancing as "impure, polluting, corrupting, debasing, spiritually ruinous, an invitation to carnality." The saxophone had been added to orchestras, shoving the violin from prominence. Its throb made the jazz music more intimate and suggestive.

There was still more to the flapper. After years of hesitation, girls really began bobbing their hair. Usually the job was done in a barber shop, since beauty parlors had not kept pace with the new fad. The boyish bob, shingle cut—barbers who had clipped only male heads found themselves struggling to shape female coiffures. Over her new bob the flapper pulled a cloche hat.

Girls also were smoking in public and cigarette sales doubled. Yes, doubled! The flapper also made lavish use of lipstick and highlighted her cheekbones with two circles of rouge. A boyish figure was the dream of every girl: thin hips, slat bottom, no visible breasts. Indeed, the girl with conspicuous bosoms was SOL, to use a wartime expression every flapper now understood.

A flapper's philosophy came straight from her boy friend: "I have a right to do anything I want to, provided I don't hurt others." She used his profanity, too, though it seldom went beyond "damn" or "hell." She delighted in shocking her elders, causing one father to complain, "My daughter will talk about anything; in fact, she hardly talks about anything else."

The flapper hummed "Three O'Clock in the Morning," the hour at which she usually arrived home. Her father and mother

172

Preceding pages: More revealing clothes made women conscious of their figures, spurred them to exercise and lose pounds—at some loss of dignity.

lay awake in bed, awaiting the sound of her footsteps on the stairs. Through sleepless hours they lay wondering if their darling daughter was one of those girls called "wild"; that is, if she had spent the hours since midnight petting in a parked car. They also wondered, as she tripped upstairs, if she had gin on her breath.

However, not all parents lay awake waiting for flaming sons and daughters to get home. At first, parents had been shocked by the excesses of the young. But these were the Roaring Twenties, and as time passed the art of having fun seemed to become the most important of endeavors. Who had the most fun? Why, the young, of course, with their heedless philosophy, hip flasks, late hours, and snappy attire. So older folk began to emulate the young. It was a notable first in human behavior, since youth had always been subordinate. Now it was on top. "Youth was the model, age the imitator," a pundit states.

There was one more major change in behavior patterns. Woman now began to stand squarely at man's side, fully expecting to share his fun and games. Gone was the double standard which had tied the female to home, no matter how far the male strayed. The female was at last free, able to vote, her daughter's independence fast rubbing off on her. In the words of Frederick Lewis Allen: "She wanted to be—or thought she wanted to be—man's casual and lighthearted companion, not broad-hipped mothers of the race, but irresponsible playmates."

Women began trying to look young. Mothers and grandmothers snipped off skirts at the knees, and if spindly, childish legs were thereby revealed, so much the better. They flattened their bosoms, bobbed their hair, puffed cigarettes.

In the mad quest for flaming youth, men and women were not content just to look young; they acted young, even childish. Nonsense songs and expressions filled the air. "So's your old man," adults said to one another. "Go cook a radish," the others snapped right back. Men dressed like schoolboys, wearing the exaggerated knickers known as plus fours. In *College Humor*, Katherine Brush described male attire: "Legs in golf stockings of blue and gray diamond pattern. Knickers, voluminous and drooping low. Coat that matched the knickers, a soft collar with a neat bow tie." A man so attired was called a sheik. To match this, a flapper was called a sheba.

The trend was caught to perfection in the flapper drawn by artist John Held, Jr. It is worthy of note that the Gibson Girl and other precursors of the John Held flapper were idealized beauties. Held's sheba was a caricature, though many girls of the time managed to look exactly like her. She resembled a precocious child dressed up in her mother's high heels and skimpy attire.

It was in the speakeasies, however, that the double standard breathed its last, as Woman placed her dainty foot next to Man's on the brass rail. Only a fallen woman would have done it a decade before.

The Silver Screen

♥ In the theater world, the once prosperous Road was leading to a dead end. Touring attractions now were confined to theaters in big cities. Vaudeville, too, was suffering at the box office. (Few were in a position to foresee it, but commercial radio, about to arrive at any moment, would sound the death knell of dear old vaude.) The reason for dog days on the road and in vaudeville was motion pictures. Scarcely older than the century itself, the flickering flicks had grown swiftly. Right now they were enjoying a golden hour.

Films at this happy time were silent. Subtitles identified characters, flashed bits of dialogue, and explained nuances in plots. This was all right with movie audiences, for no one expected the silver screen to talk. In every way the public was satisfied by films. Admission was easy on the pocketbook, theaters usually were close to home, the pictures were full of wonderful backgrounds and costume changes impossible to find in the living theater. Who could ask for anything more?

With the great success of films, the movie star made a bravura appearance on the American scene. Frequently lifted by Lady Luck from the depths of poverty and ignorance, he (or she) was in a position to earn thousands of dollars a week in the days of a small income tax.

Simultaneously fan magazines appeared to chronicle the private lives of these new stars ("The Pickford-Fairbanks Wooing"). Hollywood also experienced its baptism of newspaper headlines, as three scandals broke that muddied its name. Roscoe "Fatty" Arbuckle, ranking only just behind Charlie Chaplin as the nation's chief funnyman, underwent three sordid trials for the rape-murder of actress Virginia Rappe. Testimony showed *nouveau riche* Fatty presiding over bootleg gin parties, and told a shocked world about the Hollywood institution known as the casting couch.

While the Arbuckle scandal sizzled, ace director William Desmond Taylor was murdered in one of America's more tantalizing unsolved crimes. Among the dashing fellow's effects were lingerie and torrid love letters from two prominent stars, Mabel Normand and Mary Miles Minter. The Taylor case also revealed that movie stars were taking drugs for thrills. Soon Wallace Reid, one of the movies' most attractive stars was dead of drug addiction.

Preachers thundered that Hollywood was even more immoral than the films it made. Momentarily, the industry fell back. Then studio heads hired Will H. Hays, Postmaster General under Harding, as a much-publicized czar of morals. Pious, Hoosier-born Hays made reassuring promises to the public. The industry regained confidence and resumed its golden hour.

Movies for every taste began pouring out of Hollywood. Boys and grown-up boys

174

Annette Kellermann was famous for a diving act done in a one-piece bathing suit. But she went a step farther in 1916 movie called A Daughter of the Gods.

looked to great Western stars like William S. Hart, Tom Mix, Hoot Gibson, Jack Hoxie, Art Acord, Ken Maynard, and Buck Jones. But the career of Bill Hart, the good badman, was almost over, since he stubbornly refused to modernize his films in the light of such epics as *The Covered Wagon*. Bill's next film, *Tumbleweeds*, marked his finish. His place was filled by Tom Mix and his faithful steed Tony.

These men made feature films, but there were also Westerns among the two-reeler serials on almost every theater program. At the end of each, the hero or heroine was left in a death-defying situation. Then the words CONTINUED NEXT WEEK flashed on the screen as the audience groaned, not at all sure it could wait.

Douglas Fairbanks, King of the Silent Screen, provided more refined excitement.

Douglas Fairbanks, hanging from lintel,
displays athletic prowess in His Majesty the American.
In an age of great comics, Harold Lloyd was near top of list.
At right is famous human fly scene in Safety Last.

After beginning in light-hearted comedy (Douglas MacLean and Reginald Denny were the light comedians now), Doug parlayed his athletic prowess into super-spectacles like *Thief of Bagdad, Mark of Zorro,* and *Robin Hood.* In them, he leaped, grinned, performed feats of incredible derring-do, and clutched the heroine in a tight embrace at the end.

Doug had married Mary Pickford in 1919, and the two resided at Pickfair, Hollywood's most sanctified home. Mary had matured since the early Biograph days with D. W. Griffith. But she was still America's Sweetheart, appearing as a girl (or girl-boy) in *Pollyanna, Daddy Longlegs, Suds, Little Lord Fauntleroy.* Suddenly she reached womanhood in *Rosita* and *Dorothy Vernon of Haddon Hall.* The public didn't respond well, and she went back to *Little Annie Rooney.*

Mary Pickford was Hollywood's most popular actress, but there were others for fans to worship: Corinne Griffith, Billie Dove, Claire Windsor—there never was a trio so lovely; Pola Negri, smoldering rival of glorious Gloria Swanson; Dorothy and Lillian Gish, best in *Orphans of the Storm;* Connie and Norma Talmadge, Lila Lee, Betty Compson, Mary Philbin, Carmel Myers, Aileen Pringle, Patsy Ruth Miller, Mabel Normand, Marie Prevost, Leatrice Joy; Marion Davies and Mae Murray, two belles from the Ziegfeld Follies; Bebe Daniels, Lois Wilson, and Esther Ralston; the young crop, Mary Astor, Anita Page, Sue Carol, Mary Brian, Alice White.

Comedy! At this happy time the fun stars of two-reelers were graduating to full-length films. Charlie Chaplin had just produced his two biggest hits, *Shoulder Arms* and *The Kid.* Now he turned director, making *A Woman of Paris* in which suave young Adolphe Menjou ran away with honors. The picture was a box-office flop, for few could understand Chaplin's name on a serious story. But its naturalistic underplaying was a film milestone.

Chaplin may have been the great comedy genius, but the pictures of Harold Lloyd grossed more money. *Grandma's Boy, The Freshman, Safety Last, Why Worry?, Girl Shy*—the shekels poured in; $30,000,000, it's said.

Right behind Grandma's Boy stood Buster Keaton, in *Day Dreams, Three Ages, Frozen North, Sherlock, Jr., Go West, The Navigator, The General.* Behind him was Harry Langdon, whose forte was "adult infantilism." Also Larry Semon. Laurel and Hardy were just beginning to make an impression. Don't forget the *Our Gang* two-reelers, with fat Joe Cobb, Little Farina, and the rest.

He-men were in their prime. Milton Sills and Noah Beery staged a spectacular fight in Rex Beach's *The Spoilers.* Brawny George O'Brien was in *The Iron Horse,* an unforgettable John Ford silent about the building of the transcontinental railroad. Good prize-fighting pictures were *Patent Leather Kid,* starring Richard Barthelmess, and *Leather Pushers,* a two-reeler from the stories of H. C. Witwer.

Gilda Gray, here in Cabaret, *made shimmy famous, then appeared in De Mille epics. The trick with shimmy was to shake every muscle "like jelly on a plate."*

178

8778·31

D. W. Griffith's opulent Sorrows of Satan *stirred* 1926 audiences with daring scenes. Gentlemen in tails at left are Ricardo Cortez (seated) and Adolphe Menjou.

*Valentino rolled his eyes and always got the
girl. Douglas Fairbanks was masked swordsman in* Mark
of Zorro. *Buster Keaton devised his own gags for*
The Navigator. *Little Jackie Coogan stole* The Kid *from
Chaplin. Theda Bara was original vamp.*

Lon Chaney, man of a thousand faces, made audiences gasp and shudder in *Miracle Man, Hunchback of Notre Dame, Unholy Three, Phantom of the Opera,* and *Laugh, Clown, Laugh,* Lon not only used grotesque make-up, but twisted his body into fearful shapes.

Kid stars—Wesley Barry, Baby Peggy. Best of all, Jackie Coogan, the only person ever to steal a picture from Charlie Chaplin. On his own, Jackie was seen in *Daddy* and *Old Clothes.* The latter was the film debut of pretty flapper Joan Crawford.

In the center of it all was flamboyant Cecil B. De Mille, director of the decade. The pioneering work of D. W. Griffith was overshadowed now, for the master seemed to have spent his genius with *The Birth of A Nation* and *Intolerance,* both made before 1920. Griffith's main contribution in the Twenties was *America,* with Carol Dempster and Neil Hamilton, a story of Revolutionary days.

Artistically, De Mille was no match for Griffith, but his ornate extravaganzas opened up tempting vistas in morals and behavior. Before this, directors had been concerned only with pushing boy and girl adventurously toward the final clinch that meant living happily ever after. De Mille, however, dropped boy-girl stuff for married couples with problems. Of course, his couples had not been married long, and invariably they were young and handsome. The canny director gilded his lily by making the couples splendidly rich, so that sets and clothes awed the audiences.

De Mille titles tell his plots: *The Cheat, Male and Female, Wives and Lovers, Don't Change Your Husband, Why Change Your Wife?, Forbidden Fruit, We Can't Have Everything, The Golden Bed.* He avoided church criticism of his films by supposedly spinning a moral tale. That is to say, his characters always got in trouble at the end. De Mille fascinated audiences by showing them how not to behave.

De Mille was also a master of the semi-salacious. In almost every film the heroine entered a sumptuous bathroom and slowly disrobed, assisted by a bevy of youthful maids. It added up to a lengthy striptease, usually ending with a view of milady in the bubbly, soaping one shapely gam. From the bath, a De Mille heroine (Gloria Swanson or Bebe Daniels) moved to a canopied bed, where she slept in tousled splendor, again with one leg uncovered.

C. B.'s real inspiration was the sex orgy. He illustrated his modern morality tales with flashbacks to ancient civilizations. This permitted him to show wild parties with undraped slave girls. In *Male and Female,* Thomas Meighan quotes (by subtitle) Henley's "When I Was a Slave in Babylon" to Gloria Swanson. Instantly the scene shoots back to Babylon, where Tom and Gloria take part in a swinging orgy. In *Manslaughter,* Leatrice Joy is a heedless heiress who kills a motorcycle policeman with her car, then speeds away. By flashback, the behavior of Leatrice and her rich pals is pictured in terms of the fall of Rome. De Mille reached a glorious peak

185

Louise Brooks (in cloche) typified rolled-stockings flapper. Pola Negri was sultry Queen of the Silents. Kindly old lady is Lon Chaney, and exquisite holding court is John Barrymore as Beau Brummel.

in *The Ten Commandments* which flopped back and forth endlessly between Biblical times and modern venality.

De Mille further roused passions by scenes in which lovers pawed each other. In this, he borrowed the technique of Theda Bara, the first of the screen vamps. Nita Naldi and Barbara LaMarr were now the vamps who took part in these languorous love scenes. Today they may seem absurd, but an earlier public found them erotic. One sixteen-year-old girl told an interviewer:

"Those pictures with hot love-making in them, they make girls and boys sitting together want to get up and walk out, go off somewhere."

Rudolph Valentino, top male lover of the time—perhaps of any time—made his first hit in *The Four Horsemen of the Apocalypse,* opposite Alice Terry. He, too, was a long-drawn-out lover, whose seduction scenes often suggested two wrestlers circling one another. When Rudy did get the girl in his arms, he polished off resistance by popping his eyes at her. Recalls his Paramount boss Adolph Zukor: "Rudy's technique was largely confined to protruding his large, almost occult eyes, until the vast areas of white were visible; drawing back the lips of his wide, sensuous mouth to bare his gleaming teeth; and flaring his nostrils."

The huge success of tangoing Rudy lifted to prominence a band of actors who looked like him: Ramon Novarro, John Gilbert, Ricardo Cortez, Antonio Moreno, Gilbert Roland. Yet Rudy had pantherish

grace and a quick smile that none could ever match. In *The Four Horsemen, The Sheik, Blood and Sand,* and *Son of the Sheik,* he made women swoon. He also set the style for American males, who slicked back their hair with Stacomb and self-consciously wore slave bracelets.

Also prominent in Hollywood was Elinor Glyn, our old friend from 1907. Madame Glyn, as she now preferred to be called, had continued to write her hothouse best sellers. Inevitably, she arrived in the movie capital, where *Three Weeks* and other Glyn masterpieces proved to be excellent fodder for films. Madame Glyn was a potent figure in Hollywood, the only female able to awe Louis B. Mayer, Sam Goldwyn, Carl Laemmle, William Fox, and other studio heads. These men were badly educated; they had never traveled abroad or shaken the hand of a titled person. Madame Glyn had, often. She utilized her imposing background to full effect. She even told Rudolph Valentino how to make Latin love when he appeared in her *Beyond the Rocks.* "Do you know," she reminisced later, "he had never even thought of kissing the palm, rather than the back, of a woman's hand until I made him do it."

Madame's films bore the impressive legend, "An Elinor Glyn Production." At first she concentrated on her royal love themes. But soon—like the rest of Hollywood—she noted the enormous popularity of Jazz Age films. *Prodigal Daughters, Collegians, The Mad Whirl, House of*

Youth, Flaming Youth, The Plastic Age, The Perfect Flapper—these box office smashes were "a fast transmission belt for Jazz Age ideas," as one expert put it.

Another fondly recalls this spate of films as full of "beautiful jazz babies, champagne baths, midnight revels, petting parties in the purple dawn, white kisses, red kisses, soul kisses, pleasure-mad daughters, sensation-craving mothers."

Madame Glyn had written a novella called *It*, defined as "the strange magnetism that attracts both sexes." To the public, however, It simply meant attracting the other sex. Madame Glyn's plot focused on a man, but she shrewdly reworked it into a vehicle for Clara Bow, billed as the "Hottest Jazz Baby in Films."

Red-haired, peppy Clara had begun her rise to cinema success in 1922 when a friend sent her picture to a movie magazine. Until Clara came along, Colleen Moore, star of *Flaming Youth*, was the hottest flapper in pictures. Jazzy, boyish, flat-chested Clara looked even more like the John Held drawing than Colleen. After Madame Glyn announced her for the lead in *It*, Clara became known as the "It Girl."

"I never even had a doll," Clara recalled of her slum upbringing in Brooklyn. Now the jazz baby got $4,000 and twenty thousand fan letters every week. The It Girl lived in a Beverly Hills mansion, where she gave wild parties for movie stars and entire football teams. She bought a wire-wheeled Kissel roadster to match her flaming hair and a clutch of chow dogs of the same hue. In the red roadster, with the red dogs, her bobbed red hair flying, Clara tore up and down Hollywood Boulevard, while traffic cops looked the other way. She was the Jazz Age incarnate.

♥

The nation whirling its way through the Twenties sang and danced no less madly than it whirled. Irving Berlin ("What'll I Do?", "All Alone," "Blue Skies," "Remember," "Melody Lingers On") was the top songwriter of the decade, his straightforward songs plucking the heartstrings at which music is traditionally aimed. An unprecedented number of popular songs poured from Tin Pan Alley and Broadway. The country seemed to be enjoying its melodic peak.

To connoisseurs, the stage musical melodies of the Twenties bring the tenderest moments. At that point in history, Jerome Kern ("Who," "Look for the Silver Lining," "Ol' Man River") was the most respected composer for Broadway musicals. But young talents like George Gershwin ("Someone to Watch Over Me," "S'Wonderful," "The Man I Love") and Vincent Youmans ("Tea for Two," "Hallelujah," "I Want to Be Happy," "Bambalina") crowded him hard. Meantime, teams like De Sylva, Brown, and Henderson ("Birth of the Blues," "Black Bottom") contributed fast-paced tunes to revues like Ziegfeld Follies, George White's Scandals, Earl Carroll's Vanities.

187

Songs, songs, songs! The deluge began early in the decade. See if you remember a snatch or two of these:

"Carolina in the Morning"
"The Sheik of Araby"
"I Wonder Where My Baby Is Tonight"
"My Baby Just Cares for Me"
"I'll See You in My Dreams"
"Whispering"
"Memory Lane"
"Don't Bring Lulu"
"O Katerina"
"Kitten on the Keys"
"Mr. Gallagher and Mr. Shean"
"Limehouse Blues"

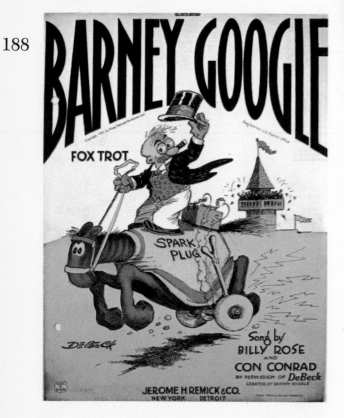

"Yes, We Have No Bananas"
"Collegiate"
"Japanese Sandman"
"Linger Awhile"
"Then I'll Be Happy"
"Barney Google"
"Margie"
"Charleston"
"Avalon"
"When My Baby Smiles At Me"
"Ain't We Got Fun?"
"All By Myself"
"April Showers"
"I'm Just Wild About Harry"
"Ma, He's Makin' Eyes at Me"

"Say It With Music"

"A Pretty Girl Is Like a Melody"

"When Francis Dances With Me"

"Chicago"

"Crinoline Days"

"Toot Toot Tootsie, Good-bye"

"Way Down Yonder in New Orleans"

"Beside a Babbling Brook"

"I Cried For You"

"Oh Gee, Oh Gosh, Oh Golly, I'm In Love"

"Swingin' Down the Lane"

"Who's Sorry Now?"

"Fascinatin' Rhythm"

"I Wonder What's Become of Sally"

"June Night"

"Why Did I Kiss That Girl,
    Why, Oh Why, Oh Why?"

"Second-Hand Rose"

"Please Don't Talk About Me When I'm Gone"

"Rose of the Rio Grande"

"Yes, Sir, That's My Baby"

"Follow the Swallow Back Home"

"Piccolo Pete"

"Hard-Hearted Hannah"

"California, Here I Come"

"Sweet Georgia Brown"

"Wabash Blues"

"When Day Is Done"

"Glad Rag Doll"

"Wonderful One"

"Runnin' Wild"

"I Love You"

"Sweetheart of Sigma Chi"

"Ten Little Fingers, Ten Little Toes"

"I Love My Baby, My Baby Loves Me"

"I Scream, You Scream, We All Scream for
    Ice Cream"

"Lonesome and Sorry"

"Gimme a Little Kiss, Will Ya, Huh?"

"Everything Is Hotsy Totsy Now"

"When My Sugar Walks Down the Street"

"I'm Forever Blowing Bubbles"

"When the Pussywillow Whispers to the Catnip"

"Dirty Hands, Dirty Face"

"Pal of My Cradle Days"

"Nagasaki"

"Ukelele Lady"

"On a Dew Dew Dewy Day"

"I've Got a Crush On You, Sweetie Pie"

"The Man I Love"

"My Sweetie Went Away"

"Somebody Stole My Gal"

"The Pal That I Loved, Stole the Gal
    That I Loved"

189

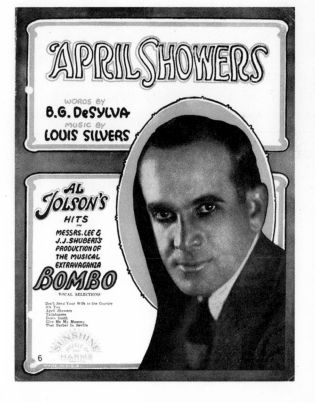

The Literary Life

♥ The hectic pace of the Twenties increased. Pelvis-to-pelvis dancing was slipping out of vogue, giving way to the wide-swinging Charleston. Here you held your partner at arm's length, hands on shoulders. Rag-doll relaxed, you performed rubbery, intricate steps with swinging legs. *Doo Wacka Doo,* wailed the mellow sax. *Vo Do Dee O Do,* people chanted.

Five years before, *Main Street* had been the book to read. Now the best seller was *Gentlemen Prefer Blondes,* by Anita Loos. A small volume, catchily illustrated by Ralph Barton, it was the semiliterate diary of Lorelei Lee, a blonde cutie from a Broadway musical-comedy chorus. The contemporary phrase for little Lorelei was gold digger, since her primary interest in life was extracting money from men. Her philosophy was neatly elucidated when a gallant Frenchman bent low to kiss her hand. "Kissing your hand makes you feel very good," she confided in her diary, "but a diamond bracelet lasts forever."

Lorelei's protector was Moe Eisman, the Button King. In *Gentlemen Prefer Blondes,* he paid for her first trip to Europe. Readers laughed at Lorelei's fractured English and gutter wisdom. But the blunt fact remains that the blonde gold digger really got along in life by selling her boyish-bobbed body. Ten years before, Lorelei would have been reviled and banned from bookstores. Now she brought nationwide enjoyment.

With fiction stressing the present, nonfiction cast new light on the past, offering history in new, exciting focus. Best sellers of the period were *Outline of History* by H. G. Wells, *Story of Mankind* by Hendrik Willem Van Loon, *Story of Philosophy* by Will Durant, and *Story of the World's Literature* by John Macy. People anxious to understand their own motivations read *Mind in the Making* by James Harvey Robinson, *Why We Behave Like Human Beings* by G. A. Dorsey, *Art of Thinking* by Abbé Dimnet, *Doctor Looks at Love and Life,* by Dr. Joseph Collins, and *Conquest of Fear* by Basil King. Information about the world at large came from *The Universe Around Us* by Sir James Jeans and *This Believing World* by Lewis Browne.

Still, this was ever the era of disillusionment. We see it again in the spate of war novels which began descending on the public. The first was *Three Soldiers* by John Dos Passos, in which one soldier says, "I've got to a point where I don't give a damn what happens to me; I don't care if I'm shot or live to be eighty; I'm sick of being ordered around."

The same theme echoed in Larry Barretto's *A Conqueror Passes,* E. E. Cummings' *Enormous Room,* Erich Maria Remarque's *All Quiet on the Western Front* and dozens of other war novels. On

190

Sinclair Lewis (at typewriter) turned sharp eye on America. Anita Loos wrote about gold diggers in Gentlemen Prefer Blondes. *Fitzgerald best caught flavor of Jazz Age. Mencken and Nathan edited mercurial* American Mercury.

the stage a pair of nonidealistic Marines named Flagg and Quirt cavorted in *What Price Glory?* by Laurence Stallings and Maxwell Anderson. Movies provided *The Big Parade,* with John Gilbert, Karl Dane, and Renée Adoree.

From all these works Americans learned a lesson the world already knew: that war is hell, and not at all the way statesmen and politicians painted it. Wrote young Ernest Hemingway, "You did not know what it was about. You never had time to learn. They threw you in and told you the rules, and the first time they caught you off base they killed you."

Nothing was sacred. The wave of disillusionment spread to nonfiction, as historians began to view formerly sacrosanct historical figures with a cold eye. This process was known as debunking. George Washington, hallowed father of his country, was debunked by both journalist William Woodward and novelist Rupert Hughes. Abraham Lincoln, paragon of Presidents, was whittled down by poet Edgar Lee Masters. John Erskine debunked history by rendering it modern and sophisticated in *The Private Life of Helen of Troy.* From overseas came Lytton Strachey's downgrading of sainted Queen Victoria. Even Jesus Christ was, in a sense, debunked. In *The Man Nobody Knows,* author Bruce Barton discovered in him the characteristics of a go-getting American businessman.

Flaming Youth—the phrase comes from *Hamlet,* of all places—was the title of a novel that gave a name to the scandalous prohibition-era behavior of the heedless young. Written by Warner Fabian (who years later was revealed as the respected Samuel Hopkins Adams), the book shocked the nation, educated it, and prepared parents for the worst.

Today *Flaming Youth* is more reminiscent of an Elinor Glyn novel than of the realistic writing of Sinclair Lewis, Ernest Hemingway, and other writers of the time who were busily crashing literary barriers. Even so, the book is of interest because it boxes the compass of jazz age sensation. In it you find rolled stockings, petting parties, drinking from hip flasks, gin marriages, companionate marriage, and what was called "going all the way."

There is also talk of abortions and premarital sex, an indication that gin-drinking and petting were not all that sheiks and shebas did. Parents took it for granted that petting parties took place in the front seats of parked cars. But they should have worried just as much about what went on in back seats.

Flaming Youth tells the story of the three flapper daughters of Ralph and Mona Fentriss, residents of Dorrisdale, a suburb of New York City. Mona is a typical mother of the time, envious of her daughters' youth. "Don't you wish you were young again?" she asked friends. The girls love Mona and say of her, "She's modern as jazz." But Mona dies. Husband Ralph sinks deeper into Wall Street moneymaking and dallying with another woman. He hardly appears again. So the three motherless flappers, Connie, Dee, and Pat, shoulder the plot of *Flaming Youth*. Connie, the family beauty, marries for money and finds it dull. As far as the book is concerned, she's through, too.

Second daughter Dee is "tall, rounded, supple, brown, redolent of physical expression." Even so, Dee is cold, perhaps frigid. Around her, girls are petting in rumble seats or "going all the way." But Dee doesn't even like the touch of a man's hand. She's really in love with the family doctor, an older man who worshiped mother Mona.

Fortunately for the story, kid-sister Pat is made of hotter stuff. She's fifteen at the beginning of the book and because of her youth is banished to bed during a wild party in the house below. The precocious brat steals into Dee's room, borrows a knee-length frock and high heels, and slips downstairs. Immediately a boy gives her a gulp of bootleg hooch from a flask and pulls her toward the nearest petting ground. Pat is more than willing, but her sisters catch her. So it's back to bed for jazzy little Pat.

The socko scene of the book—a nude bathing escapade that rocked the nation's readers—comes early. At a country club evening a daring group decides on a nude dip in the pool. One participant is man-hating Dee, who agrees only when the others ridicule her. A tennis net is dropped in the pool to keep the bare sexes apart and the half-drunk revelers jump in for a segregated dip. But the fun ends almost as soon as it begins. A handyman, hearing the happy shouts, switches on the flood-lights. Simultaneously, a drunken girl almost drowns. Bashful Dee is saved from scandal. She has just begun to undress when the lights go on.

Dee feels she has to do something with her life, and agrees to a companionate marriage with her most eligible suitor. This means no sex activity until the pair has decided the union is sure to work. But Dee's husband quickly violates the agreement and climbs into bed with her. The man-hating girl despises him for it. Next she's pregnant, and after an abortion she loathes him even more.

Time creeps on, with young Pat growing up to have "a dark, exotic radiance, like a flame among flowers. She exhaled a delight, like a perfect perfume of her ardent soul." Pat is still wild. "I've been a terrible petter since I began to grow up," she boasts.

Pat is happily traveling the downhill path when one night the Fentriss doorbell rings. Outside is Cary Scott, once in love with mother Mona. Unaware of her death, his shock is so genuine that he is quickly made a member of the household.

Cary must be forty, even forty-five. Pat has just touched eighteen, but the wild flapper makes a play for him. Amused at first, Cary suddenly succumbs to "the lucious huskiness in her voice, the gleamy mist of her hair, her strong, super-vitalized

193

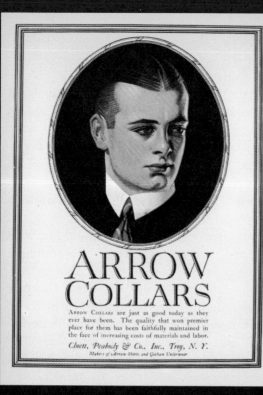

ARROW COLLARS

ARROW COLLARS are just as good today as they ever have been. The quality that won premier place for them has been faithfully maintained in the face of increasing costs of materials and labor.

Cluett, Peabody & Co., Inc., Troy, N. Y.
Makers of Arrow Shirts and Gotham Underwear

"And then, and then, came Spring and Rose in hand. My threadbare Penitence apieces tore" OMAR

OMAR
TURKISH
BLEND
CIGARETTES
EXCEPTIONAL QUALITY
THE AMERICAN TOBACCO CO.
OMAR

The economy of OMAR Turkish Blend is only incidental. More enjoyment has given OMAR its lead over the All Turkish cigarettes **20 for 15¢**
ADVT.

Holeproof Hosiery

STOCKINGS selected for beauty need not disappoint in their wearing qualities — not if you will ask for Holeproof. For in this famous hosiery, sheer, lustrous appearance is united with a fine-spun, woven-in strength that withstands long wear and repeated launderings. Moderate prices put Holeproof Hose within the reach of all, both for dress and every-day wear.

Holeproof Hosiery is offered in a wide variety of styles in Silk, Wool, Silk and Wool, Silk Faced, and Lusterized Lisle for men, women and children
If not obtainable locally, write for price list and illustrated booklet

HOLEPROOF HOSIERY COMPANY, Milwaukee, Wisconsin
Holeproof Hosiery Company of Canada, Limited, London, Ontario

Advertising discovered the inferiority complex, picturing products as symbols of success and style. For example, the Arrow Collar man was the embodiment of assured masculinity.

TIME TO RETIRE?

BUY FISK

THE FISK RUBBER COMPANY

Norman Rockwell

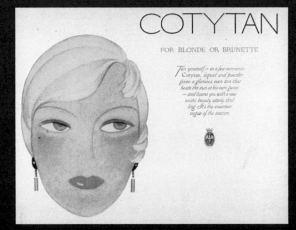

COTYTAN

FOR BLONDE OR BRUNETTE

Tan yourself — in a few moments Cotytan, liquid and powder gives a glorious even tan that beats the sun at his own game — and leaves you with a new exotic beauty utterly thrilling. It's the smartest vogue of the season.

HANDEL LAMPS are noteworthy examples of master craftsmanship. Each is designed and made for permanence, to give life-long service as well as to enhance the attractiveness of the room it adorns. The lamp pictured above illustrates the unusual in decorative treatment, the rare artistry of line and fine balance between shade and standard that make Handel Lamps so distinctive and so desirable.

hand with colors that are fadeless. All standards and metal parts specially treated to afford a decorative finish as enduring as the metal itself.

Floor lamps, electroliers, pendants, wall sconces, boudoir lamps and torcheres—a few of which are shown—provide a Handel Lamp for every purpose, for every room. They, or other styles and designs, may be purchased at stores of the better sort. Ask to see them.

THERE'S A TOUCH OF TOMORROW IN ALL COLE DOES TODAY

Sportster

Cole Aero-EIGHT

THE CRITERION OF MOTOR CAR FASHIONS
GREATER PERFORMANCE EFFICIENCY

COLE MOTOR CAR COMPANY, INDIANAPOLIS, U.S.A.

Creators of Advanced Motor Cars

young body." Roughly, he hauls her to a sofa. Pat is taken aback by this mature reaction to her gin-set flirting. To the panting Cary she says, "I'm terribly in love with you—tonight." Soon, after a passionate kiss, the two "go all the way."

When it's all over, deflowered Pat leaps to her feet. "I'm not sorry," she pants, "I'm not! I'm not! I'm glad!"

What of Dee during all this? Well, she is all set to run out on her noncompanionate marriage when her husband is carried home after an auto smashup. It's a life sentence for Dee. The husband she loathes will be an invalid the rest of his life, and she must nurse him.

Cary Scott returns to Europe, where he is a big shot with the League of Nations. Pat goes back to running wild. Petting parties, up-ended flasks, broken engagements, an almost-affair with a Greenwich Village violinist—all these founder as the specter of Cary Scott rises to spoil her pleasure.

Cary Scott comes back to Dorrisdale. He has not been able to forget his eighteen (now nineteen)- year-old love. Nor has she found anyone better than Cary, old though he is. The two discuss marriage and for a mad moment ponder the companionate kind. This would never work for *them*.

All through *Flaming Youth* Pat has talked fast and loose, like the wildest flapper. But her behavior, except for that one lapse, has really been all right. It's that way now. On the last page she tells Cary, "As a husband, you'll have to be a terribly on-the-job lover. There are so many men in the world!"

We know the jazz baby doesn't mean it.

♥

With such freedom in literature, there was bound to be freer talk. Intellectuals now sprinkled conversation with references to the theories of Dr. Sigmund Freud, while magazine writers made telling points with psychoanalytical jargon. To the average person, psychoanalysis was still baffling, but one semiprofessional term lodged in the public mind: inferiority complex. America, somewhat appalled at its own behavior, was quite willing to admit it suffered from feelings of inferiority.

Advertising moguls were among the first to become aware of this, and swung the great power of their industry behind a type of advertisement designed to work upon people's latent insecurities.

Magazines and newspapers might still feature tasteful ads for commodities like autos and fur coats. Ultra-smart folk might be urged, "Be Nonchalant—Light a Murad." But other advertising copywriters concentrated on the realm of the mind, the emotions, and the mysterious psyche. Skillfully they juggled human fears and hopes. Writes Frederick Lewis Allen: "The copywriter was learning to pay less attention to the special qualities and advantages of his product, and more to the story of what the mass of unregenerate mankind wanted—to be young and desirable, to be rich, to keep up with the Joneses, to be envied."

In 1919, one Listerine ad began: "The prompt application of Listerine may prevent a minor accident from becoming a major infection." In the mid-Twenties, a similar ad opened: "Spring! For everyone else but her . . . " Cleverly conjuring up inadequacies people never before suspected, the ads wound up by offering instant remedies. As always, the slogans left no doubt: "Always a Bridesmaid But Never a Bride," "Even Your Best Friends Won't Tell You," "Four Out of Five Have It."

Still more ads promised a smooth highway to popularity. One method was a correspondence course in the piano: "They Laughed When I Sat Down at the Piano, But When I Started to Play!" Learning a language was another way. An ad for French At Sight recounted the social ostracism of a rolled-stockings flapper who thought filet mignon was a kind of fish. The same course brought triumph to a young man introduced to a pretty girl: "*Comment ça va?* She Said With A Laugh, and I Astounded Her With My Reply!"

Accumulation of knowledge was another path to popularity. An ad for the Pocket University showed a strong-jawed young man at a party: "Ali Baba? I sat forward in my chair. I could tell them all about this romantic, picturesque figure of fiction." On the other hand, an elderly man in evening dress was pictured cowering in the back seat of a limousine. His young wife snarled at him, "I was so embarrassed. You sat there like a dummy. You didn't say a word all evening."

The answer to this man's problem was to buy Elbert Hubbard's *Scrapbook* and dig up nuggets of knowledge. Or perhaps Dr. Eliot's Five Foot Shelf of Books would do as well. Others might favor Emily Post's *Book of Etiquette,* which guaranteed to tell you "Exactly What To Do, Say, Write, or Wear on Every Occasion." Rugged males might prefer to find the secret of popularity in the muscle-building course offered by Lionel Strongfort.

Another advertising innovation of the time was the testimonial in which the rich and famous swore (for a fee) to the use of a cigarette, beauty cream, or bedspring. Ordinary folk, anxious to be bracketed with the rich and famous, rushed to buy the product. The first testimonials appeared over the slogan "Lucky Strike, It's Toasted," but the most diligent user of testimonials turned out to be Fleischmann's Yeast. Celebrities at first, then average citizens vowed, "For Years I Was Tired, Now I Take Fleischmann's Yeast 3 Times A Day."

With all this, historian Allen believes, American advertising hit its low point. Beginning as a business, advertising had risen to be a profession. Now it turned into a racket. Few objected. Intellectuals had great fun mocking the ads, but millions of other people believed them and eagerly bought the advertised products.

It made everyone happy.

Thrills & Sensations

♥ From Mah-Jongg, to Ask Me Another, to Crossword Puzzles, the nation was swept by craze after craze. It was a time when people played the same games, thrilled to the same crimes, idolized the same celebrities. Sensations were rapid-fire—more than ever before or since in a given time span. While occupying the front page, each sensation commanded the undivided attention of the population. When swept aside by the next thrill, it was forgotten, leaving only the residual material for historians of the wacky Jazz Age.

Strange to relate, a cynical population was also enormously gullible, swinging into mass madness over men like Dr. Emile Coué, a French medico who thought up what he called Autosuggestion. "Imagination is vastly more powerful than will," Coué told the world. He urged people to flex the imagination by repeating over and over, "Day by day, in every way, I am getting better and better."

When Coué arrived here in January, 1923, the nation grabbed him to its bosom, seeking a fast cure for the inferiority complex that advertising had given it. Police saved him from crowds who regarded him as a messiah. The doctor toured the major cities, establishing Coué institutes in each.

The next big sensation was the visit of the Prince of Wales, first glamour boy to take America by storm. The Prince did not go on tour, but stayed in the effete East.

There he rode, played polo, and fox-trotted on the Long Island Riviera. Even so, the public devoured details of his visit. At times the playboy Prince visited New York night clubs, and newspapers hinted that some of the demitasse cups he sipped from were filled with Scotch whiskey.

The 1924 visit of the Prince of Wales also called attention to the sob sister, the female tabloid reporter who wrote stories with tears in them. The girls—usually young and pretty—had quite a time with the susceptible young Prince, who liked to dance. "Yes, the Prince of Wales danced with me," a sob sister gushed in print. Another only spoke to His Royal Highness, but that was enough. "The heir to the throne of England," she wrote, "wears a

Prince of Wales with Mayor John Hylan of New York

four-in-hand tie of pink, purple and red in diagonal stripes. He told me he tied it himself. I think he has excellent taste."

Thrills had tremendous variety in the teeming Twenties. Sport sensations began in 1921, with the first million-dollar gate in boxing history. World's champion heavyweight Jack Dempsey, known as the "Manassa Mauler," took on "Gorgeous Georges" Carpentier of France in a dull fight at Boyle's Thirty Acres, in Jersey City. One expert called it "an afternoon waltz." Yet skillful ballyhoo made the country go wild over it. Two years later the Mauler was knocked out of the ring (he climbed back) by Luis Firpo, the Wild Bull of the Pampas.

It was a time of fine fighters in all divisions. Benny Leonard ruled the lightweights, Mickey Walker the welters.

"Big Bill" Tilden was supreme in tennis. Sober Helen Wills—"Little Miss Poker Face"—was scoring the first of her string of women's championships.

Pitcher "Babe" Ruth came to New York from the Red Sox, was switched to the outfield, and promptly launched baseball's home-run era—and a Yankee dynasty. Man o' War retired in 1921, after two victorious years that convinced many fans he was the greatest race horse ever. Handy Earl Sande was most people's favorite jockey. And Coach Knute Rockne brought a small Indiana college to national football prominence with a spectacular 1924 backfield known forever after as "the Four Horsemen of Notre Dame."

Competing with sports thrills was crime.

William T. Tilden

199

In 1922, two bodies were discovered under a crab-apple tree in De Russey's Lane, outside New Brunswick, New Jersey. This was the beginning of the Hall-Mills case, first of the decade's "crimes of the century." Two years later the nation reeled in shock over the thrill slaying committed in Chicago by Nathan Leopold and Richard Loeb. These two college-age boys, sons of wealthy families, considered themselves superintellects and to prove it murdered fourteen-year-old Bobby Franks. A jigger of homosexuality was part of the brew. Rather than supersmart, the boys were stupid and quickly got caught. The great Clarence Darrow was persuaded to take

200

the case, and in a trailblazing defense branded the boys mentally sick rather than insane. The thrill killers got life imprisonment.

Darrow also figured in the Monkey Trial at Dayton, Tennessee, where he volunteered to serve as defense counsel for high-school teacher John Scopes, who was charged with violating state law by teaching the theory of evolution. Opposing Darrow was William Jennings Bryan, three times presidential candidate, onetime Secretary of State. Bryan believed every word of the Bible; Darrow was an agnostic. During those hot days, so many people crowded into Dayton that the proceedings moved to the courthouse lawn. Under Darrow's sharp examination, Bryan became befuddled and pedantic. Five days later he died of a stroke. Scopes got a small fine; Darrow won further eminence as a liberal lawyer.

Next, a spelunker named Floyd Collins

was trapped underground by a landslide near Cave City, Kentucky. Newspaper editors of the day clamored endlessly for human interest stories and here was a towering one: a single man at the mercy of God and nature eight hundred feet underground. Above, at the entrance to the cave, experts argued heatedly over the best method of rescue. Feature reporters took over Cave City and for eighteen days the nation lived in suspense. When help finally got to him, Floyd Collins was dead.

Newspaper headlines brought escapist excitement or increased disillusionment.

On the witness stand in a law suit, Henry Ford was questioned about his knowledge of American history. His ignorance was appalling. He called Benedict Arnold a writer and the War of 1812 a revolution. Boastfully he said, "I live in the present," then admitted only scanning the headlines of newspapers. He wound up by stating, "History is bunk!" The younger generation looked scornfully at the older. "Is this the kind of person you ask us to admire?" it demanded bitterly.

Added disillusionment came from the power of gangland elements which had risen to distribute liquor and brew illicit beer. Crime empires raked in hundreds of millions a year. Chicago was a crime center, with Al Capone, formerly of the AEF, mercilessly rubbing out rivals with machine-gun bullets. Capone and his gunsels had taken over the entire town of Cicero, Illinois, and all but ran Chicago from headquarters in a downtown hotel.

Other cities had prohibition gangsters, but not on the scale of Chicago, with Capone, Johnny Torrio, Dion O'Banion, Bugs Moran, and Hymie Weiss. New York boasted Owney Madden, Dutch Schultz, Big Frenchy DeMange, Legs Diamond, and the like. They never had the finesse of the Chicagoans, who believed in spending $15-$25 for silk shirts. Hearing this, Dutch Schultz gave a snort, "Silk shirts! A guy's a sucker to spend fifteen or twenty bucks for a silk shirt. Hell, I can buy a good shirt for two bucks."

One who observed all this with total

Al Capone

lack of surprise was H. L. Mencken, who with George Jean Nathan had begun to publish his green-covered *American Mercury* magazine. Baltimore-born Mencken was an iconoclast willing to believe the worst of the world. A pungent thinker, his ideas exploded like fireworks in impressionable minds. Mencken had a genius for the striking word and phrase, and coined such terms as "boobus Americanus" and "the booboisie."

Mencken promoted lusty talents like one-time hobo Jim Tully in the pages of the *Mercury*, but he himself always remained the stellar attraction. "President Harding," he once wrote,

"writes the worst English I have ever encountered; it reminds me of a string of wet sponges; it is so bad that a sort of grandeur creeps into it. Almost I yearn for the sweeter song, the rubber stamp of more familiar design, the gentler and more seemly bosh of the late Woodrow."

Of William Jennings Bryan at the Scopes trial, the redoubtable Mencken declared:

"Once he had one leg in the White House and the nation trembled under his roars. Now he is a tinpot pope in the Coca-Cola belt and a brother to the forlorn pastors who belabor halfwits in the galvanized iron tabernacles behind the railroad yards."

The *American Mercury* sold for fifty cents, a lot of money for a magazine without pictures. Few of the booboisie ever got to read it, but intellectuals embraced it as a living Bible. From highbrow readers Mencken's irreverent philosophy filtered down through the population to the roots of American thinking.

Cartoons & Comics

♥ Everything changed in the Twenties. Comic strips were no exception. For this, the main credit goes to Captain Joseph Medill Patterson, the man who founded the tabloid *Daily News* in New York in 1919. Burly Joe Patterson was a member of the family which already owned the Chicago *Tribune*. With the *Daily News* established, the Captain wasted no time in starting a News-Tribune Syndicate. It sold features to other newspapers, promising a readership of four million.

Captain Patterson was fascinated by comic strips, which were turning out to be a financial gold mine for syndicates like King, Bell, NEA, and McNaught. In the early days, only city readers had seen comic strips, but with the rise of syndicates the strip became a nationwide institution. Kid strips, bizarre strips, domestic strips—you name it, somebody had 'em!

In the syndicate pattern, successful artists were corralled and their strips sold to as many papers as possible. Captain Patterson had a more individualistic approach. He dreamed up his own ideas and sought the right artist. Or he took a minor facet of an established strip and developed it into a new one.

"Patterson dug deep down to the simplest, rock-bottom instincts of the masses and built a strip on each one," writes authority Stephen Becker. "He considered cartoonists important, and felt that they would be even more important with the benefit of his own judgment."

Each Patterson strip was close to a segment of American life: the Gumps were family life; Harold Teen, youth; Smitty, kid stuff; Winnie Winkle, girl stuff; Moon Mullins, rough humor; Gasoline Alley, suburban life. Perusal of them today exposes one curious fact. In these top-success strips of the Twenties there is none of the high jinks associated with the decade. Never does cute, popular Winnie Winkle drink from a hip flask or dance the Charleston. Nor does Harold Teen. From this it is possible to deduce that during the Twenties some folk went on living quietly. Perhaps only the wealthy and the well-to-do did the roaring.

"The comic strip was vitalized by Captain Patterson," the books tell you. But other influences were visible. One was the single drawing, where everything takes place in one outsize panel.

Top practitioner in the panel form was Fontaine Fox, with his "Toonerville Trolley That Meets All Trains" (with the Terrible Tempered Mr. Bang, Powerful Katrinka, Mickey McGuire, Tomboy Taylor, Aunt Eppy Hogg). Fox's Toonerville was a zany locality, a considerable distance removed from reality. Closer to life were the cartoonists who neatly and humorously exposed the soul of the average man, woman, and child. Perhaps the best here was Clare

Bachelor Walt Wallet's adventures with foundling Skeezix was theme of "Gasoline Alley," one of many family-life comics that burgeoned during Twenties.

The Gumps

Smitty

Moon Mullins

Bringing Up Father

Winnie Winkle

Harold Teen

Briggs, who alternated between "Ain't It a Grand and Glorious Feeling?" "When a Feller Needs a Friend," "Far Into the Night," and others. Briggs also did the Sunday strip, "Mr. and Mrs.," featuring Joe and Vi.

Somewhat gentler than Briggs (and often confused with him) was H. T. Webster, who drew "The Thrill That Comes Once in a Lifetime," "How to Torture Your Wife," and so on. His Sunday strip was the "Timid Soul," the immortal Casper Milquetoast.

Denys Wortman gave the world "Mopey Dick and the Duke," "Metropolitan Movies," and "In and Out of the Red with Sam." The single-panel drawing, originally appearing in this country in *Puck* and *Life,* reached new peaks of wit and sophistication in *The New Yorker,* which commenced publication in 1925.

Comic-strip characters usually overshadowed their creators, but a few artists became more famous than their strips. One was Rube Goldberg, who attained immortality by his insane inventions, most of them the work of his Professor Lucifer Butts. Another man more famous than his strip was Robert L. Ripley, of the amazing "Believe It or Not."

Milt Gross, too, was famous. Beginning as assistant to T. A. Dorgan, Gross branched out on his own with "Banana Oil" and "Count Screwloose from Toulouse." His weird situations were embellished with garbled Jewish dialect. Even stone-faced Calvin Coolidge, who seemed amused by nothing, was a Gross fan.

Milt Gross had so many ideas that he abandoned strips in midstream to begin others. He wrote the best-selling books *Nize Baby* and *Hiawatta.* Journeying to Hollywood, he created comic situations for Charlie Chaplin. At the same time he kept producing strips like "Dave's Delicatessen," "Grossly Xaggerated," "Looey Dot Dope," and "That's My Pop."

1920's CARTOONS

Wash Tubbs (with Easy, Rip O'Day)
S'Matter Pop?
   (with Despr't Ambrose, tha deteckativ)
The Nebbs
Toots and Casper (with Buttercup)
Banana Oil
Just Kids (Mush Stebbins, Ignatius Conway)
Reg'lar Fellers
   (Puddin'head, Pinhead, Jimmy Dugan)
Freckles and His Friends (notably Tagalong)
Little Mary Mixup
   (with Bunny and horse Vanilla)
Tillie the Toiler (and Mac)
Ella Cinders (with Lotta Pill, Prissie Pill)
Clarence (with wife Mary and Uncle Walt)
Betty (with Lester De Pester)
Peter Rabbit
Boots and Her Buddies
   (with Cora and Professor Tutt)
Betty Boop
Bungle Family
Barney Google (with Spark Plug)
Thimble Theatre
   (with Olive Oyl, Ham Gravy,
   Castor Oyl, Cole Oyl, Nana Oyl)
Just Kids
Boob McNutt
Elmer
G. Whizz Jr.
That's My Pop

206

1900 1905
1905 1910
1910 1915
1915 1920
1920 1925
♥ **1925 1930**
1930 1935
1935 1942

ERA OF WONDERFUL NONSENSE

♥ The 1920's have been given many nicknames: the Jazz Age, Roaring Twenties, Turbulent Twenties, Teeming Twenties, Whoopee Era, Fabulous Decade, Lawless Decade. But maybe the best designation of all is the Era of Wonderful Nonsense.

The peak of the nonsense—wonderful or not—came after 1925. The second half of the glorious decade produced such wacky characters as Alvin "Shipwreck" Kelly, the flagpole sitter. Calling himself the Luckiest Fool Alive, this ex-sailor first perched atop a pole on a St. Louis building for seven days. Over succeeding months, he more than doubled that time to become, despite considerable competition, the nation's No. 1 flagpole sitter. Most of the flagpoles Shipwreck adorned were at least fifty feet high. In the words of that bright new magazine *The New Yorker,* he sat up there "etched in magnificent loneliness."

How did the fellow do it? Shipwreck's chair was a rubber-covered wooden seat strapped tightly to the round flagpole ball. He took only fluids—milk, coffee, broth—hoisted up to him in a bucket. He slept with thumbs anchored into two holes bored into the wooden seat. During one sleet storm he used a hatchet to chip ice from his body.

The flagpoles were usually atop hotels, for Shipwreck's endurance feats brought much business. People peered up at him from the street, and any who paid fifty cents could ride to the roof for a closer view. One who did this was a redheaded flapper, aged eighteen. As she stood there, the man next to her said, "He's nothing but a damn fool." "He is not," she replied angrily. "He knows just what he's doing." She then slapped the man's face.

Informed of this episode by a note in his food bucket, thirty-two-year-old Shipwreck expressed a natural desire to meet the girl. She was hoisted up to him by a rope around her midriff, and the two pitched woo in mid-air. When Shipwreck climbed down they got married.

More madness came from the high-powered activities of promoter C. C. Pyle, whose many stunts included a transcontinental foot race, starting on the West Coast. Newspapers dubbed it the Bunion Derby. In New York, another promoter hired Madison Square Garden for a multi-event marathon. In one corner was a group of nonstop talkers; newspapers called this the Noun and Verb Rodeo. In another, a rocking-chair derby. And so on. These assorted marathons were open twenty-four hours a day and in the early hours of the morning revelers from New York's five thousand speakeasy night clubs dropped in to gape at the fun.

Not all was nonsense in the Nonsense Era. For unabashed sadism there were the dance marathons in which young couples danced around and around, with only a

Flagpole sitters, like this now unidentified daredevil perched atop a Keith theater, held public's attention until new and giddier fads diverted it.

208

few minutes of each hour for sleep. Often dancers passed out from sheer exhaustion in partners' arms. By the rules, they had to be awakened and they usually came up screaming and clawing. "This," one reporter stated, "is known as 'going squirrelly,' and it gives everyone lots of laughs."

♥

The top nonsense story of the Era of Wonderful Nonsense was the saga of Peaches and Daddy. Each of its wildly publicized installments turned out to be goofier than the one before. Daddy was millionaire Edward West Browning, elderly New York real-estate dealer. He had a penchant (the word one newspaper used) for very young girls, on whom he liked to bestow pet names. The night he met pudgy fifteen-year-old Frances Belle Heenan, Daddy announced, "I'm going to call you Peaches, because you look like peaches and cream to me." Then he instructed her to "Call me Daddy." He married Peaches in the spring of 1926. A horde of reporters, photographers, and sob sisters followed them everywhere. CROWDS TRAMPLE PEACHES, a tabloid shrieked when the bride celebrated her sixteenth birthday by shopping along Fifth Avenue. Six months later Peaches packed her finery and departed dear old Dad. Naturally, reporters covered the event.

Daddy and Peaches had turned into what Damon Runyon called Homo Saps. That is, they'd do anything for publicity.

Instead of racing home to mother, Peaches went to the office of a top-flight ghost writer. She gave him material for a scorching story called "My Honeymoon With Daddy." Daddy, too, dug up a ghost writer, to give his side of the drama to another tabloid. Next, the pair hired relays of ghost writers to whom they told new and differing stories. "Nothing more sensational or fantastic has ever appeared in newspapers," says an authority.

Peaches sued for a legal separation, asking $300 a week in alimony. The Peaches-Daddy trial at White Plains, New York, in January, 1927, became the silliness sensation of the decade. The *New York Times* carried the testimony on page one, while the tabloids whipped up lurid coverage. A mob seethed outside the courthouse, with women abandoning baby carriages in order to push inside.

Courtroom testimony alternated between the funny and the salacious. Peaches turned out to be a typical flapper, while Daddy bounded to the witness chair like an actor taking a curtain call. His lawyer immediately asked, "You are a sane man, aren't you?" Daddy answered with an emphatic, "Yes." With Peaches crying bitterly, the judge decided against her, and the whole business sank into oblivion.

Mass hysteria swept to a morbid crest in 1926, with the death of movie actor Rudolph Valentino, the Sheik of Sheiks. Despite his slinky appearance, the screen lover in private life was a quiet fellow; he liked to call his wives "Boss." The latest of

Peaches and Daddy Browning typified Era of Wonderful Nonsense. When married, she was sweet sixteen, he in mid-fifties. After that, only headlines mattered to the antic pair.

these had persuaded Rudy to break his lucrative contract with Paramount Pictures. Restless without work, in need of money, he began a personal-appearance tour of big-city theaters. He collapsed when he reached New York and was rushed to a hospital. In an operation for appendicitis, doctors also found two perforated gastric ulcers. With this, pneumonia, pleurisy, and peritonitis set in. Glossy-haired Rudy was doomed.

When he died, hysteria broke loose. Thirty thousand people, their emotions churned higher by skillful press-agentry, descended on Frank E. Campbell's Memorial Chapel, where the actor lay in state attired in immaculate evening dress. Plate-glass windows were smashed and women trampled. With order restored, one hundred and fifty persons a minute began filing past the bier. The line of mourners never seemed to slacken.

♥

Nonsense songs, fads, silly sayings reflected the atmosphere. On the vaudeville stage, comedians got laughs with the brand new She-Was-Only jokes: "She was only a farmer's daughter, but she sure did know her oats"; "She was only a doctor's daughter, but my how she operated"; "She was only a bootlegger's daughter, but I love her still"; "She was only a cab-driver's daughter, but oh, you auto meet her."

College boys in raccoon coats raced the roads in Model T flivvers, the sides covered with slogans like Rattle of the Century, Girls Wanted, Plus-Four Brakes, Ain't She Sweet?, Handle With Hooks—No Care. Sheiks and shebas bought bright yellow slickers, spent hours stenciling them with contemporary catch phrases: Thanks for the Buggy Ride; Don't Step On It, It Might Be Lon Chaney; Show Me the Way to Go Home. Flappers and boy friends brought the ukelele into prominence, as fingers whipped the elementary instrument through a frenzied "Sheik of Araby" or "Who Stole My Heart Away?"

New slang popped up. A cute flapper was "a beaut," or "the cat's meow," "cat's

Dance marathons were cruel tests of endurance. Opposite: Valentino's death unloosed an orgy of grief. Admirer kneels at bier as Great Lover lies in state.

whiskers," or "cat's pajamas." Her boy friend was a "cakeater," "jazzbo," "jellybean," or "lounge lizard." Anything a flapper or jellybean liked was "nifty," or "the nuts." Rapture was expressed by "hot diggity dog," or "hot diggity." A tough guy was a "hard-boiled egg"; a stupid girl a "dumbbell," or "Dumb Dora." At a wild party, the flapper who hoisted skirts in a wicked Charleston was urged on by cries of "Get hot! Get hot!"

At the close of a happy date, a flip flapper would say to her sheik, "Thanks for the buggy ride." To tell him off, she'd snap, "Go fly a kite." If the cakeater made her laugh, she'd giggle, "Ooo, you slaughter me!" A pet expression of disbelief was, "It's the bunk." Or, "Banana oil." "Well, for crying out loud," meant incredulity.

Liquor, bathtub gin, or bootleg hooch, was "booze," "giggle water," "giggle soup." Speakeasies were "whoopee parlors." Anything strange was "goofy," anyone strange a "goof." To add emphasis a sheba breathed fervently, "I should hope to tell you!" or "And *how!*" The girl never said yes or no. Sometimes she'd give a long-drawn-out "Ab-so-lute-ly," or "Pos-i-tive-ly." Other times it was a scramble of both "Abso-*tive*-ly," or "Pos-a-*loot*-ly."

THE LONE EAGLE

♥ America needed something exceptional to pull it out of an abyss of tastelessness. That exceptional something came out of the Midwest in the person of a blond young man named Charles Augustus "Slim" Lindbergh, ex-airmail pilot and all-around flying wizard. Slim was the image of the All-American Boy. His fresh face radiated boyish modesty and calm self-confidence. The general look of clean-cut youthfulness was increased by a semi-military outfit of khakis, leather flying jacket, and leather puttees or woolen knee socks. Slim was quiet, but there was nothing impolite in his silence. He was merely a self-sufficient young man who preferred his own thoughts.

Public excitement over the exploits of aviators had been generated in 1926, when Commander Richard Evelyn Byrd and pilot Floyd Bennett flew over the North Pole.

Now the time seemed right for someone to earn the $25,000 prize that had been offered in 1919 for a nonstop flight between New York and Paris. Already the famous Commander Byrd was awaiting good weather at Roosevelt Field on Long Island. So was the relaxed, experienced flier Clarence Chamberlin. These two men would fly with crews—Byrd with three men besides himself, Chamberlin with one. Lindbergh also planned to compete for the prize. He would fly alone.

At 7:52 on the morning of May 20, 1927, Lindbergh daringly took off, leaving the others behind. A nation hypnotized by sordid scandals and general silliness raised its eyes reverently to the realm of the Lone Eagle. Thirty-three and a half hours later the suspense ended. He landed in Paris. "I am Charles Lindbergh," he stated, unaware of the world's breathless interest in him. Back home, America exploded. It had suddenly found something to worship.

The whole world enthused over Lindbergh. In America newspapers affectionately dubbed him Lindy, Lucky Lindy, Plucky Lindy, the Flying Eagle, the Flying Kid. Tabloids used the Flying Fool, a nickname Lindy resented, since there had been nothing foolish about his flight or his meticulous preparations for it.

Paris, Brussels, and London gave the Lone Eagle roaring receptions. He did aerial stunts over Paris while throngs gasped and cheered. But America wanted its hero home as fast as possible and President Coolidge sent the cruiser *Memphis* to fetch him. His first reception was in Washington, with broadcaster Graham McNamee crying, "Here comes the BOY!" New York outdid Washington; as Lindy entered the bay fireboats shot up fountains of water. Mayor Jimmy Walker for once arrived on time, and at his side stood official greeter Grover Whalen. New York's reception for Lindy has never been

214

Charles A. Lindbergh made bold solo flight across the Atlantic, brought a breath of fresh air into the inane Twenties. "Lucky Lindy" was idolized around the world.

surpassed anywhere for mass worship. Throngs who saw him downtown raced uptown to see him again.

While the nation idolized Plucky Lindy, the aviation thrills went on unabated. Indeed, the summer of 1927 has been called the Big Parade in the Air. Lindbergh's flight was only the first, though the greatest, of its aviation feats.

Clarence Chamberlin took off, carrying his financial backer Charles A. Levine as passenger. Since Lindbergh had gotten to Paris, Chamberlin hoped to fly as far as Berlin, thus setting a new long-distance record. He missed Berlin, but set a record anyway by landing in a farmer's field one hundred miles short of his goal.

Commander Byrd flew next. His three-motor Fokker encountered foul weather from the beginning. It was impossible to glimpse Paris through the pea-soup fog and the plane crisscrossed helplessly over the city. Suddenly pilot Bert Acosta cracked from the strain. Commander Byrd knocked him out with a blow from a heavy flashlight. Co-pilot Bernt Balchen took over until the plane ran out of fuel. Finally, it set down in the English Channel, so close to the shore the crew waded in.

The Big Parade in the Air! On the West Coast, Army lieutenants Maitland and Hegenberger covered the forty-two hundred miles from San Francisco to Hawaii, longest overwater flight to date. A pair of intrepid civilians named Smith and Bronte followed. Next came the $25,000 Dole Race to Hawaii which Commander Byrd

and others called "needless and ill-advised." Art Gobel won, with Martin Jensen runner-up. Nine other men and pretty teacher Mildred Doran drowned as one plane after another disappeared into the Pacific.

The big challenge remaining was a flight from Europe to America. Princess Lowenstein-Wertheim and pilot Leslie Hamilton set off from Croydon, England, and never were heard of again. From Germany two low-winged monoplanes, *Bremen* and *Europa*, took off. Bad weather sent them back, but next year *Bremen* made it.

Detroit businessmen Edward Schlee and

Lindy's plane, Spirit of St. Louis, *is surrounded by crowd at London's Croydon Field. Above: New York gives hero (seated with Mayor Walker) a ticker-tape parade.*

Billy Brock were quietly hopping around the world. They got as far as Tokyo, where the American Navy refused them fuel for the dangerous Pacific hop. William Randolph Hearst subsidized a transatlantic flight piloted by Lloyd Bertaud, with passenger Philip Payne, editor of the New York *Mirror*. The plane vanished. Flying alone, Paul Redfern left Brunswick, Georgia, for Rio de Janeiro. He too was lost, and rumors still persist that he may be alive with Central American aborigines.

The ocean flying season supposedly ended in mid-September. Yet Ruth Elder took off on a transatlantic hop with pilot George Haldeman on October 11. If Lindy was the All-American Boy, Ruth was an All-American Girl, a peaches-and-cream Southern belle. Ruth's plane landed beside a Danish tanker and she got to Paris by ship and train.

In December—repeat, December—eccentric Mrs. Frances Grayson badgered experienced Oskar Omdal into taking off from Roosevelt Field on a flight to Denmark. From them came one radio message, "We are in trouble." No one heard from them again.

At year's end, Lindbergh was getting an enthusiastic reception in Mexico City, after covering the United States on an aviation promotion tour. He stopped only at the major cities, but even when he circled over the airports of smaller towns, schools were let out and crowds gathered just to see him wave from the cockpit of his famous *Spirit of St. Louis*.

218

Following Lindbergh, many aviators extended airplane's potential. Above: Ruth Elder. Opposite: Richard E. Byrd (center) and Floyd Bennett being honored by President Coolidge. Bottom: Bernt Balchen (left) and Clarence Chamberlin.

IDOLS OF THE AIRWAVES

♥ The books tell you that in the late Twenties radio was just moving out of its infancy. People listening at the time thought radio was a fascinating, never-ending wonder. The day of the head-set and crystal had grown into the era of twisting dials and the swan's-neck loud-speaker (RCA Radiola, eight tubes, $275). Not everyone in the country owned a radio, but those who did were fully satisfied.

Over the magic of airwaves, the public heard the New England twang of Calvin Coolidge on his inauguration in 1924. Radio carried major prize fights, receptions for Lindbergh and other transatlantic fliers, political conventions, symphony concerts, jazz, comedians, and stage head-liners. Up to now, New York had been the country's capital for sophistication, but radio's great contribution was to help the whole nation catch up to New York.

January 1, 1927, was the date of the first nationwide hookup. At three o'clock that afternoon, nineteen stations across the land joined to broadcast the Rose Bowl Game between Stanford and Alabama. Needless to say, the silver tonsils of Graham McNamee described this stirring contest. "And he did it! Yessir, he *did* it! *Boy,* I want to tell you, this is one of the finest games. . . ."

Radio was still so new that people actually pondered the content of programs. It seemed to sober thinkers that a football game was an unsuitable event for the pioneering cross-country broadcast. So the networks diplomatically scheduled another nationwide for eight o'clock that night. This was a concert by the New York Symphony Orchestra, conducted by Dr. Walter Damrosch. With him was a splendid galaxy of musical luminaries, among them John McCormack, Rosa Ponselle, Mischa Elman. In New York this was heard over station WEAF, which, with WJZ, was the important outlet in the area. In Pittsburgh the station was KDKA, over which the very first broadcast had been made on November 2, 1920.

In the words of author Paul Sann, "Radio didn't grow; it flew." As it did pioneer broadcasters tried to figure out what the public really wished to hear. Soon those who preferred symphonies and serious lectures found their taste shoved aside by a wave of popular entertainment. "The saxophones begin at seven," longhairs complained, as radio's prime time was increasingly given over to light music.

Radio also produced new personalities in the Happiness Boys, Billy Jones and Ernie Hare ("We two boys without a care/ Entertain you folks out there"); the Gold Dust Twins; Little Jack Little; Smilin' Ed McConnell; the Silvertown Masked Tenor; Arthur Tracy, the Street Singer; Wendell Hall, the Red-Headed Music Maker, and others.

Radio stars in days of swan-neck speakers
were singer Jessica Dragonette and announcer Norman
Brokenshire (above), the Happiness Boys,
Billy Jones and Ernie Hare (left),
and newsman Floyd Gibbons.

With them came those talented girls—Vaughn de Leath and Jessica Dragonnette. It is worthy of special note that Vaughn de Leath was the first girl to sing over radio. The soprano was told to hold her voice down to keep from shattering tender tubes. So the art of crooning was born.

With radio-based entertainment came additional talent from vaudeville and the Broadway stage: Will Rogers, Moran and Mack, Eddie Cantor, Elsie Janis, Irene Franklin, Ed Wynn, Ruth Etting, Al Jolson, Harry Richman. Balancing the radio-oriented orchestras were famous bands from outside: pioneering Vincent Lopez ("This is Lopez speaking"); Paul Whiteman, the King of Jazz; Jan Garber, Idol of the Airlanes; the Jean Goldkette Orchestra (from Detroit); Wayne King, the Waltz King; Isham Jones, and Paul Tremaine.

Early announcers? They were Milton Cross, Norman Brokenshire, Graham Mc-Namee, Phillips Carlin, Ted Husing, David Ross, assorted others. In the kiddie field you had Uncle Don, Nila Mack's Let's Pretend, and Irene Wicker, the Singing Lady. Dr. S. Parkes Cadman delivered inspiring Sunday sermons, with a stimulating question-and-answer period afterward. And never forget Roxy (S. L. Rotha-fel) and his beloved Gang—Erno Rapee, Jimmy Melton, Wee Willie Robine, Gambi (Maria Gambarelli), and Roxy himself, with his city-slicker folksiness.

Radio statisticians of the time figured that major stations broadcast 56 weekly hours of talk, 42 hours of classical music, and 259 hours of jazz and popular entertainment. All of this was free; it was what the world of entertainment had feared since the Year One. Radio was not only keeping people at home, but also competing with the theater, movies, and vaudeville. Already, hallowed vaude was dying, while stage and screen would never again bring in the profits they had before radio.

But to the public it was exciting! There were, after all, new things under the sun.

The vibrant, enthusiastic voice of Gra-

ham McNamee reported every major event occurring in the United States during the early days of radio. His flavorsome delivery and vivid description caught all the drama of the scenes he watched. Here is his description of the beginning, the controversial "Long Count" (of which McNamee seems unaware), and the decision in the second Dempsey-Tunney bout:

"Good evening, ladies and gentlemen of the radio audience—This is a big night—Three million dollars' worth of boxing bugs are gathered around a ring at Soldier Field, Chicago—Burning down on us are forty-four 1000-watt lamps over the ring—All is darkness in the muttering mass of crowd beyond the light—The 'mike' is fixed on the ring floor in front of us—The crowd is thickening in the seats—There's Jim Corbett—Mayor Thompson of Chicago in a cowboy hat—Irvin Cobb—John Ringling—Tex Rickard in a beige fedora—It's like the Roman Coliseum—

"Here comes Jack Dempsey, climbing through the ropes—white trunks, long bathrobe—Here comes Tunney—He's got on blue trunks with red trimmings—Hear the roaring of the crowd—Both men are in the ring now—They're getting the gloves out of a box tied with a pretty blue ribbon—The announcer shouting in the ring—trying to quiet 150,000 people—Robes are off—

(Round 7): "Gene is stabbing Jack off—oh-oh—Jack is wandering around Gene—Dempsey drives a hard left under the heart—Jack pounded the back of Tunney's head with four rights—Gene put a terrific right—hardest blow of the fight—Gene beginning to wake up—like a couple of wild animals—Gene's body red—hits Dempsey a terrific right to the body—Jack is groggy—Jack leads hard left—Tunney seems almost wobbling—they have been giving Dempsey smelling salts in his corner—Some of the blows that Dempsey hits make this ring tremble—Tunney is DOWN—down from a barrage—they are counting—six-seven-eight—

At this point, Tunney got to his feet. Few were aware of it, but by the time the referee—after pushing Dempsey into a corner—had begun his count, the official timekeeper at ringside had already reached the count of four. Thus, some maintained, Tunney was down for more than the full count. As it was, he rose on the referee's count of nine and went on to beat Dempsey.

(At end): "Yes, Tunney, I feel sure, retains his championship because at the last moment Dempsey was practically out on his feet. And, ladies and gentlemen, I assure you there were no fouls in this fight—There were no fouls here—There was nothing questionable that I saw —TUNNEY WINS—GENE TUNNEY IS STILL WORLD'S CHAMPION—GENE! GENE! Here is Tunney come to say something—"

Tunney: "Hello, everybody! It was a real contest all the way through. I want to say hello to all my friends in Connecticut and elsewhere. Thank you!"

McNamee: "And now Jack comes out of the ring half beside himself with anger, and we hope he is not going to knock all the typewriters and telegraph operators over—Well, at the last moment—JACK! JACK!—Well, we wanted Jack to say hello too—He boxed a real good fight. Gene Tunney managed to master him, but by no great margin and there was one time when Tunney might have taken the long road himself back to oblivion."

Gate for the fight was $2,600,000. Tunney got $990,000 as champion and winner. Dempsey was paid $430,000. He never fought again.

Jack Dempsey, the Manassa Mauler, downs Gene Tunney at Soldier Field, Chicago, in 1927. Referee Jack Barry is about to begin disputed long count that lost Dempsey his title.

MADNESS EVERYWHERE

♥ Madness was everywhere. In Chicago Mayor "Big Bill" Thompson needed a re-election issue that would distract voters from the vice and rum-running rampant in his bailiwick. Big Bill decided to accuse the King of England of attempting to occupy the Windy City. In florid orations, he demanded that all mention of King George V be expunged from Chicago's library and schoolbooks. It was a smart caper. Big Bill was royally re-elected.

New York had its crowning glory in Jimmy Walker, playboy Mayor. The Late Mayor he was also called, since he seldom turned up on time for appointments. No wonder, for dapper Jimmy (also known as the Night Mayor) liked to stay up late in night clubs, enjoying the company of pretty girls from Broadway shows. Walker thoroughly typified a heedless era. "He wore New York on his lapel like a boutonniere," wrote Gene Fowler.

Fanning the flames of sensation were the tabloid newspapers which pioneered in keyhole journalism, with accompanying keyhole photos. In New York, the *News*, *Mirror*, and *Graphic* engaged in deadly circulation warfare, the ammunition being journalistic dirt. Chicago and other cities spawned the get-the-story heroics immortalized by Ben Hecht and Charles McArthur in *The Front Page*.

Nor were the tabloids the only headliners of sensation. The dignified *New York Times* carried many scandals of the era

conspicuously on its front page. Alert readers soon noted that the vaunted *Times* coverage often carried more juicy details than the shorter, jazzed-up tabloid stories.

There was no pause for the sensation-seekers. On the very morning of the Peaches-Daddy verdict, newspapers carried a front-page story of a Queens Village housewife named Ruth Snyder, who was accused of killing her sleeping husband with a sash weight. Next day her lover, Judd Gray, was implicated and arrested.

The Snyder-Gray case turned out to be the most sordid sensation of all those in the turbulent Twenties. It was a crime without subtlety. The Dumbbell Murder, Damon Runyon called it, "because it was so dumb."

Yet the nation wallowed in its messy details. The principals became "Ruth and Judd." In jail, meek little Judd Gray received so much fan mail that two extra cells were needed to hold it. A new breed, known as feature writers—among them stage producer David Belasco, mystery author Mary Roberts Rinehart, evangelist Aimee Semple McPherson, film director D. W. Griffith, and much-married Peggy Hopkins Joyce—were commissioned to write about the day-to-day proceedings.

One of these feature writers stated that the trial promised "Hot love, the throbbing of jazz and the tawdry splendor of night clubs, the rhythmic beat of the heart's desire." It produced none of this, for if

John Gilbert and Greta Garbo in Flesh and the Devil. *Passionate film introduced soul kiss to movie public. Religious groups branded it "Gilbo-Garbage."*

*Great athletes of Twenties were
(from left): Johnny Weismuller, Suzanne Lenglen,
"Babe" Ruth, and "Red" Grange.*

nothing else Ruth and Judd were ordinary folk, people-next-door types gone hideously wrong. The case was important only because the country's preoccupation with it marked a low point in America's cultural life. A nation wallowing in the mire with Ruth and Judd, sociologists say, could sink no lower. And indeed, the worst of sensational nonsense was past.

A somewhat healthier excitement was provided by sports. It was a decade of superlative performers, and Americans found new heroes and heroines to admire in sports events.

Sprinter Charley Paddock, of the University of Southern California, was "the world's fastest human." Johnny Weismuller was the holder of a dozen swimming records. Willie Hoppe was the master of the billiard cue. Golf, tennis, baseball, boxing, six-day bicycle racing, ice hockey, wrestling all had their fans.

Promoter C. C. Pyle caused a stir by persuading the French tennis star, Suzanne Lenglen, to turn professional. He then got the nation's most famous football player, Harold "Red" Grange, the Galloping Ghost of Illinois, to turn pro with the Chicago Bears. Pro football was still a fly-by-night sport, but people flocked to see Red. The Bears paid him at the rate of $1,000 a minute. This, plus his lucrative testimo-

nials, earned him $3,000,000 in three years.

Jack Dempsey lost his world's heavyweight boxing championship to Gene Tunney, at Philadelphia, in 1926. Babe Ruth hit sixty home runs for the 1927 Yankee juggernaut, a mark that would stand for thirty-four years.

And recording these feats was an all-star generation of sports writers: Grantland Rice, Ring Lardner, W. O. McGeehan, Heywood Broun, and Westbrook Pegler.

Hollywood, meanwhile, was not to be outdone. Early in 1927 people turned their attention to the Swedish actress Greta Garbo, who had been paired with dashing John Gilbert in *Flesh and the Devil*. This romantic duo had introduced the soul kiss to the screen. Pious groups were outraged, and called the film Gilbo-Garbage. Their thunder was drowned out in the fall of that year, when Al Jolson sang and talked —yes, sang and talked!—in *The Jazz Singer*, by means of a new process known ·as Vitaphone. The movies now had a voice.

Some vestiges of Wonderful Nonsense remained even as the decade drew to a close. "Quick, Henry, the Flit!" became the advertising slogan and the favorite expression of the moment. The Charleston gave way to the black bottom and the varsity drag. Over the horizon was the lindy hop—and the Crash.

*It was too good to last! After sending out
many unheeded distress signals, the stock market
crashed in October, 1929. Losers jammed Broad Street
entrance to Exchange, where the action was.*

THE CRASH

♥ Money—easy money—made the Twenties whirl as they did. For the Stock Exchange, once the exclusive province of the highly prosperous, had like everything else come within reach of the average citizen. Brokerage houses, succumbing to the idea of mass consumption, sought the little accounts as well as the big.

The stock market shot upward. Coolidge prosperity, followed by Hoover prosperity, brought the ordinary man paper profits and easy-money ideas. Of 1928, *The New York Times* declared, "It has been a year of wonderful prosperity." This was no exaggeration. Stocks had made a gain of over eleven billion dollars, and it was fondly expected that the figure would be higher in 1929. In his election speeches, Herbert Hoover had promised two cars in every garage and two chickens in every pot. And the people believed him.

By the last years of the decade, Prosperity was the new God.

The people had tried breaking the prohibition law and relaxing moral standards. Neither brought real happiness. Now they tried Prosperity.

Americans began gambling on the country's prosperity, and the place to gamble (or at best speculate) was the stock market. The plumber who came to fix a faucet discoursed on blue-chip stocks and offered financial advice to housewives. Chauffeurs of rich men kept ears cocked for tips that would make them richer than the men they drove. People bought on margin, hoping to double or triple their savings on a rising market. Hundreds of thousands played the stock market as if it were a gigantic Kentucky Derby, with comfortable seats in every brokerage office and an oracle at the end of every telephone. "No race track plunger ignored the form charts as recklessly or listened to the tipsters as credulously as did the little speculators," writes Joe Alex Morris.

There was, of course, good reason for the average man's belief in the national prosperity. A soaring stock market seemed no more than a happy manifestation of our ordained progress. The American Dream was, as expected, coming true. Weren't national wages at an all-time peak? Wasn't America the most efficient industrial nation the world had ever known? The years since 1920 had showed an amazing growth in physical (or consumer) goods. From 1910 to 1919, they had increased ten per cent. From 1920 to 1929, the increase was ninety-three per cent!

On all sides prominent men used statistics to paint the clouds with sunshine. President Hoover and Secretary of the Treasury Andrew Mellon promised better times. When John J. Raskob of General Motors spoke optimistically of the auto industry, GM stock rose twelve points. Newspapers began to carry closing stock prices as prominently as baseball scores.

Upward, upward went the stocks. General Electric stood at a mighty 396; AT&T 304; U.S. Steel 261. Even new stocks like Auburn, Grigsby Grunow, and Kolster Radio shot up. In 1926 and 1928, two recessions gave warning that things were overextended, but the public looked on these as lucky breaks rather than warnings. A recession gave a man (or woman) the chance to rush in and buy at low prices, then sell later at high. Only most people didn't sell, they held on and bought more. The result was paper profits, paper riches.

An occasional unheeded voice rose to warn of danger in the swelling balloon of prosperity. Overseas Europe's economy lagged, a bad sign. Our own economy—if you looked closely—was dangerously overexpanding. Newfangled installment buying brought overproduction. Wall Street profits, in turn, increased installment buying. It was a vicious circle. Capital and business were bloated. Price levels for most commodities were far too high.

Air began seeping out of the balloon of prosperity in late September, 1929. U.S. Steel, at a sky-high 261, suddenly tumbled to 215. Why? No one could figure it. Other stocks fell, but few paid heed. Once again, a slump seemed a glorious opportunity to jump in and buy blue chips at bargain prices. Experts at the time saw the recession as no more than a slight attack of economic indigestion. Years later Thurman Arnold called it "the first outbreak of a wasting economic fever."

Over the next month steel failed to rally. Nor did other stocks rise. By now the air was whistling out of the balloon, and the public sensed it. The big crash began on Thursday, October 24, 1929, as steel fell to 193. The big wheels of banking—Morgan, Guaranty, First National, Chase, Bankers—were as alarmed and bewildered as the smallest buyer. Calling a hasty meeting, they ordered Stock Exchange Vice President Richard Whitney, a Morgan man, to buy all the U.S. Steel shares possible at 205. Altogether, Whitney bought some $20,000,000 worth.

This was an attempt to bolster public confidence, and over the weekend it worked. But on Monday, things again fell apart. The next day—Black Tuesday—was even worse. Huge blocks of stock were thrown on the market by panicky owners to be sold for anything they would bring. Anything! Bankers, brokers, clerks, even messengers were inundated by orders to sell, not buy. Cross-country phone and telegraph wires were clogged with brokers' demands for margin payments. American Can sank from 181 to 86, AT&T from 304 to 197, New York Central from 256 to 160.

The Big Bull Market was over, and down the drain went billions in profits and paper profits. People everywhere were wiped out; in every town families took the terrible drop from affluence to debt. Men who had dreamed of comfortable retirement now hoped for work beyond the retiring age. Newspapers carried grim news of a rise in suicide rates.

In the midst of national confusion there was nothing to do but listen to soothing words from the country's leaders. "There has been a little distress selling on the Stock Exchange," said Morgan partner Thomas W. Lamont, in one of the understatements of all time. Nicholas Murray Butler, president of Columbia University, took a broader view. "Courage will end the slump," he pontificated. From Washington, President Hoover and Treasury Secretary Mellon issued vague but hopeful statements.

The collapse went on, its sources uncomprehended then and still not thoroughly understood today. Possibly the trouble lay in the fact that the bustling country had never stopped to work out a real conception of the industrial revolution of the twentieth century. Heedless America had allowed representatives of the old order—men schooled in the era of trusts—to guide its economy into a new, bursting era. The Government politely stood aside, allowing it to happen. The current of American life had swung into new channels. New pilots were necessary, but the old were still in service. Economist Stuart Chase thought the country had allowed the successful banker-industrialist-businessman to become "the dictator of our destinies . . . ousting the statesman, the priest, the philosopher, as creator of standards and ethics."

Pundit Mark Sullivan offered the theory that the Crash really began in 1921, when President Harding whimsically appointed

248

his boyhood playmate, Henry Cressinger, as head of the Federal Reserve System. Cressinger proved to be an ignorant, unqualified man for the post. His incompetence, Sullivan thought, ignited the fuse that finally led to the explosion of 1929.

But no one really knows. As the Roaring Twenties ended, the nation once so sure of itself peered into a grim unknown.

The American Dream had turned into a nightmare.

Each paper headlined the Crash in its own way. Variety's has become a classic.

Popular songs still poured from Tin Pan Alley in the second half of the Tumultuous Twenties. (At the end of the decade *Variety* listed the decade's top sellers: "Prisoner's Song," "My Blue Heaven," "Three O'Clock in the Morning," "Valencia," "Whispering," "In a Little Spanish Town," "Sleepy Time Gal," "Blue Skies.")

With the advent of talking pictures, the world had one more rich source of popular songs. Many of the early talkies were lavish musicals, abounding in hit tunes by top Broadway composers imported at fabulous Hollywood salaries. Other dramatic films had theme songs calculated to sustain the mood of the picture.

232

Among Hollywood's early hit songs—theme or otherwise—were "Am I Blue" (*On With the Show*), "Sonny Boy" (*Singin' Fool*), "My Sweeter Than Sweet" (*Sweetie*), "Sunny Side Up," "If I Had a Talking Picture of You" (*Sunny Side Up*), "Pagan Love Song" (*The Pagan*), "Broadway Melody," "You Were Meant for Me" (*Broadway Melody*), "Singin' in the Rain" (*Hollywood Revue*), "My Love Parade" (*Love Parade*), "Tiptoe Through the Tulips" (*Gold Diggers of Broadway*), "I'm in the Market for You" (*High Society Blues*), "It Happened in Monterey" (*King of Jazz*), "Sing You Sinners" (*Honey*).

Other hit songs of the Twenties were—

Five Foot Two, Eyes of Blue
Chloe
I Love My Baby, My Baby Loves Me
Dinah

Baby Face
Breezin' Along with the Breeze
Moonlight on the Ganges
Dancing With Tears In My Eyes
Ain't She Sweet?
Among My Souvenirs
Ramona
Side by Side
Crazy Rhythm
Button Up Your Overcoat
She's Funny That Way
I Wanna Be Loved By You
Sweet Sue
That's My Weakness Now
I Kiss Your Hand, Madam
Should I?
S'posin'
You Do Something to Me
It Had to Be You
The Song Is Ended But the Memory Lingers On
Lover Come Back to Me
Old Man River
Hallelujah
Let a Smile Be Your Umbrella
Bye Bye Blackbird
Just a Gigolo
Always
Me and My Shadow
What Is This Thing Called Love?
I Can't Give You Anything But Love, Baby
Sunny Side of the Street
Exactly Like You
I'm Sitting on Top of the World
Jeannine, I Dream of Lilac Time
I've Got a Feeling I'm Falling
Just a Cottage Small By a Waterfall

1900 1905
1905 1910
1910 1915
1915 1920
1920 1925
1925 1930
♥   **1930 1935**
1935 1942

Troubled Thirties

♥ As the nation reached the threshold of the Troubled Thirties, the national economy lay terrified and paralyzed, a patient surrounded by medical men who had recently given rich assurances of superb good health. Now the medicos were hopelessly baffled by the sick man's debilitation and ragged pulse.

What had happened to the robust U.S.A.? For thirty years American capitalism had led a charmed life. Now the national credit system was endangered, a threat to loans, mortgages, corporate structures. Plainly these had been supported by inflation, and there was no more inflation. The sum of $30,000,000,000 appeared to have gone up in smoke. Yet few could believe that the slump would last. "Prosperity is just around the corner" became the national catchword.

It was a curious kind of Depression, with the rich suffering first. As Wall Street fortunes shriveled, the rich stopped patronizing jewelry stores and high-priced dress shops. The field of luxury services felt it next. Maids, gardeners, valets, chauffeurs lost jobs as the ripples widened. Next the middle and the poorer classes felt the pinch. By the end of 1930 every fourth factory worker was out of a job. The mortality among white-collar workers was nearly as great. Men without hope trudged from office to office, factory to factory. "We'll let you know if anything turns up,"

they were told. Most of those fortunate enough to keep jobs were forced to accept salary cuts. Oddly enough, these cuts in salary hastened the advent of the five-day week, long advocated without great success. Now employers gave Saturdays off as sweetening for thinner pay envelopes.

The national mood remained one of bafflement. Yet there were no signs of violence, even among the starving. As men began selling apples on street corners the voices of the President and his advisers sank lower. Soup kitchens opened in cities and shanty towns known as Hoovervilles appeared in vacant lots. The word *unemployed*, once an adjective, became an ominous noun.

A new class of migrant evolved; journalist Meyer Berger called them the white-collar destitute. Doctors, lawyers, artists, writers, clerks, architects, engineers—they gathered their families and took to the national highways in a desperate quest for nonexistent jobs. Berger pictured them living like primitives on the edges of great cities, searching garbage cans, pawing among discarded fruit and vegetables in city markets.

It was a bleak and wretched time, perhaps the lowest moment the country has ever known. Still, a bit of back-patting may be in order for the way most people took it. America faced up to adversity with great intestinal fortitude. It's true that

234

*Citizens who could spare
a dime in dark Depression days were
supposed to do their part by buying apples
at the stands of the formerly employed.*

some men committed suicide, but most stood firm. Top entertainment figures did their best to distract their countrymen. Eddie Cantor, his life savings lost, wrote a humorous book called *Caught Short: A Saga of Wailing in Wall Street*. Groucho Marx and other big losers told Depression jokes over the radio. Critic Alexander Woollcott dropped $100,000 and retaliated by working harder and upping his prices for articles and book reviews.

The entire country seemed to retain a sense of humor. People laughed at a slender volume called *Oh, Yeah!* which collected the glib prophecies of statesmen, Government officials, and bankers at the onset of the Depression. There was further laughter over the joke about the hotel clerk who asked a registering guest, "Do you want the room for sleeping or jumping?" There was also the one about the two men who jumped off a building hand in hand because they held a joint account.

Magazines also helped. At this low moment, *The New Yorker* entertained with hilarious stories and drawings by James Thurber. Other *New Yorker* stalwarts were E. B. White, Clarence Day, Donald Moffatt, and artist Peter Arno. *The New Yorker* in five years had reached full flowering. More amazing, perhaps, was the instant success of two magazines actually spawned in Depression days. One was *Ballyhoo,* an irreverent fifteen-cent publication which was the brain-child of Norman Anthony, former editor of *Life* and *Judge. Ballyhoo's* masthead listed O. Zilch as editor and

members of this prolific family up to Z. Z. Zilch filled other responsible positions. *Ballyhoo's* editorial page was covered with the word *Blah;* its early issues came wrapped in cellophane. The magazine joyously spoofed advertisements in other magazines and carried bawdy cartoons, some the bathroom variety. "Buy a *Fresh* Magazine," it urged, borrowing from the slogan "Buy a *Fresh* Cigarette."

A nation anxious to laugh at anything swept 150,000 copies of the first issue of *Ballyhoo* off the newsstands. Later issues of a million copies vanished just as rapidly. At least twelve competitors to *Ballyhoo* sprang up, one of them named *Hooey*.

The success of the second Depression-born magazine is harder to explain. It was *Esquire*, price fifty cents. *Esquire* was jumbo-size, its paper stock the best. First issues were Rabelaisian on the order of *Ballyhoo,* with dignified lacings of *The New Yorker* and high-toned *Vanity Fair. Esquire* cost far more than people were accustomed to pay in those days; there was nothing truly remarkable in its content. Yet it caught on in the deepest days of the Depression. Possibly its secret lay in the use of Ernest Hemingway, F. Scott Fitzgerald, and other big-name authors. Editor Arnold Gingrich roped them in by offering Depression prices, but promising fast payment, sometimes in advance of delivery. Somehow the males of the country were ready for this Magazine for Men. *Ballyhoo* died after some five years; *Esquire* is still around.

As Depression ground on, all kinds of people took to the road in search of work: white collar workers and professionals, and farming families who sheltered themselves wherever they could.

Humor and new publications were unable to blunt the shocks as scandal was added to financial hopelessness. Officers of the Bank of the United States, with sixty branches and deposits of $160,000,000, were convicted of gross mismanagement of funds during the tall days of prosperity. Ivar Kreuger, the world-famous Match King, shot himself in Paris, leaving behind evidence of gigantic swindles. His Kreuger & Toll stocks, which appeared to come through the crash unscathed, suddenly were worthless. Richard J. Whitney, the man who acted for J. P. Morgan in efforts to stave off the crash, had become the respected head of the Stock Exchange. Even so, he was headed in the direction of Sing Sing prison, for misappropriation of funds. In Chicago, Samuel Insull saw his utility empire overextended and fled to Greece.

Everyone felt the sobering effects of the slump. People began reading more books than ever, with public libraries invaded by those who had never before set foot in them. A businessman in Middletown, Ohio, put it this way: "Big things are happening that are upsetting us, our businesses, and some of our ideas, and we want to try to understand them. I take a lot of books out of the library and sit up reading them."

The divorce rate fell as feuding couples paused to consider the costs of court action. (Later, the divorce rate rose again.) College graduates, crisp diplomas in hands, had as much trouble as anyone finding jobs. Faces of men young and old showed the dragging responsibilities of family support. As for the American girl, she seemed to improve. No longer the bored, thrill-seeking flapper of the decade before, she suddenly became alert and aware—much like the girl of today. Nor was there much talk of sex; the national economy was a more important subject.

Life went on, even if skies had switched from blue to gray. Tension, disquiet, and fear permeated the atmosphere, but people managed to hum "Life Is Just a Bowl of Cherries" as often as the more realistic "Brother, Can You Spare a Dime?" It was like a war, but this time the war was on the home front. The foe was something vague, and no giant propaganda campaign rallied spirits. But each American in his way fought to maintain himself in a time of incomprehensible Depression.

Magazines proliferated during the Depression.
Long-lived Esquire *was born
and even then cost readers half a buck.
Several monthlies chronicled the
foibles of the rich and powerful, while movie
magazines made the gossamer world of
Hollywood a second home to everyone.*

Radio's Golden Age

♥ "The best things in life are free," caroled a song of the madcap Twenties. It was truer than ever in the Thirties, as the country grabbed at any kind of free diversion to keep its mind free of life's misery. Now, as if on heavenly cue, radio stepped forward to enjoy its Golden Age. Radio brought humor, news, information, culture, and all-around entertainment into American homes. In doing so, it also made the country more sophisticated, and began to eradicate what has been called the regionalism of America.

In ten short years, radio had leaped from a hobby to the country's fourth major industry. Sales of sets had jumped an astonishing four hundred per cent. Every third American family now owned one. This added up to a total of sixteen million radios, providing a listening audience of about sixty million people.

Radio had become an entrenched part of American life. Humorist Will Rogers, who was taking full advantage of the medium himself, put it this way: "Radio is too big a thing to be out of."

Best of all, however, radio was an escape hatch for a dispirited population. It became the custom in the dark days of Depression for American families to serve dinner at six o'clock, so that when seven rolled around all of them could assemble before the loudspeaker to listen to "Amos 'n' Andy," with Madame Queen, Kingfish,

and the Fresh Air Taxi Company. Other listeners preferred popular music to "Amos 'n' Andy," and for them the hour provided Arthur Tracy, the Street Singer, who opened his program with "Marta," (Rambling rose of the wild wood); tenor Morton Downey, who began his fifteen minutes with "Carolina Moon"; or Kate Smith, whose theme was "When the Moon Comes Over the Mountain." Statistics compiled by cross-country telephone companies showed that almost no one used the phone between seven and seven fifteen on weekdays.

Yet radio did far more than entertain. Citizens who had never read any more than hometown newspapers began getting the full drama of world news from Floyd Gibbons, first of the famous news broadcasters. On his heels came H. V. Kaltenborn, Lowell Thomas, Boake Carter, Gabriel Heatter, and Edwin C. Hill, the last of whom offered "the human side of the news."

On Sunday night people who liked to gossip with back-fence neighbors got the low-down on film and theater celebrities from staccato-voiced Walter Winchell. With his success, Hollywood columnists like Louella Parsons and Jimmy Fidler began to reveal the shimmering secrets of the film city. Tony Wons and his Scrapbook ("Are you listenin'?") provided culture of a sort. So did Ted Malone. Alexan-

240

O rare Fred Allen! His biting wit was one of the ingredients of radio's Golden Age. That, and the fact that the medium was free for the listening.

der Woollcott began as the Early Bookworm, became the Town Crier ("Hear ye! Hear ye!"). He carried the art of the raconteur to top level, sent Americans scurrying to the dictionary for the esoteric words he used. Irvin S. Cobb, a more folksy fellow, offered a southern drawl and the superb timing of the born storyteller.

"People used to pay fifty cents to see Eddie Cantor, but now they can hear him for nothing," a small-town movie owner complained. It was so. With radio, the greatest talent in American show biz was anyone's at the twist of a wrist. You couldn't see, of course. But you could hear, and for the moment that was sufficient.

Eddie Cantor, who had received $100 a minute for early Eveready broadcasts, got more as star of the Sunday night Chase and Sanborn Hour, bouncing jokes off violinist David Rubinoff and announcer Jimmy Wallington. Ed Wynn was the hilarious Texaco Fire Chief, with Graham McNamee as straight man, telling nonsense stories that began with a drawn-out "So-o-o."

Radio's first hour-long variety show was the Fleischmann Hour, hosted by Rudy Vallee, with his Connecticut Yankees ("Heigh-ho, everybody"). The first hour-long musical show with a cast of regular characters was the Maxwell House Showboat with Charles Winninger, Lanny Ross, Annette Henshaw. Fred Allen, the most literate comedian of all, was first the star of the Linit Bath Club Revue, with Portland Hoffa, the girl he married. Chester-

field's Music That Satisfies boasted Ruth Etting, the Street Singer, and the Boswell Sisters. The Lucky Strike Program had B. A. Rolfe's Orchestra, with a loud, metronomic beat. Favored guest stars on all programs were the Mills Brothers. Early crooners were Russ Columbo and Bing Crosby. Ozzie and Harriett brought youth to a youthful medium.

Paul Whiteman earned astronomical sums for appearances as the King of Jazz. Just behind him in popularity came Vincent Lopez, Fred Waring's Pennsylvanians, Isham Jones' Orchestra, George Olsen and His Orchestra, featuring Ethel Shutta, and Will Osborne and His Orchestra. Other popular radio orchestras were led by Leo Reisman, Abe Lyman, Phil Harris, Nat Brusiloff, Harry Sosnik, Peter Van Steeden, and Meredith Willson. Ohman and Arden were the top two-piano team.

On the symphony side, Dr. Walter Damrosch still conducted the dignified Philharmonic. Radio's own symphonies were led by Dr. Frank Black, Alfred Wallenstein, Wilfred Pelletier, Erno Rapee, Rosario Bourdon, Andre Kostelanetz. Ferde Grofe was a composer-conductor. Serious artists favored by the public were Lawrence Tibbett, Lily Pons, Gladys Swarthout, Nino Martini, José Iturbi, Lauritz Melchior, and John Charles Thomas, who habitually signed off with the words, "Good night, mother."

Broadway star Joe Cook arrived with his nonsense stories. From the same locality came Walter O'Keefe (the Man on the

242

Bouncy Eddie Cantor had one of the first big-time variety hours. Full-throated Kate Smith, crooner Bing Crosby (at NBC mike), and mellow Morton Downey made music for the millions.

The Mills Brothers, with
their silken rhythms, were the guest
stars every radio host wanted.

Flying Trapeze), and Jack Pearl as Baron Munchausen, with Cliff Hall as Sharlie. George Burns and Gracie Allen scored first with vaudeville-type dialogue. Jack Benny, ever relaxed, was building a durable comedy framework with Mary Livingstone and Rochester, and his faithful Maxwell auto. Belle Baker sang throatily for Eveready Blades. Julia Sanderson and Frank Crummit, husband and wife, appeared for Blackstone Cigars. Phil Baker played his accordion and traded gags with stooges. Ben Bernie, the Old Maestro, signed off for himself and All the Lads with an intimate, "Au revoir, a fond cheerio, a bit of a tweet-tweet, God bless you, and pleas-ant dreams." The Old Maestro's feud with Walter Winchell was a sensation of early radio—was it real or wasn't it? Later, Fred Allen and Jack Benny borrowed the feud formula.

Radio's big-time entertainment stemmed from Broadway and vaudeville. Highly polished, it was delivered by performers with years of experience before live audi-

ences. Radio got it simply by putting up the money.

Yet radio also developed its own humor, and it is not surprising to find it more down-to-earth and pithy than the glossy professional product. Radio's humor was heard at its best in certain daytime series in which two people (two guys, two girls, or a married couple) coped with problems of contemporary existence.

Today the names of these programs are coated with a rich frosting of nostalgia: "Fibber McGee and Molly," "Easy Aces," "Myrt and Marge," "East and Dumke" (Sisters of the Skillet), "Stoopnagle and Budd", (remember Phoebe B. Beebe and her Canoe Canal in Canarsie?), "Lum and Abner," "Vic and Sade."

These programs offered humor, earthy wisdom, and trenchant comment on the minutiae of American life. Indeed, it has been said that a historian of the future, eager to find the true flavor of American life in the Thirties and Forties, might well exhume the scripts or recordings of these day-to-day programs.

Far below the level of such programs lay the soap operas, likened by James Thurber to a sandwich: "Between thick slices of advertising, spead twelve minutes of dialogue, add predicament, villains, and female suffering in equal measure, throw in a dash of nobility, sprinkle with tears, season with organ music, cover with rich announcer sauce, and serve five days a week."

Daily, the nation's housewives suffered

244

along with "Pepper Young's Family," "Just Plain Bill," "When a Girl Marries," "Ma Perkins," "One Man's Family," "Guiding Light," "Young Widder Brown," and "Life Can Be Beautiful." Remember them? "True Story," with Mary and Bob, was the most polished of the soapers.

Singin' Sam, the Barbasol Man (Harry Frankel) was a native radio product, his deep voice injecting passion into "No brush, no lather, no rub in/Just wet your face and then begin." So was Phil Cook who, after many roles, wound up as the Musical Chef. Frank Parker and Frank Munn were radio's favorite singers of popular ballads. The "American Album of Familiar Music" was a cherished program. So, in a different way, was "Gang Busters." The West Coast had Captain Dobbsie and Reverend Bob Schuler. The Midwest loved Little Jack Little. National Barn Dance, and the Sinclair Minstrels had fans by the million.

There was more, much more. John J. Anthony and his "Good Will Hour," "Professor Quiz," and other question-and-answer programs. A radio day opened at an early morning hour with Don McNeill's "Breakfast Club," or Ed and Pegeen Fitzgerald chatting over the breakfast table. Comedians Joe Penner and Bob Burns used radio as a stairway to fame and fortune. Vera Vague lived up to her name. Roy Atwell stuttered, usually with Fred Allen. "The Lone Ranger" came along in 1934 and after him "Buck Rogers," "Captain Midnight," and "Superman."

For years the most popular of night programs was the "Major Bowes' Amateur Hour," with the benign host offering words of gentle encouragement or clanging his cruel shut-off gong. "Round and round she goes, and where she stops nobody knows," the Major intoned at the beginning of each program. When CBS lured the "Amateur Hour" from NBC, it marked the first big talent raid in radio history.

After 1935 radio grew more sophisticated, with Mae West and Charlie McCarthy trading dialogue that shocked the country. Bibulous W. C. Fields and Charlie also engaged in masterly, mature invective. But in early Depression days, radio was just right for the country—and the country was just right for radio.

Every radio entertainer's dream was to find a catchword which immediately made the listening public think of him. Here are a few that sank deep in the public consciousness:

Amos 'n' Andy—"I'se regusted!"
Joe Penner—"Wanna buy a duck?"
Ben Bernie—"Yowza."
Rudy Vallee—"Heigh ho, everybody!"
Tony Wons—"Are you listnin'?"
Gracie Allen—"Oh, George, I'll bet you say that to all the girls."
Jack Pearl (Baron Munchausen)—"Vas you dere, Sharlie?"
Jimmy Durante—"I've got a million of 'em!"
Jack Benny—"Jello again."
Walter Winchell—"Good evening Mr. and Mrs. America and all the ships at sea."
Major Bowes—"All right! All right!"
Alexander Woollcott—"Hear ye! Hear ye!"
Lone Ranger—"Hi yo, Silver."

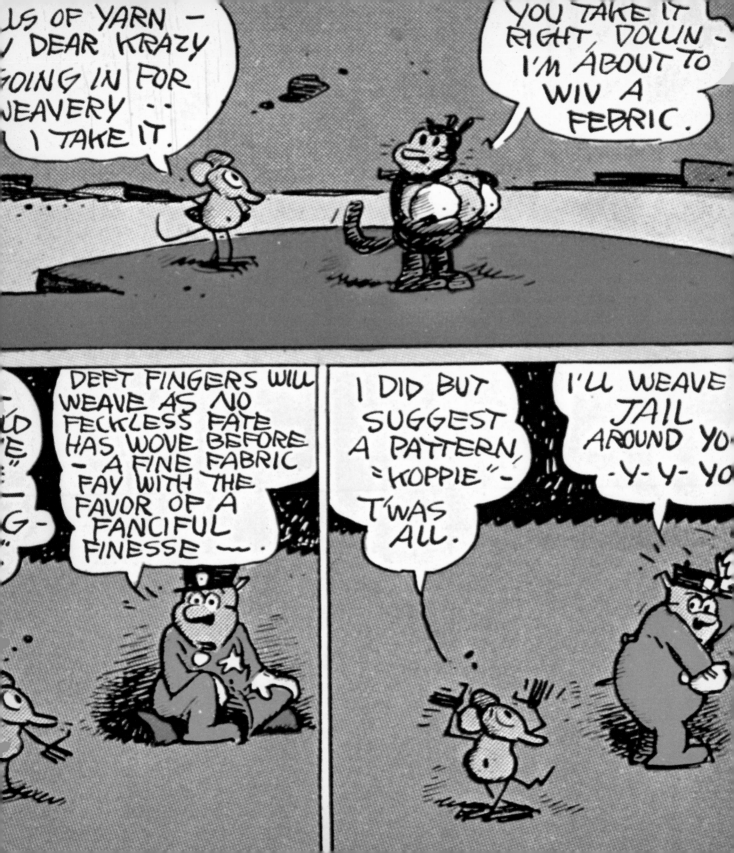

Comic Strip Heroes

♥ Captain Joe Patterson, demon creator of comic strips, was restless again and this brought more escape to a Depression-ridden population.

Many famous strips of the Twenties and before were still going strong. (Some still are, but the classic Krazy Kat expired with the death of creator George Herrimann in 1944.) The most successful still featured the Gumps, Harold Teen, Winnie Winkle, and other Joe Patterson inspirations of a decade before. Blondie, Li'l Abner, and Joe Palooka were recent arrivals, but the Gumps remained the most famous comic-strip family in America.

Captain Patterson, with his instinct for timing, felt the time was ripe for a new kind of strip. The nation might be in the cold clutch of Depression, yet there was violent activity in the field of crime. Al Capone was in Alcatraz, but gangsters still rubbed each other out on city streets. Beyond the cities, a new type of murdering, kidnapping, bank-robbing criminal had risen. John Dillinger, Pretty Boy Floyd, and Alvin Karpis typified the breed.

With artist Chester Gould, who had suggested a strip based on crime busting, Patterson worked out an idea which Gould christened "Plainclothes Tracy." Patterson used his blue pencil to make this "Dick Tracy," and added Tess Trueheart for romantic interest. "Dick Tracy" became the first newspaper strip of realistic violence,

unlike the nonsense, brick-throwing kind.

Adventure heroes multiplied, including Flash Gordon, Barney Baxter, Tim Tyler, and Captain Easy. But Patterson was still not satisfied. He and artist Milton Caniff worked out an adventure strip with a new dimension; it painted an aspect of the modern world in old, romantic colors. Caniff named the result "Tommy Tucker," but the indefatigable Captain changed it to "Terry and the Pirates," adding such characters as the humorous George Washington Confucius (Connie). "Terry and the Pirates" became the most imitated of all comic strips, and started another cycle in the art form that began back in 1896 with the gap-toothed Yellow Kid.

Still, it is comforting to know that the most popular comic strip character of the Thirties wasn't unlike the Yellow Kid.

He was Skippy, generally considered the greatest of all strip kids. With his checked hat, huge white collar, flowing tie, and sagging socks, Skippy hit America's humor nerve as has no other. Perhaps his popularity came from a mixture of pure humor and adult philosophy distilled in the words and actions of a sloppy kid. Or perhaps, in a time of national uncertainty, it was because Skippy seemed both self-confident and self-sufficient, ever in command of a situation.

Skippy's creator was a character, too. Percy Crosby, artist, painter, author, holder

Comic strips had entered a new, exciting phase, but old-fashioned "Krazy Kat" went on forever —perhaps because artist George Herrimann was a genius with weird words as well as with his pen.

of idiosyncratic opinions, made enough money from Skippy to take full-page ads in major newspapers attacking prohibition and other things that riled him.

Crosby and Skippy. They proved that hard times couldn't get everyone down.

Here are some other comic strips of the Thirties. Some are still going strong. Remember:

Blondie (with Dagwood, Baby Dumpling)
Joe Palooka
Popeye (from Thimble Theater)
Joe Jinks (later Curly Kayoe)
Dick Tracy
Li'l Abner (Pappy and Mammy Yokum,
    Jack S. Phogbound, Henry Cabbage Cod,
    Sir Cecil Cesspool, Lower Slobbovia)
Etta Kett
Pottsy
Don Winslow of the Navy
Mickey Finn
Scorchy Smith (derived from Lindbergh)
Captain Easy
Dixie Dugan
Barney Baxter
Tarzan
Smokey Stover (with Cash U Nutt)
Abbie 'n' Slatts (with Becky Groggins,
    Bathless Groggins)
Cap Stubbs and Tippie
Little Annie Rooney (with dog Zero)
The Phantom
Radio Patrol (originally Pinkerton Jr.)
Smilin' Jack
Little Joe (and Sheriff Utah)
The Lone Ranger
King of the Royal Mounted
Brutus (Hot Dog Ranch, Sampson, Sooky)
Apple Mary
Mary Worth
Pete the Tramp

Little Orphan Annie

Secret Agent X-9
Napoleon and Uncle Elby
Dolly Dimple and Baby Bounce (with cat Cumfy)
Silly Milly (with Yuk, Yuk, Yuk, the
    Wild Bust of Lafter)
Buck Rogers (with the Tiger Men of Mars)
Brick Bradford (with the Time Top)
Flash Gordon (with the planet Mongo, ruled
    by Ming the Merciless)
Mandrake the Magician
Prince Valiant

Skippy

Gasoline Alley

Dick Tracy

Depression Days

♥ Life rolled along, even during the black days of the Depression. It's hard to believe, but the nation still had the appetite for a few fads, nonsense songs, and games. As early as 1930, the country was swept by the miniature-golf craze. This was no more than golf played on midget roadside courses, but for a brief time the industry was rated at $125,000,000. A little over a year later, miniature golf was practically gone, but jigsaw puzzles were ascendant. Meantime, college students tried to make tree-sitting a cross-country stunt. Walt Disney's first "Silly Symphony" came along in 1930.

Aviation continued to provide thrills. One-eyed Wiley Post and Harold Gatty flew around the world in the plane *Winnie Mae* in the miraculous time of eight days, fifteen hours, and eight minutes. Jimmy Doolittle and Captain Roscoe Turner engaged in a battle for the transcontinental speed mark. Other speed kings were Captain Frank Hawks and Al Williams. In 1932, Captain James Mollison, an Englishman, made the first solo westward crossing of the Atlantic, landing in New Brunswick, Nova Scotia, after a thirty-hour flight from Ireland. Mollison flew in a single-engine sports plane, top speed 120 mph.

Still, the big news in aviation was the prominence of women fliers. In fact, 1932 was Women's Year in the Air. Amelia Earhart, a girl who resembled Lindbergh, picked the fifth anniversary of Lindy's flight to fly solo from Harbor Grace, Newfoundland, to Londonderry, Ireland. Where Lindbergh's flight weather had been good, Amelia's was awful. In addition, a broken exhaust pipe threatened her fuel line. Yet she made it, and soon after the flight was fox-trotting with the Prince of Wales in London. Returning home, the intrepid aviatrix set a long-distance record for women by a flight between Los Angeles and Newark. Next, Ruth Nichols established an altitude record of 21,350 feet. Louise Thaden and Frances Marsalis set a refueling endurance record for the fair sex by staying up in the air eight days. Mae Heaslip set a speed record of 252 mph.

In sports, too, new records were being set by track stars such as miler Glenn Cunningham. At Daytona Beach, Sir Malcolm Campbell bettered his own speed of 245 mph in his two-and-a-half ton racing car, *Bluebird*. Heavyweight Jack Sharkey won a decision over Germany's Max Schmeling. The Davis Cup was still in France, but lanky, youthful Ellsworth Vines beat the hitherto invincible Henri Cochet in the singles championship. Helen Wills Moody had decided to retire, allowing sturdy Helen Jacobs to take her place. Babe Ruth was still the most colorful figure in baseball. In the World Series of 1932 he took two strikes, then pointed to a spot in the bleachers to show the crowd and the

Chicago Cubs just where the next ball would land. On the next pitch he whammed it to just that spot.

Los Angeles was host to the Olympic Games in 1932. Here Mildred "Babe" Didrickson emerged as the big attraction "A one-woman track team," she was called. She won the javelin and hurdle events, tied for first place in the high jump. Many muttered when Olympic officials prevented Babe from participating in other events. Journalists marveled at her co-ordination and reflexes, then turned to report that she looked pretty in a dress and could dance a mean lindy hop. "I never liked dolls," she confided.

Book readers still patronized public libraries, but the growth in lending libraries, plus the heavy advertising of the Book-of-the-Month Club and the Literary Guild, made the country increasingly conscious of the best seller. Every month, it seemed, brought a new book you *had* to read.

In early Depression days the over-all best seller was *The Good Earth* by Pearl S. Buck. Others were *The Fountain* by Charles Morgan, *Tobacco Road* by Erskine Caldwell, *Water Gypsies* by A. P. Herbert, *I Went to Pit College* by Lauren Gilfillan, *State Fair* by Phil Stong, *A Fortune to Share* by Vash Young, *The Epic of America* by James Truslow Adams, *While Rome Burns* by Alexander Woollcott, and *100,000,000 Guinea Pigs*. Sensation-book of the moment was *Washington Merry-Go-Round*, whose anonymous authors eventually stood revealed as Drew Pearson

Mildred "Babe" Didrickson

and Robert S. Allen. In 1933, *Anthony Adverse* by Hervey Allen came along to become top best seller of the time, and after that it was Margaret Mitchell's *Gone With The Wind*.

The movies were just getting back to normal after the shock of 1927, when sound was introduced by Al Jolson in *The Jazz Singer*. Overnight an industry basking in its Golden Age had begun to founder. Careers were ruined as Vitaphone revealed top actors with voices that failed to jibe with screen personalities. Virile John Gilbert, filmdom's top lover, turned out to possess a high, squeaky voice; his career ended. Clara Bow spoke Brooklynese, which detracted from her cute, pepper-pot

252

Boffo moments from the movies: Edward G. Robinson gets tough, Muni and Dvorak mix emotions, Harlow practices seduction, Lombard spurns Barrymore, and the Marx Brothers dream up madness.

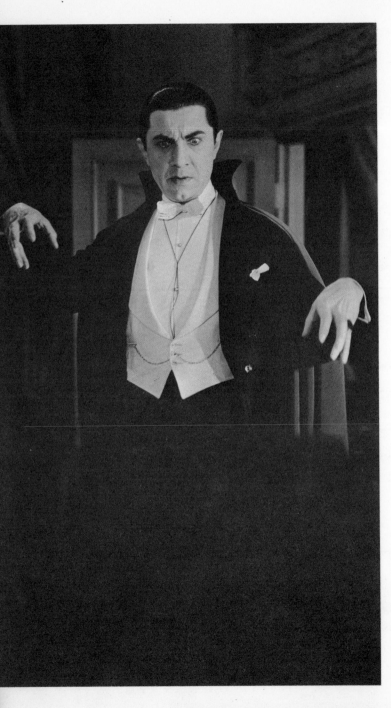

Hollywood in the Thirties produced classics in genre of the weird and fantastic. Bela Lugosi's Count Dracula and gigantic gorilla, King Kong, had movie-goers all atremble.

personality; her career began a downward slide. Actors from Broadway poured into Hollywood, their pear-shaped tones earning them juicy roles while big-name screen stars were shoved aside. Frantic directors could think only of photographing Broadway plays. Producers pinned hopes and fortunes on star-studded musical revues with hundreds of chorus girls hoofing in unison.

In 1931, *Frankenstein* was a box-office smash. And the great gangster cycle began. *Little Caesar*, starring Edward G. Robinson; *Public Enemy*, with James Cagney shoving a grapefruit in Mae Clarke's face; *Scarface*, with Paul Muni—these and other gangland films not only provided gripping entertainment, but helped Hollywood adjust to sound. For the first time, sound became functional, with the clatter of machine-gun fire, the squealing of tires, and the grinding of brakes all adding to suspenseful scripts.

Gangster films were simple to create, since their plots depended heavily on sensations straight from the headlines. *Scarface*, for instance, combined Chicago's Al Capone and the St. Valentine's Day massacre with a hospital-room shooting of New York's Legs Diamond.

But with the gangster movies, the industry outsmarted itself. The pictures brought millions of customers to the box offices of the land, but they also aroused protest because they tended to glorify the life of crime. After a year, movie czar Will Hays advised the industry to de-emphasize gangsters and their molls.

Thrown back on its resources, the newly confident medium began making really distinguished films. It was the era of *Grand Hotel*, with Greta Garbo, John and Lionel Barrymore, Joan Crawford, and Wallace Beery; *The Phantom President*, with George M. Cohan and Jimmy Durante; *A Farewell to Arms*, with Helen Hayes and Gary Cooper; *A Bill of Divorcement*, with John Barrymore and Katharine Hepburn (her film debut); *Maedchen in Uniform*, an import from Germany; *I Am A Fugitive From A Chain Gang*, with Paul Muni; *Dr. Jekyll and Mr. Hyde*, with Fredric March and Miriam Hopkins; *Rasputin and the Empress*, with the three Barrymores; *The Guardsman*, with Alfred Lunt and Lynn Fontanne; *The Champ*, with Wallace Beery and Jackie Cooper; *The Thin Man*, with William Powell and Myrna Loy; *Of Human Bondage*, with Leslie Howard and Bette Davis; *Topper*, with Roland Young and Constance Bennett; and *Twentieth Century*, with John Barrymore and Carole Lombard. The fabled *King Kong*, a film in a category of its own, came along in 1933.

The Thirties produced a new crop of movie stars, and never has the breed seemed more glamorous: Bette Davis, Joan Crawford, Myrna Loy, Carole Lombard, Norma Shearer, Jean Harlow; Clark Gable, Spencer Tracy, Humphrey Bogart, Gary Cooper, William Powell, Cary Grant, James Stewart, Lee Tracy.

But with all these, the most famous

actress in the country was Mae West, who first appeared in *Night After Night*. "She stole everything but the cameras," muttered co-star George Raft, after a preview. Every line Mae uttered seemed to have a double entendre. "I used to be Snow White, but I drifted," was one. Her second film, *She Done Him Wrong*, actually saved Paramount Pictures from bankruptcy, amassing more than $2,000,000 in three months' time. Ranking just behind raucous Mae was Jean Harlow, who first appeared in *Hell's Angels* in 1931. These two would remain on top until the success of child star Shirley Temple, innocent as ice cream, signaled a change in the national mood.

♥

Yes, life rolled on, even though times were grim and getting grimmer. There were fourteen million unemployed now. Banks in many parts of the country had begun to close. Hoovervilles had increased on the outskirts of towns and cities. The ominous term *dust bowl* was beginning to appear in newspapers and magazines. From the security of his millions, J. P. Morgan, son of the great financier, advocated a nationwide, block-to-block drive to collect $1 from every employed person, the money to be channeled to the jobless. One random statistic showed that neighborly visiting had fallen off. Call it pride, listlessness, or misery, people just did not want to see other people, preferring to stay home with the radio.

But as if to provide distraction for a despairing public, some of the great news stories occurred in early Depression days. Just look at these, which took place between 1930-35:

Disappearance of Judge Crater, still one of the world's great question marks.

Death of Knute Rockne in an airplane crash.

Mysterious death of beautiful Starr Faithfull, speakeasy playgirl.

Investigation of Mayor James J. Walker of New York, followed by his resignation under fire.

Massie rape case, in Hawaii.

Arrival of the *Graf Zeppelin* on a flight from Germany.

Kidnapping of the Lindbergh baby, the crime of the century.

Suicide of Ivar Kreuger, the Match King.

Trial of trunk-murderess Winnie Ruth Judd.

Mysterious death of tobacco-heir Smith Reynolds, young husband of torch singer Libby Holman.

March of the Bonus Army on Washington.

Attempted assassination of President-elect Franklin D. Roosevelt in Miami.

Opening of the Chicago World's Fair, saluting a Century of Progress.

Fall of the dirigible *Akron* in a storm.

Election of colorful Fiorello La Guardia as Mayor of New York.

Rise of Adolf Hitler in Germany.

The continuing battle between the G-Men and "Public Enemy Number One."

Burning of the cruise liner *Morro Castle*.

Birth of the Dionne quintuplets, heart-throb story of the era.

Arrest of Bruno Richard Hauptmann, for the Lindbergh crime.

*Whatever the Thirties had, it was not an "even tenor
of existence." We thrilled to capture of Public Enemy John
Dillinger, gave our hearts to Mickey Mouse, rooted
for prosecution of Lindbergh kidnapper Bruno Hauptmann (right).
Nonstop flights to Lisbon were new, art of Sally Rand was not.*

The New Deal

♥ All these notable news events, however, were topped in 1932 by the election of Franklin D. Roosevelt as President of the United States. For with this event, the American people bade lasting farewell to a segment of the American Dream which had existed for over one hundred years. Until the advent of the Thirties the country had displayed a naïve belief in the wisdom of financiers, industrial leaders, bankers. Especially cherished was the image of the ruthless, self-made man. But where had the assorted wisdom of these first-class people led the country? Only down the thorny lane to Depression.

With the election of Roosevelt, America finally rejected the leaders of the past. In FDR people saw a man who, like themselves, distrusted the old wisdom. Roosevelt was prepared to rely on college professors and liberal thinkers rather than on Wall Street insiders and banker-businessmen. In the campaign of 1932, he spoke in generalities, his plans for a New Deal perhaps unresolved in his own mind. Yet voters sensed in him a vigorous man who stood ready to revolutionize government by building recovery from the bottom up. In November, 1932, FDR was triumphantly voted in.

Where would Roosevelt have been without radio in 1933? It's a staggering thought, for radio took his inaugural speech of March 4 into every corner of the land. The speech, in turn, brought a surge of returning hope to a desolate country. In confident, ringing tones, FDR served notice that he planned to slice through the Gordian knot of Depression, where the Hoover administration tried to untie it. Years later his personal secretary Grace Tully wrote that the man she called The Boss was one of those rare persons who enjoy heavy responsibility. "My shoulders are broad," he liked to say. "I'll carry the load."

Over the next hundred days, Roosevelt subjected an awed Congress to a barrage of bills and messages which sharply altered the shape of American life. First he produced the Agricultural Adjustment Act, providing for crop curtailment and the refinancing of farm mortgages. In rapid-fire order came the Civilian Conservation Corps, offering young men employment in reforestation; the Federal Emergency Relief Act, giving $500,000,000 to states in the greatest welfare program in history; the Civil Works Administration allocating $400,000,000 to get the jobless back to work; the Tennessee Valley Authority; Federal supervision of information on new investment securities.

There was all this, and the National Recovery Act, too. Quickly shortened to NRA, it was the most famous of New Deal measures, FDR's do-or-die attack on Depression. Among other things, NRA gave

Voters liked confidence of campaigner FDR, felt their spirits lift when he told them on Inauguration Day, 1933, "The only thing we have to fear is fear itself."

the Government power to shorten the work week, enforce a decent minimum wage, prevent unfair competition, and control production by means of fair-practice codes for each industry. Once an industry code was approved, members were awarded Blue Eagles to post in store windows or feature in newspaper ads. "We Do Our Part," the eagle sign said.

In charge of NRA was bluff General Hugh Johnson, a West Pointer, author of boys' books, lawyer, expert on the wartime draft, bearer of the nickname "Old Iron Pants." In Washington, Johnson talked turkey to industry leaders, bullying them into signing industry codes. "Like captured peasants, sweating businessmen were led before him," one account says.

Not everyone was happy about it. Conservatives, seeing the Government veer to the left, began to call FDR every name in the book. Traitor to his class was the least of the epithets. Programs like the CWA and WPA, which created all varieties of new jobs, were disparaged by the opposition as boondoggling. Whoever heard of a government making jobs for painters, writers, and actors, the vocal right demanded. As Eleanor Roosevelt began traveling the country, acting as her husband's eyes and ears, opponents had another target for vicious abuse.

Seldom has a President been vilified as much as FDR. Most of the nation's newspapers opposed him. Big business also. "No one likes him but the people," someone cracked.

Roosevelt's honeymoon with Congress ended with his first hundred days in office, and he began meeting stiff opposition to some of his programs. There also were rumors that the Supreme Court, most of its members over seventy years of age, was upset by the New Deal. The lunatic fringe also was on Roosevelt's trail, with Father Coughlin, Francis Townsend (advocating pensions for the aged), and Senator Huey Long keeping malcontents churned up. The year 1934 was one of continuing political crises, but Franklin Roosevelt handled them with characteristic enjoyment. He still seemed delighted at being President, still grinned the happy grin, continued to be stimulated by challenge and responsibility.

Then, in 1935, the Supreme Court, in a unanimous decision, declared the NRA unconstitutional. It said: "Extraordinary conditions may call for extraordinary remedies. But extraordinary conditions do not create or enlarge constitutional power."

Perhaps Roosevelt should have been happy, for the tough old NRA had outlived its usefulness and was beginning to creak. But the Supreme Court decision was a blow to his pride and his image. More, it put the future of the entire New Deal in jeopardy. FDR turned his supple mind to evolving a plan for thwarting the Nine Old Men. As he did, the New Deal stood stalled.

Yet the spirit of the people remained high. America had touched rock bottom. Now it was intent on climbing back.

1900 1905
1905 1910
1910 1915
1915 1920
1920 1925
1925 1930
1930 1935
♥
1935 1942

Second Term

♥ The year 1935 ushered in the better half of the Depression decade. It was the year that brought an end to the sixteen-year marriage of America's Sweethearts, Douglas Fairbanks and Mary Pickford, with Doug announcing plans to marry the glamorous international beauty, Lady Sylvia Ashley. In the same year the sleek French liner *Normandie* arrived in New York after a maiden voyage of four days, three hours, thirteen minutes. Admiral Richard E. Byrd, of transatlantic flight fame, returned to the United States after extraordinary Antarctic explorations.

The trial of Bruno Richard Hauptmann for the kidnap-murder of the Lindbergh baby started on January 2, and the courtroom drama ran grippingly until February 15. Drama of another sort came later on when Louisiana's Huey Long, combination buffoon and demagogue, was assassinated in the ornate lobby of his skyscraper state building in Baton Rouge.

Immortal Babe Ruth quit the Yankees— the pillars of baseball's past were tottering! —and accepted a three-year contract as vice president and assistant manager of the Boston Braves. Soon the name Joe DiMaggio began to be heard. The dirigible *Macon,* which cost $4,000,000 to build, dropped into the Pacific and sank off Point Sur, California. This disaster marked the end of American interest in lighter-than-air craft, though the world still retained its faith. Wasn't Germany's *Hindenburg* still in successful operation?

Joe Louis defeated man-mountain Primo Carnera, and the Detroit Tigers won the World Series, with Hank Greenberg as hero. Books of the year were *North to the Orient* by Anne Morrow Lindbergh, *Personal History* by Vincent Sheean, *Butterfield 8* by John O'Hara (based on the death of Starr Faithfull), *Of Time and the River* by Thomas Wolfe. Film of the year was Alfred Hitchcock's *39 Steps;* top Broadway show, Gershwin's *Porgy and Bess.* A popular dance band was Ted Weems, with soloist Perry Como.

At the end of 1935, the Associated Press picked the six new names-in-the-news that had most livened the year. They were Emperor Haile Selassie of Ethiopia; prize fighter Joe Louis; Governor Alf Landon of Kansas; child actor Freddie Bartholomew; Elaine Barrie Barrymore; and Alice Jane McHenry. Sweet Elaine, of course, was the girl from Hunter College who caught the roving eye of actor John Barrymore, becoming a sprightly Ariel to his aging Caliban in a ludicrous cross-country chase. But who was Alice Jane McHenry? Why, she was that youngster whose upside-down stomach was righted in a much-publicized operation.

The next year, 1936, brought one of the most romantic stories of all time, when King Edward VIII (remember him as the

In 1936 campaign, Roosevelt asked crowds, "Do you want the Depression back?" His popularity, plus ineptness of Republican Alf Landon, brought FDR a rousing victory.

264

boyish Prince of Wales?) abdicated the throne of England for the love of Wallis Warfield Simpson, a divorcée from Baltimore, Maryland. Never before had there been such a universal heart throb! Americans were first to learn about this incredible love affair, since *Time* and other magazines dared to print items about it, while British magazines and newspapers did not. Great Britain got more publicity when Charles Lindbergh and his wife moved there, sickened by the hoopla surrounding the kidnapping of their son and the trial and execution of the kidnapper. Thomas E. Dewey, the very image of a young crime buster, sent Lucky Luciano to Sing Sing prison in his drive to clean up New York. The 1936 Olympic Games were held in Berlin. To the intense discomfiture of race-conscious Nazis, Negro Jesse Owens was the star.

Yet most of all, 1936 was a political year. For one thing, it saw the long-range accomplishments of the New Deal supplant the rapid remedies passed to halt the Depression. It was the year when Social Security, unemployment insurance, and the WPA (which lasted until 1943) came into being. More, 1936 was a year of Presidential election, with FDR running for the first time on past performance as well as on hopes for the future.

The President was still vilified by the nation's economic royalists and conservatives. The majority of the nation's newspapers opposed him. On one tour as President he was booed at Harvard, his aristocratic alma mater. But the people appreciated him more than ever, seeing in him the embodiment of a better life. This was recognized by the Chief Executive himself. "There's only one issue in this campaign," he told

Sports excitement continued: Jesse Owens was supreme at 1936 Berlin Olympics, Joe Louis humbled all opponents, Joe DiMaggio hit 46 home runs in 1937.

advisor Raymond Moley. "It's myself. People will be either for me or against me."

The Republicans helped him by nominating Governor Alfred E. Landon of Kansas, a mild, colorless man. (Senator Vandenberg of Michigan, and other top Republicans didn't want the nomination.) Landon surrounded himself with amateur advisors, while Roosevelt's were seasoned pros. Alfred E. Smith and his archconservative Liberty League also helped by hurling charges at FDR. The charges only improved the President's image.

In October, Roosevelt set out on a campaign swing that resembled a Roman triumphal march. Big-city bosses hustled out crowds to jam the presidential route. FDR grinned delightedly and waved his battered campaign hat. His tactic for beating the Republicans was simple. "Do you want the Depression back?" he asked.

He won, of course. Republican Landon carried only Maine and Vermont.

By now the calendar read 1937. In that year John D. Rockefeller died at age ninety-seven. Amelia Earhart vanished in an attempt to circle the globe. The *okies* had materialized out of the barren dust bowl. Tragedy came when a mysterious spark ignited hydrogen in the 803-foot zeppelin *Hindenburg* as it touched the mooring mast at Lakehurst, New Jersey. A shattering blast followed, then a sheet of flame devoured the fabric covering the steel skeleton. News shots of the disaster rank with the most dramatic ever taken. By contrast, the coronation of George VI and Queen Elizabeth of England was a relaxing, colorful spectacle.

On Broadway, playwright Clifford Odets was the man. In his successful *Golden Boy* were Luther Adler, Lee J. Cobb, Morris

267

Carnovsky, Elia Kazan, Jules (later John) Garfield, and Karl Malden. The ingenue was Frances Farmer. Movies stood tall in the entertainment saddle. In 1934, the double feature had arrived, bringing new prosperity. In addition to double bills, some theaters had Bank Nights and Dish Nights ("Get a complete set of this genuine gold-bordered china in only six weeks").

Mae West was still screen queen, earning the second highest salary in the nation. (William Randolph Hearst was first.) Shirley Temple, actress at three and star at five, was the talk of Hollywood. Other child stars included the Dead End Kids, Bobby Breen, Deanna Durbin, Mickey Rooney, Judy Garland, Jackie Cooper, Baby LeRoy. Grace Moore was starring in superior films with operatic flavor, while Fred Astaire and Ginger Rogers were tops in musicals.

Some of the finest screen comedies of all time were being released, among them *It Happened One Night, My Man Godfrey, The Awful Truth, Nothing Sacred, Mr. Deeds Goes to Town* (remember "pixillated"?). It was also the vintage of *Lost Horizon,* with Ronald Colman. One Hollywood event of the year was the marriage of Jackie Coogan, age twenty-three, to Betty Grable, age twenty—and who but the principals recalls *that* wedding?

Double features had brought special problems to Walt Disney, who was making twelve Mickey Mouse and six Silly Symphony features a year. The long programs began to crowd his shorts off the bill. Disney realized that he must advance to full-length cartoons, or quit. He began *Snow White and the Seven Dwarfs,* and took three years to draw and photograph its quarter of a million sketches. As the world knows, it was a smashing success, with the country happily whistling "Heigh-ho, Heigh-ho, it's off to work we go." A cheerful Disney looked out on the world of 1937, a man with no worries.

Dance of the year was the big apple ("Do that stomp with lots of pomp"). Ray Eberle and Helen O'Connell were top singers of pop. *Gone With The Wind* won the Pulitzer Prize for fiction. Hemingway's *To Have and Have Not,* price $2.50, was a big seller. Self-help books were the nonfiction talk of the day: *Live Alone and Like It* by Marjorie Hillis, *Wake Up and Live* by Dorothea Brande, *How to Win Friends and Influence People* by Dale Carnegie, the perennial *Life Begins at Forty* by Walter Pitkin, the *Importance of Living* by Lin Yutang.

Coronet magazine was launched by the publishers of *Esquire* (as was the forgotten *Ken). The March of Time* hit movie screens. The contract bridge craze made Ely and Josephine Culbertson famous. Monopoly was the big parlor game; another game called G-Man failed to click. All of a sudden the country was swept by one of the maddest games ever. "Knock, knock," you'd say to the person nearest you. "Who's there?" came the quick response. "Olive." "Olive who?" "Olive you!"

Cafe Society

♥ Cafe society, that gay group of social madcaps, from 1936 on helped keep the public mind diverted from the fact that the Roosevelt prosperity was something of a twilight prosperity, remaining so until the advent of world war. There were still at least eight million unemployed.

It was much more exciting to read about the mad Manhattan social whirl and the fun people involved. The playground of cafe society comprised a few nighttime New York blocks, but the entire nation was aware of its existence. Blank-faced Brenda Frazier, a reluctant debutante polished and perfected by an ambitious family, was the acknowledged belle of cafe society. The term Glamour Girl was coined just for her (out in Hollywood, the Oomph Girl was Ann Sheridan). Husky Lucius Beebe, his attire as mannered as his prose, was cafe society's gentleman chronicler. Jerome Zerbe, first of the cabaret candid cameramen, snapped photos of his friends and got well paid for it. Prissy Maury Paul, who wrote society chit-chat as Cholly Knickerbocker, dreamed up the name cafe society. *Town & Country* magazine was the bible of the select set.

El Morocco, if you could get past maitre d' Carino, was the place to be. The dance floor, small to begin with, dwindled through the night as new tables were put around the edge. Two crack orchestras alternated, while electric stars twinkled in a cerulean sky, and patrons relaxed on the zebra-stripe upholstery.

Next to El Morocco came the Stork Club, so called because all the pretty babies went there. The Stork was favored by newspaper celebrities and prom-set rich kids. Journalists like Walter Winchell and Westbrook Pegler made its exclusive Cub Room a home away from home. So did entertainers like George Jessel and Morton Downey. Meanwhile, the more sedate members of cafe society had late supper at the Persian Room of the Plaza or the Iridium Room of the St. Regis.

For gracious dining *sans* dancing, there were the Colony, Theodore's, and the Rainbow Room atop the RCA building. In a class by itself—and still in one—was 21, haunt of the front-page celebrity.

A few critics accused cafe society of being shallow, saying its members behaved as heedlessly as the jazz babies of the Twenties. But look hard and you see something remarkable about cafe society. It shoved aside the old social criteria of wealth and an oak-like family tree. Achievement plus personal attractiveness, not background and inherited wealth, were the requisites for this brave new world. In cafe circles, an Irving Berlin rated higher than a Brokaw.

"Cafe society," wrote the elegant Beebe, "is the only society of the day that amounts to a hill of *haricots verts*."

♥ In 1938, Americans were attempting to look in two directions at once. At home lay the many fascinations of the home front. Abroad, World War II was brewing, and nothing like the suspense of this time has ever been known. The actual events of the fighting war may have made us forget the world-scale drama as war clouds gathered, then collided in a thunder of conflict.

Not the least dramatic factor in this cliff-hanger was the presence on the center of the stage of a deep-dyed villain. Usually the causes of great wars are obscure, but in this case the world had one man to hate. He was Adolf Hitler. In appearance Hitler might resemble Charlie Chaplin, but in words and actions he seemed evil incarnate. Hitler persecuted the Jews, purged political enemies, burned books, broke his word to heads of other nations, used brute force to terrify the strong and weak. All this he did to the accompaniment of wild speeches which inflamed the German people, left the rest of the world cold.

The Hitler drama began as America wallowed in the Depression. It was easy to overlook him then, and call him a mountebank whose National Socialist followers were ludicrous goose-steppers. But even through the fog of Depression, his menace began to be felt. The first chilling warning was the burning of the Reichstag in 1933, five days before Franklin Roosevelt's inauguration. This baffling conflagration made sense only after the Nazis won the national election a few days later. The world suspected the Nazis had set the fire themselves, to place suspicion on the Communists and capitalize on the resulting fury and panic. It also showed that Hitler and his National Socialists were prepared to act with gangster ruthlessness to attain their ends.

Further proof came when Hitler, as Chancellor, ordered the murder of his Storm Troop Commander Ernst Roehm and a thousand of his men. Informed that this purge had been successfully carried out, the Fuehrer said, "This has been the hardest day of my life." The Hitler hand was next visible in the murder of Chancellor Engelbert Dollfuss by Austrian Nazis. Only bungling after the killing kept the Nazis from gaining control of Austria at this time.

From the first, correspondents like Dorothy Thompson, John Gunther, and H. R. Knickerbocker warned America that Hitler's plan was world conquest. Journalists like Raymond Clapper and Marquis Childs now traveled abroad, saw the gathering German might, and sounded further alarms. Radio also played a vital part. The era of the news commentator had dawned, with world-minded experts like H. V. Kaltenborn, Elmer Davis, and Raymond Gram Swing alerting listening millions. Last, radio correspondents like Edward R. Mur-

270

From Europe, the strident tones of Adolf Hitler were heard. At first America thought him a joke, but by mid-decade he was a serious international threat.

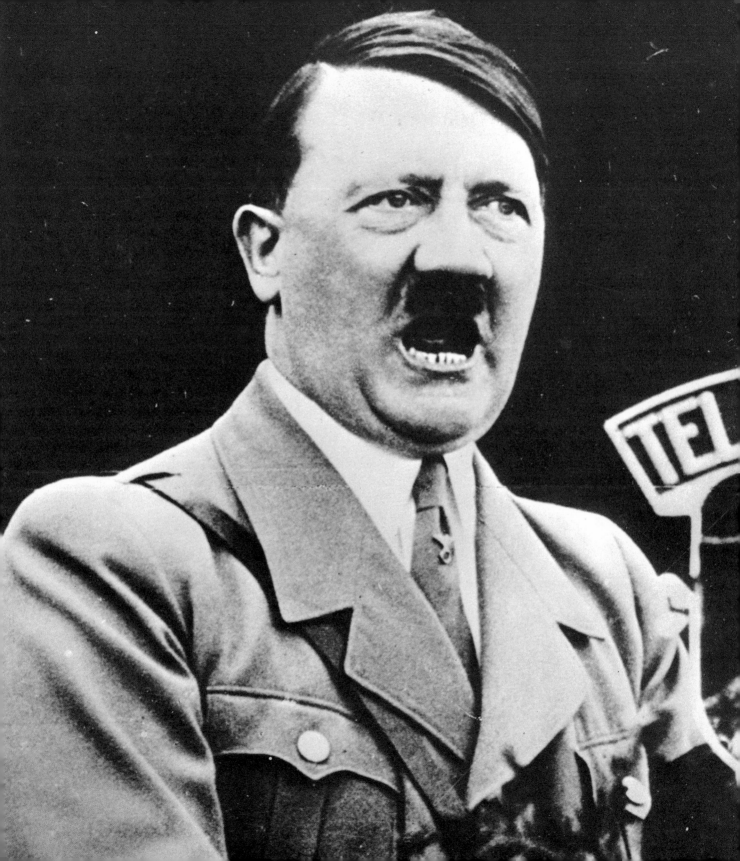

row, William Shirer, and Howard K. Smith began reporting directly from Europe.

There was much to report, for the Hitler villainy continued. Beginning in 1936, the Germans (and Russians, as well) used the Spanish revolution as a testing ground for the efficacy of aerial warfare and the bombing of cities. At the same time, the Spanish conflict diverted attention from the fact that Hitler was creating a massive war machine, every bit as formidable on land as in the air. In 1938 the dictator stood ready to test his plan of conquest. Determined on *anschluss* (union) with Austria, he ranted that the majority of Austrians desired it, too.

The world thought it brilliant when Chancellor Kurt Schuschnigg of Austria replied by calling a national election, which the Nazis were sure to lose. But the Fuehrer was a madman who couldn't tolerate being thwarted. He moved his armed might into Austria, claiming that he was rescuing the people from brutal oppression.

Was Hitler bluffing? If the great powers had risen for a showdown at this point would he have pulled back? No one knows. With his projected election, Schuschnigg had sought to rouse the conscience of Europe. He failed. England and France quietly sat out Hitler's ruthless show of force. Benito Mussolini, the original fascist dictator, found himself out-dictatored by the little man with the funny mustache.

Hitler now believed—why not!—that by show of mechanized might he could win

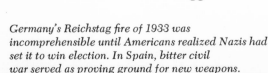

Germany's Reichstag fire of 1933 was incomprehensible until Americans realized Nazis had set it to win election. In Spain, bitter civil war served as proving ground for new weapons.

any territory he wanted. Czechoslovakia was next on his pattern of conquest and he began to demand the Sudetenland, a section of Czech territory in which three million Germans lived. The German press told daily of intolerable oppression of pro-Nazi Czechs. Hitler's speeches at the Nazi Party rally at Nuremberg outdid the press. In London, Prime Minister Neville Chamberlain became so alarmed that he requested a meeting with the rabid Fuehrer. World tension rose as Chamberlain traveled to Germany for a late-night conference. At its conclusion he urged the Czechs to submit to German demands for the Sudetenland. In agreement with him was French leader Edouard Daladier.

274   Returning humbly to Germany for a second conference—the pitch of world drama soared high again—Chamberlain found Hitler upping his demands. Again the Prime Minister gave in, but the Czechs were stubborn. Chamberlain was in the midst of a speech to the House of Commons when a terse message from Hitler summoned him to Munich. Here Hitler, Mussolini, Chamberlain, and Daladier presided over what has been called the rape of Czechoslovakia. This Munich pact gave Germany eleven thousand square Czech miles and more than three and a half million people, together with seventy per cent of the national iron and steel, seventy per cent of electrical power supplies, eighty-six per cent of gas and chemicals, eighty per cent of cement and textiles. Back home again, Chamberlain told crowds, "I believe it is peace in our time." Most Britishers were with him. They hated Hitler, but didn't want Englishmen killed in a war.

Hitler had given his word to Chamberlain that Czechoslovakia would be his final territorial demand in Europe. But now he swung toward Poland, uttering the familiar cries of intolerable acts and warlike provocations. Even the patient, fumbling Chamberlain could take no more. He announced that Britain and France would back the Polish Government if Germany attacked. "I'll cook them a stew they'll choke on," the Fuehrer ranted.

He did. Hitler had always feared that Russia, France, and England would band against him in military alliance. While England and France hesitated over this, the Fuehrer signed a ten-year nonaggression treaty with Russia—a cynical, sinister pact of Right and Left which made the world gasp. Now Hitler had no need to fight on two fronts. He was free to overrun Poland, turn to France and England.

It was August 23, 1939, and the week became one of the strangest that ever was. Europe knew war was inevitable, and acted like it. "Our continent seems about to commit suicide in a frightful war," said King Leopold of Belgium. None could gainsay him. Britain mobilized army and navy, called up reserves. London streetlights were hooded in case of air attack, the crown jewels moved from the city for safekeeping. Paris closed the Louvre, ordered troops to the heavily fortified Maginot Line. Berlin closed railroads to civilian

Benito Mussolini, posturing proudly as world's first fascist dictator, soon found himself overshadowed by Hitler. Italy's invasion of Ethiopia was unheeded warning of conscienceless deeds to come.

In 1938 at Munich, Hitler got Daladier of France and Chamberlain of England to agree to "rape of Czechoslovakia." English cheered arrival of "peace" document.

travel, and Germany gazed in awe at the masses of bombers flying overhead. In Poland, fortifications were hastily constructed, windows darkened. In the United States, Franklin Roosevelt appealed to Hitler, ordered Americans home from Europe.

Not a shot was fired, but for a week Europe was on war footing. Then on September 1, Hitler stood in the Kroll Opera House to shout that Poles had attacked and mutilated German citizens. Then he piously revealed, "Since 5:45 this morning, enemy fire has been returned." He had gone too far—probably he wanted to, anyway. England and France, forced to de-

clare war, did so two days later.

Russia sat back, licking its chops, eyeing Finland and other neighbor countries. In the East, Japan affirmed the Tokyo-Berlin Axis and stepped up its own war fever. Japan's dreams encompassed all of Asia and even the United States.

For the second time since 1900, the world had gone up in flames.

The month of September, 1938, culminating in the Munich Pact, may well be the most suspenseful the world has ever known. On-the-spot radio reports from Europe pulled the nerves of civilization taut. At the CBS studios in New York, commentator H. V. Kaltenborn remained on duty in the studio for eighteen consecutive days, sleeping on a cot and eating sandwiches. The multilingual Kaltenborn was the only analyst able to translate Hitler, Daladier, and Mussolini as heard over short wave. In one hundred and two broadcasts of two minutes to two hours in length, he gave America an instant summary of what had just been said.

Americans had never listened so intently to radio news before, and the broadcasts of Kaltenborn and his fellow commentators sold more radios during the crisis weeks than ever before.

Here is the march of events in the Munich month:

September 12
At a Nuremberg rally, Hitler hysterically demands that the rights of self-determination be given to Sudeten Germans.

September 13
Rioting in the Sudetenland causes Czech Government to impose martial law; Czech Nazis give Government six hours to cancel decree.

September 14
Prague ignores Nazis and sends additional troops to Sudeten area.

September 15
Prime Minister Chamberlain dramatically flies to Berchtesgaden for nighttime meeting with Hitler.

September 16
Chamberlain returns to London to report on Hitler's demands.

September 17
Prague puts all Czechoslovakia under martial law.

September 18
Premier Daladier and Foreign Minister Bonnet of France fly to London to confer with Chamberlain.

September 19
Britain and France agree to Hitler's demands for all predominantly German areas of Czechoslovakia.

September 20
Prague calls Anglo-French plan to partition Czechoslovakia unacceptable.

September 21
Pressure from London and Paris forces Czechs to agree to cede Sudetenland.

September 22
Chamberlain flies to Bad Godesberg to tell this to Hitler.

September 23
Hitler ups his demands, threatening invasion if not met; Czechoslovakia orders general mobilization; Paris talks of partial mobilization.

September 24
Chamberlain flies back to London; Mussolini assures Hitler of support; Britain prepares to mobilize.

September 25
Daladier and Bonnet join Chamberlain in London; Czechs reject new German demands.

September 26
President Roosevelt appeals to Hitler to negotiate.

September 27
Chamberlain calls Hitler's Godesberg demands "unreasonable" and makes further appeal to German dictator; Britain partially mobilizes fleet; Roosevelt makes another appeal.

September 28
Europe seems on the verge of war; Hitler calls four-power conference in Munich.

September 29
Chamberlain, Daladier, Hitler, Mussolini meet in Munich.

September 30
In all-day conference, the four powers reach agreement allowing Hitler to occupy Sudeten areas; Czechoslovakia, betrayed, gives in.

World's Fair

♥ What did it have, that New York World's Fair of 1939-40? Even at the time it seemed to possess a rare aura. Those who visited it just never forgot. *"That* was a Fair," they tell you. At the later Fair of 1964-65, held on the same grounds, you heard, "It's not like the old one."

Even writers felt its magic. Frederick Lewis Allen, usually the most controlled of historians, waxed eloquent over the 1939 Fair. "Gardens, fountains . . . music resounding everywhere. At night the splendor of superb lighting. Miracles of invention and of industrial efficiency to goggle at. A sense of festival!" To fellow author James D. Horan, it was "That wonderful, wonderful Fair."

What, then, did it have?

Well, it had beautiful, wide walks, some twenty-five miles of them. It had horns on Fair vehicles that gently tooted the first notes of "Sidewalks of New York." It had impressive modern architecture, severe and spacious at the same time, which offered the first chance many Fair visitors had to see what such design could do. It had fine restaurants, with French, Belgian, and other pavilions offering what the haughty magazines call superb cuisine. More than this, it was a comfortable Fair, achieving a neat balance between information, education, and amusement. After a day of absorbing knowledge, a family could dine well, then press on to the pop-

ular parachute jump, the Billy Rose Aquacade, or Frank Buck's Jungleland.

Perhaps, though, the Fair got its biggest assist from history. For it bravely called itself the World of Tomorrow, with its trylon and perisphere symbolic of glowing faith in the future. The Fair featured a Court of Peace, Lagoon of Nations, Democracity, and Futurama. It tried to embody the American dream of a better life, together with international peace. On this, it followed through. At the World's Fair of 1939 no international tensions were visible (Nazi Germany was the only major nation not represented); there were no social barriers; no sectional feuds; no hints of poverty or slums; no memorabilia of the Depression. Those who traversed its walks saw sweet harmony represented by General Motors and Remington Rand cheek by jowl with Russia and the WPA.

On the opening day of the Fair on April 30, 1939, Franklin Roosevelt spoke glowingly about the World of the Future. Another speaker said, "No Superman is going to build the World of Tomorrow for you. You must build it yourself. Here are the tools with which it is to be built."

Yet four months after these words were spoken, hopes for the beautiful World of Tomorrow were shattered by a madman in Europe. Not for a long time would people be able to use the tools offered by the Fair, for the world was again at war.

Trylon and perisphere of New York's 1939 World's Fair hopefully symbolized a peaceful world and technological wonders of future. But hopes fell as war engulfed Europe.

278

*Question that touched almost everybody:
To fight or not to fight. World's Fair time capsule
(right), to be opened in 5000 years, symbolized
hopes for peaceful future. America First Committee,
championed by Charles Lindbergh (here with
Senator Burton K. Wheeler at his right,
novelist Kathleen Norris and Norman Thomas
at his left) advocated isolation.
Edward R. Murrow, broadcasting from embattled
London, sympathized with Allies. Meanwhile
we watched machinations of Japan's War
Minister Tojo, kept arms factories
humming . . . just in case.*

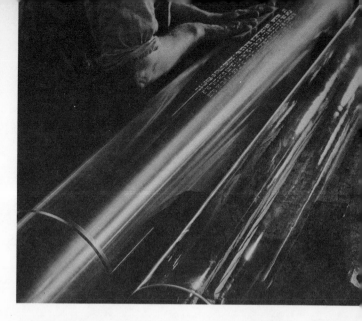

The Present Arrives

♥ It was 1940, only four decades after the Turn of the Century.

Never in all history had forty years wrought such stunning changes in the world. In 1900, the automobile was an infant, the airplane a dream, the wireless a mechanical toy. Now the world treated all three as absolute necessities. Cities which had been clusters of low buildings had blossomed into forests of skyscrapers. Graceful suspension bridges stretched across bays and rivers, mighty dams harnessed and disseminated power.

There had been so many changes on the whirling planet that no one could enumerate them. Some, of course, were political. A swing of the world pendulum had made Germany dominant on the Continent. This had shifted power from the democratic bloc led by Britain to the brooding authoritarian bloc dominated by Hitler. At the far end of a totalitarian axis, Japan rose supreme.

Where did America stand in this changed order? As long as anyone at the time could recall, Great Britain had controlled the seas, serving as the unofficial policeman of the world. As such, Great Britain had also provided America's first line of defense. Now the United States stood unprotected in the vast game of power politics. Even so, it was determined to pursue a policy of strict neutrality combined with pro-Ally sympathy. President Roosevelt saw the primary need of keeping the British fleet afloat and operative. "All assistance short of war" was our promise to Britain. But some thought a country as big and powerful as the United States had no right to claim neutrality. Others considered neutrality impossible.

President Roosevelt had long been outspoken in warning of fascism's danger to democracy. His words appeared to say that he thought American participation in the war both necessary and inevitable. Yet this world leader also had to function as a domestic President. In Congress, important Senators—William E. Borah of Idaho, David Walsh of Massachusetts, Burton K. Wheeler of Montana, and Gerald P. Nye of North Dakota—were determined isolationists. Other Congressmen hated Roosevelt on general principles. War and Navy Departments were riddled by isolationist sentiment. The vocal America First Committee, with Charles A. Lindbergh among its members, agitated against American involvement. The majority of the population wanted to see Hitler defeated. But like the English in the Chamberlain crisis, they did not want American men killed in the process.

America's isolationist movement provided the pressure needed to make FDR decide on the unprecedented step of a third term. In 1908, Theodore Roosevelt could

Men who made the sound of the early Forties: young vocalist Frank Sinatra, funny man Ed Wynn and suave pianist Eddy Duchin, swing men Benny Goodman and Gene Krupa, band leader Duke Ellington.

have—perhaps should have—run for a third term but his conscience wouldn't let him. FDR felt no such qualms. He had already considered running a third time to preserve his New Deal policies. He feared a Republican victory if another Democrat ran.

His opponent in 1940 was Wendell Willkie, a formidable man with a tremendous drive to victory. A Republican in the Roosevelt image, Willkie had been nominated by popular acclaim. But lamentably lacking in him was the commodity of experience. FDR was a man born with politics in his blood, who in get-togethers with local politicos ceased to be the aristocrat, sank comfortably to precinct level. He was one pro working with others. Willkie, on the other hand, alienated the Republican pros, some of whom came to hate him more than FDR. Willkie relied on big-business friends and publishers.

Willkie was defeated, though he pulled a large popular vote. He had warned that Roosevelt policies would end in war. But after a trip abroad, he returned believing the President was not moving fast enough.

Political news of 1940 was third term for FDR. His opponent was Wendell Willkie (above), a strong but losing candidate. In Europe, English army was heroically rescued from Dunkirk.

A terrifying year, 1941! After a winter of mock war, Europe exploded into the most awful conflict civilization had ever known. Dive bombers rained death on defenseless cities as the Nazis overran Denmark, Holland, Belgium, Luxembourg, and pushed toward Paris. At the end of May came the heroic evacuation of Dunkirk, when 900 craft, most of them from England, rescued 338,226 men of the British and French armies. Next the Germans captured Paris, with Hitler joyously stamping his foot for newsreel cameramen. The Luftwaffe remorselessly bombed Britain for seventy-two consecutive nights, sometimes with a thousand planes. The RAF hit back. Nightmare became delirium as Hitler swung on his pact-partner Russia to declare war in the east.

In Washington the atmosphere was strained, tinged with guilt. One observer thought the city's activities resembled a

slow-motion movie taken in a lunatic asylum. Democrats had resoundingly won the election; Democrats supposedly wanted America in the war. Still, action was delayed.

In a way, it was reminiscent of 1917. Once again a President dared not lead the country into war without extreme provocation. In the meantime, FDR worried about the fate of Britain. Warily eyeing the powerful isolationists in Congress, he went ahead with the draft, Lend-Lease, and other measures short of war.

The nation was tense. At night people gathered around radios to hear Ed Murrow's sepulchral "This is London." In the background could be heard the noise of bombs and the shouts of fire wardens. After Murrow, people turned to Raymond Gram Swing and H. V. Kaltenborn.

Life went on. Magazines carried colorful Matson Line ads for luxury cruises to Hawaii. Young folk reveled in the fabulous era of the Big Bands: Benny Goodman, Tommy Dorsey, Glenn Miller, Harry James. A youthful Frank Sinatra quit the James band to join Dorsey; in the back of his mind were thoughts of going out on his own. As always, nonsense songs enlivened the national spirit: "Hut Sut Ralston," "Flat Foot Floogie," "Cement Mixer," "Three Little Fishes in an Itty Bitty Pool." Most topical was Spike Jones' defiant jingle about laughing in der Fuehrer's face.

But the nation at peace all but stood on a wartime footing. The civilian draft had swelled the army from one hundred and seventy-five thousand enlisted men to a million and a half. Factory assembly lines produced tanks and war planes. Shipyards worked overtime to build ships.

The overt act which alone could shift the balance toward war came with a vengeance on Sunday, December 7, 1941. President Roosevelt, informally attired in a turtleneck sweater, was lunching from a tray in his White House study when word of Pearl Harbor came at 1:50 P.M. He uttered an incredulous, "No!" Word of the sneak attack was relayed to the country at 2:25 P.M., EST.

Roosevelt already had a war plan in his mind and quickly summoned Secretary of State Cordell Hull, Secretary of War Henry E. Stimson, General George C. Marshall, the Army chief of staff. In other parts of Washington, diplomats and military men raced to offices. Still wearing the turtleneck sweater, FDR functioned effortlessly. "I have seen many statesmen in times of crisis," recalls one man present, "but never have I seen one so calm and steady. Roosevelt was completely relaxed."

Before going to bed that night, the President spoke with Ed Murrow, home on leave from London. "Did the Pearl Harbor attack surprise you?" the Chief Executive wanted to know.

"Yes, Mr. President."

"Maybe you think it didn't surprise *us!*"

So, on wings of tragedy and surprise, the past departed. The present had arrived.

Washington expected an overt act from the Axis, but nothing as sudden or violent as the sneak attack on Pearl Harbor, December 7, 1941. America declared war next day.

PICTURE CREDITS

AC—Allen Churchill collection
BB—Brown Brothers
CP—Culver Pictures
LC—Library of Congress
UPI—United Press International

Cover and 2-3—Albert Squillace and David Namias.

1900   1905
9-CP. 10-CP. 12-BB. 13-BB. 14(top)-BB; (bottom)-New-York Historical Society. 15-UPI. 16(both)-LC. 17-BB. 19-(all but bottom, right)-CP; (bottom, right)-Erie Lackawanna Railroad Co. 21-BB. 22(both)-CP. 23-CP. 25-CP. 26-27(left)-BB; (right)-CP. 28-29(all)-CP. 31-BB. 32(top; bottom, left)-BB; (bottom, right)-CP. 33-UPI. 34-BB. 35-BB. 37(both)-CP. 39-BB. 40(left)-CP; (right)-BB. 41(both)-CP. 42-AC. 44-45(all)-CP. 47(top, left)-LC; (top, right; bottom)-CP. 48(all)-CP. 50-BB.

1905   1910
52-LC. 55-CP. 57-CP. 61(top, left)-BB; (top, right)-New York Public Library; (bottom, left)-AC; (bottom, right)-CP. 62-63(both)-AC. 65-BB. 66(top, left; bottom, center)-AC; (top, right; bottom, left and right)-CP. 67-BB. 69-BB. 70-BB. 71-CP. 72-CP. 75(all)-UPI. 76(top, left; bottom, right)-CP; (top, right)-BB; (middle and bottom, left)-LC. 79(all)-CP. 80-81-CP. 82-BB. 84-85-LC. 86-CP. 87-CP. 88(top, left)-CP; (top, right; bottom)-BB. 91-BB. 92(both)-CP. 93-CP. 94-Historical Society of Montana, Helena. 96-Tom Burnside, from *Treasury of the Automobile* by Ralph Stein. 97-BB. 98-CP. 99-CP. 102(all)-CP. 104-105-CP.

1910   1915
106-BB. 111(top)-BB; (bottom, left)-AC; (bottom, right)-CP. 114(top, left)-New York Public Library; (bottom, left)-AC; (right)-CP. 115(all)-CP. 117-AC. 118(both)-AC. 120(top)-reprinted by permission of Bill McClure Syndicate, copyright © 1966 by Aedita S. de Beaumont; (middle, left)-*Chicago Tribune,* New York News Syndicate; (middle, right)-AC; (bottom)-King Features Syndicate. 123-BB. 124-CP. 125-CP. 126(left)-CP; (right)-BB. 127-CP. 128(top)-CP; (bottom, left and right)-BB. 129(top, left)-New York Public Library; (right; bottom, left)-CP. 132-LC. 133(right; top, left)-BB; (middle and bottom, left)-LC. 135-CP. 136-137(left)-CP; (center, top)-"September Morn," The Metropolitan Museum of Art, anonymous gift; (center, bottom)-"The Storm," The Metropolitan Museum

of Art, Bequest of Catharine Lorillard Wolfe, 1887; (right)-"Nude Descending a Staircase, No. 2," 1912, Philadelphia Museum of Art: The Louise and Walter Arensberg Collection. 139(both)-CP. 140-BB.

1915   1920
142-CP. 144-145(all)-CP. 149-BB. 154-CP. 155-CP. 156(all)-LC. 160-161-BB. 162-BB.

1920   1925
165-CP. 166-Long Island Automotive Museum, from *Treasury of the Automobile* by Ralph Stein. 167(top; bottom, right)-BB; (bottom, left)-CP. 168-169(all but top, right)-CP; (top, right)-BB. 170-171-BB. 175-CP. 176-CP. 177-CP. 179-CP. 180-181-CP. 182(all)-CP. 183(left)-CP. 184(top, left and middle)-AC; (top, right; bottom)-CP. 188-189(all)-CP. 191(all but top, left)-CP; (top, left)-BB. 194-195(all but bottom, left)-CP; (bottom, left)-AC. 198-BB. 199-BB. 200-LC. 201-BB. 203-*Chicago Tribune,* New York News Syndicate. 204-205(all)-*Chicago Tribune,* New York News Syndicate.

1925   1930
209-BB. 211-CP. 212-CP. 213-CP. 215-CP. 216-217(both)-BB. 218-CP. 219(all)-CP. 221(all but bottom, left)-CP; (bottom, left)-National Broadcasting Co. 222-BB. 225-CP. 226(left)-UPI; (right)-CP. 227(both)-CP. 228-BB. 231-CP.

1930   1935
235-BB. 236(top, left)-CP; (top, right; bottom, left)-LC; (bottom, right)-BB. 238-CP. 239(all)-CP. 241-CP. 243(all)-CP. 244-CP. 246-King Features Syndicate. 248-*Chicago Tribune,* New York News Syndicate. 249(top)-King Features Syndicate; (middle; bottom)-*Chicago Tribune,* New York News Syndicate. 251-UPI. 252-253(all but bottom, left; middle)-CP; (bottom, left; middle)-BB. 254-255(both)-CP. 258-259(top, left)-BB; (top, middle)-Wide World Photos; (bottom, left)-Pan American World Airways; (bottom, middle; right)-CP. 261-UPI.

1935   1942
265-UPI. 266(left)-CP; (right)-UPI. 267-UPI. 271-BB. 272-UPI. 273(both)-Wide World Photos. 275-UPI. 276(left)-UPI; (right)-Wide World Photos. 279-Wide World Photos. 280(top)-BB; (bottom, left and right)-UPI. 281(top)-Wide World Photos; (bottom)-UPI. 283(all but bottom, right)-CP; (bottom, right)-BB. 284-CP. 285-Wide World Photos. 287-CP.

Remember When

The End